D1329665

Black Literature
in White America

Black Literature
in White America

BERNDT OSTENDORF

Professor of American Cultural History
University of Munich

THE HARVESTER PRESS · SUSSEX

BARNES & NOBLE BOOKS · NEW JERSEY

First published in Great Britain in 1982 by
THE HARVESTER PRESS LIMITED
Publisher: John Spiers
16 Ship Street, Brighton, Sussex

and in the USA by
BARNES & NOBLE BOOKS
81 Adams Drive, Totowa, New Jersey 07516

British Library Cataloguing in Publication Data

Ostendorf, Berndt
    Understanding black culture in white America. – (Harvester
    studies in contemporary literature and culture; 7)
    1. American literature. – Afro-American
    authors – History and criticism
    I. Title
    810.9′896073   PS153.N5

    ISBN 0-7108-0041-X

Library of Congress Cataloging in Publication Data

Ostendorf, Berndt.
    Understanding black culture in white America.

    1. American literature – Afro-American authors – History
and criticism.   2. Afro-Americans – Race identity.
I. Title.
PS153.N508   810′.9′896073   81-19089
ISBN 0-389-20257-6   AACR2

Typeset in 11/12 pt Bembo by Inforum Ltd, Portsmouth
Printed in Great Britain by
Mansell Limited, Witham, Essex

CONTENTS

Introduction   vii

I   Rediscovering an Invisible Culture   1

II   Double Consciousness: The Marginal Perspective
in Language, Oral Culture, Folklore, Religion   14

III   Minstrelsy: Imitation, Parody and Travesty in
Black-White Interaction Rituals 1830–1920   65

IV   Social Mobility and Cultural Stigma: The Case
of Chicago Jazz 1920–1930   95

V   Oral Tradition and the Quest for Literacy:
The Crisis of Black Writers from Phillis
Wheatley to Ralph Ellison   118

VI   Contemporary Afro-American Culture: the
Sixties and Seventies   148

INTRODUCTION

Black Studies, a relatively recent academic concern, have a strong European connection. Janheinz Jahn, Joachim Ernst Berendt and Eva Hesse in Germany, Eric Hobsbawm, Paul Oliver, and Chris Bigsby in England, Hugues Panassié, André Hodeir, Jean Wagner and Michel Fabre in France have for many years been promoting interest in black culture. In fact, European attention may well have increased its visibility at home. This book is a child of that European interest, which in my case was corrected or buttressed much later by American training. After World War II my age group was introduced to black culture through jazz. Devoted fans all over Europe listened nightly to Willis Connover's jazz hour on the Voice of America, and no one in this conspiracy of fans would have doubted the seriousness or legitimacy of this American contribution to modernist culture. Built into our appreciation of jazz was a strong bias in favour of its black creators, Louis Armstrong, Duke Ellington, Lester Young, Charlie Parker, Bud Powell and many more. In fact, jazz became the tape by which we tended to measure all things American. This pre-academic basic training in black music influenced my understanding of America, but most of all it prevented any exclusively literary reading of black culture. When Ralph Ellison suggested in a *Time* essay of April 1970 that all American culture is 'jazz-shaped' those European listeners of Willis Connover might be found to agree more readily than many Americans who were not subverted by the American information agency and who remained happily oblivious of this mainspring of American culture.

The most encompassing thesis of this book is that American culture is a hybrid – full of contradictions – which owes its vitality to a long history of imitation, travesty, parody and productive misunderstanding between its various cultures. While socially and politically there has been strong pressure towards assimilation, in culture there has been an increasing 'ethnification'. In this process the relationship between black and white America has ben particularly significant for the development of an American vernacular style.

A quest for literacy, freedom, and respect characterizes the development of black culture, a quest which used any strategy to overcome oppression, circumvent legal and institutional barriers, and subvert the canon. Robert Stepto in his recent book *From Behind the Veil* (1979) charts the internal history of that quest, the inner logic in the development of narrative genres. This book focuses on the historical and structural contingencies which defined its course and which gave shape to a black aesthetic grammar; the contingencies of race, class, and poverty, and the cultural gamesmanship of affirmation, rejection, and subterfuge which make for a specific black style. By necessity the book had to neglect large parts of the black literary and cultural corpus; for its aim was not quantitative. Instead it pays attention to key metaphors and key issues of the black cultural experience in America. Discrete cultural artefacts, say, a novel or the blues, are meaningful as self-contained symbolic systems and may be understood from a variety of cultural perspectives. But they acquire their full resonance from their form–giving context. In my view the rich resonances, ambiguities, and ironies of black culture have all too often received short shrift in our attention to discrete forms of that culture. Therefore the word 'literature' in the title should be taken in a catholic and comprehensive sense. As every text is part of a culture, the culture is part of the text. Though their guise is 'literary', texts are much more.

Two black writers were my chief guidance, W.E.B. DuBois and Ralph Ellison. Their works, notably *The Souls of Black Folk, Invisible Man,* and *Shadow and Act* inspired the sympathetic and celebratory pattern of immersion which characterizes this particular narrative. My other debts are many. Richard Dorson, Herbert Gutman, Jules Chametzky, Bernard Bell, Michael Harper, Daniel Aaron discussed parts of the manuscript. Rita Stoephasius read the entire manuscript and Ortrun O'Connor typed it.

Permission to use previously published materials was kindly granted by the following editors and publishers: Martin Christadler and *Amerikastudien:* 'Black Poetry, Blues, and Folklore. Double Consciousness in Afro-American Oral Culture', *Amerikastudien*, 20 (1975); Marta Sienicka and Adam Mickiewicz University, Poznan: 'Reinventing an Invisible Culture. New Directions in Black Oral Tradition', *Proceedings of a Symposium on American Literature* (Poznan, 1979); Simone

Vauthier and RANAM: 'Contemporary Afro-American Culture: The Sixties and Seventies,' *Recherches Anglaises et Américaines*, X (1977); Hans Bungert and Reclam Verlag: 'Die afroamerikanische Literatur der Gegenwart: Tendenzen und Aspekte', *Die amerikanische Literatur der Gegenwart* (Stuttgart, 1977); Peter Freese and Erich Schmidt Verlag: 'Ralph Ellison 'Flying Home', *Die amerikanische Short Story der Gegenwart* 'Berlin, 1976); Jules Chametzky and *The Massachusetts Review* for 'Ministrelsy and Early Jazz', *The Massachusetts Review*, 3 (Fall 1979).

Quotations from works by the following authors and publishers were made possible by the kind permission of their respective publishers and representatives:

I   REDISCOVERING AN INVISIBLE CULTURE

The scholarship of black culture has been unpredictable and ideologically confusing. The recent wave of revisionist writing in black history reflects the deep ambiguity of the subject matter and the uneasy position of black and white scholars in a changing political climate and in the attendant academic market. Particularly in the fifties and sixties 'the problem' weighed heavily on the conscience of all liberal white scholars, and their work shows it. It is not surprising that the evolving Civil Rights struggle of the fifties and sixties re-directed black studies in an extraordinary manner, sometimes into eccentric and contradictory positions. An extreme instance of such revisionist ping-pong is the diametrically opposed assessments of slavery in the work of Elkins and Fogel/Engerman respectively.[1] The former saw the black slave as a pathological victim of a closed system, similar to the concentration camp. The latter rebuilt him into a well-fed Horatio Alger with a puritan work ethic. Both works had tacit political implications and background assumptions; the first was swept along by the neo-abolitionist fervor of the fifties, the second reflected the morale-boosting temperament of the late sixties.

However, in recent years the social and cultural sciences in America have taken a self-reflexive turn and have begun to question the tacit background assumptions buried in their paradigms. As a consequence students of folklore, anthropology, musicology, social history, and linguistics have taken a second look at Afro-American culture and have challenged the presumptuous manner in which social scientists and cultural critics had over the past half century solved the 'black problem'.[2] Background assumptions, particularly those that are identical with the self-image of the dominant group, are strong epistemological filters.[3] While seemingly objective, revisionist critics may cull from past history or present society a plausible justification of their current assumptions. This approach seems to have worked for what LeRoi Jones called the 'mainline' culture of America (thus calling attention to the narcotic nature of self-images), since it innocently endorses the

1

obvious success of the dominant ideology of which the critics themselves are heirs.[4]

Such revisionism in cultural studies is merely a symptom of a real historic movement: namely of a quiet and often unnoticed change in political priorities and thus in background assumptions. Oscar Wilde mocked the historicist dilemma: 'The one duty we owe to history is to rewrite it.' However, we rewrite it in terms of the winners; for we are much better equipped to explain current victors and the status quo, i.e. the manifest and providential *telos* of history, than victims and defeated causes which went under or became invisible.[5] In America a deep-seated cultural narcissism has failed to do justice to the 'unsung black army of men and women' who were not consulted when the American Dream was fashioned and who were not able, except vicariously and at the price of self-denial, to participate in the heady Horatio Alger myth. Few blacks would have conceived of themselves as a 'redeemer nation' when they were still waiting to be redeemed into basic Civil Rights. Fernand Braudel remarks in his study of material culture that historians generally trail behind the victorious and literate parties of history while paying little or no attention to the unwritten history of the illiterate folk.[6] There is a compulsive or inevitable quality to such historiography: 'Die jeweils Herrschenden sind die Erben aller die je gesiegt haben,' (Dominant groups are heirs to all previous victories) writes Walter Benjamin; and the Southern historian Vann Woodward reminds the American Historical Association at bicentennial time that winners often have a 'skewed and eccentric perspective on history.'[7] At their worst, winner historians will tacitly and gratefully accept the status quo as the providential result of historic progress, rename it norm or normal and call all departures from this standard deviant. Much of winners' writing on the losers of American history has to be seen in this light. Historians and social scientists of the consensus school assumed that the anonymous masses had no culture of their own and either shared the dominant cultural values or aspired to them. If they didn't, the implication ran, they surely ought to. Failure on the part of the have-nots to fall in line with the dominant cultural trend has been interpreted as a sign of inferiority (cynics will call it self-inflicted) or as social pathology, an opinion which often implied a blueprint for therapeutic and compensatory action. Franklin Frazier, a member of the cultural inferiority school, wrote that 'the most conspicuous thing about the Negro is his lack of culture.' Gunnar Myrdal called the Negro 'characteristically American' who is 'not proud of those things in which he differs from the white American.' This notion of cultural deprivation or infantization hardened to political orthodoxy in the Moynihan report of 1960 which declared that the Negro 'has no values or culture to guard and protect.'[8] Though Frazier, Myrdal and Moynihan proposed these claims to strengthen a pro-black political argument, few blacks recognized themselves in their books, or trusted the politics based on them.[9]

In the late sixties a black reaction set in, equally absolute and understandably strident, which projected a militant self-image of blacks into the Afro-American past and which constructed an abstract African lineage above and outside the historical involvement of blacks and whites in America.[10] While the first party of consensus historians had no use for data that suggested cultural difference, or interpreted any such difference in terms of inferiority or deprivation, the new Africanists (reacting to the obvious political success of the inferiority school) equally reject large parts of their own multifaceted culture which grew out of 350 years of black-and-white shared history.

Until the late sixties few revisionist white scholars and even fewer militant black scholars asked the blacks to speak for themselves or tried to reconstruct on the basis of available data what the black masses felt or what they did during and after slavery. The excuse was: (1) they left no documents, (2) they have no culture as we understand it, (3) they are not sufficiently in control of their own destiny. This was said with a good deal of conviction. When historians did go hunting for new sources off the beaten track they found to their delight that the alleged lack of documents on the black masses was a myth. In 1969 Lawrence Levine complained that the history of black culture could not be written since there were so few reliable documents to go by;[11] in 1977 he is overwhelmed by the sheer mass of unanalyzed material which rests in collections of black folklore and in archives all over the United States. Herbert Gutman collected so much evidence disproving one of the most popular myths on the black family that his publisher would not print all of it.[12] Scholars believed for a long time that the current instability of the black ghetto family and its 'deviance' from the nuclear family pattern had its roots in slavery. The assumption was that normal family behavior had been socialized out of black males and females by the extreme conditions of slavery. Gutman admits his own amazement that so much material which flies in the face of this most popular academic prejudice should have remained invisible for so long. Folklorists knew this material, but they collected it without much further analysis. And anthropologists who had the analytical tools were much better informed about Africa and the South Seas than about their own exotic minorities. Melville Herskovits, who dealt with the touchy question of African retentions, was strongly attacked by most of his colleagues, particularly by the Chicago sociologists.[13] The latter explained the 'irregularities' of black culture and behavior as social wounds; they were seen as negative symptoms of a deficient culture, not as positive items of a full-grown native Afro-American culture. Since the sixties anthropologists and folklorists have come up with material which is evidence of an immensely rich, diversified oral cultural tradition. The more we find the more we must reject the claims of the pathology school. Ralph Ellison wrote in 1944 in his critique of Myrdal's book *The American Dilemma*:

> But can a people . . . live and develop for over three hundred years simply by *reacting*? Are American Negroes simply the creation of white men, or have they at least helped to create themselves out of what they found around them? Men have made a way of life in caves and upon cliffs, why cannot Negroes have made a life upon the horns of the white man's dilemma?[14]

If we accept that black culture is not a deficient copy of white American culture, that it is not a hand-me-down culture, nor exclusively a culture of pathology or poverty, why did it take historians and social scientists so long to accept this culture as a positive achievement? How could Gunnar Myrdal, brilliant man that he was, spend 800 pages denying the existence of an affirmative Afro-American culture and how could Glazer and Moynihan second him as late as 1960 — five years after the death of Charlie Parker? And why would scholars when they did see items of black culture label these 'deviant' or 'pathological'? Let me speculate about some of these barriers or censors (in the Freudian sense) that made this culture and its people 'pathological' or 'invisible' to the academic and cultural establishment.[15]

Ralph Ellison's novel *Invisible Man* is a classic case of art being in the vanguard of social thought. Historians and social scientists today second his critique of Myrdal (unpublishable in 1944) and follow the many clues of his novel of 1952. His protagonist introduces himself, but he might just as well be speaking about the dilemma of studying black culture:

> I am an invisible man. No, I am not a spook like those who haunted Edgar Allan Poe; nor am I one of your Hollywood-movie ectoplasms. I am a man of substance, of flesh and bone, fibre and liquids — and I might even be said to possess a mind. I am invisible, understand, simply because people refuse to see me. Like the bodiless heads you see sometimes in circus sideshows, it is as though I have been surrounded by mirrors of hard, distorting glass. When they approach me they see only my surroundings, themselves, or figments of their imagination — indeed, everything and anything except me.
>
> Nor is my invisibility exactly a matter of bio-chemical accident to my epidermis. That invisibility to which I refer occurs because of a peculiar disposition of the eyes of those with whom I come in contact. A matter of the construction of their *inner* eyes, those eyes with which they look through their physical eyes upon reality.

What caused this blindness? What censors or filters went into the construction of the 'inner eyes' Ellison speaks of?[16] And why is such a great deal of black culture suddenly quite visible in 1977? The major factor is quite clearly political: The change of political consciousness, a sea change in basic attitudes, which swept over the United States. Other reasons, though they seem to hinge on questions of method or scholarly accuracy, are equally political: some have to do with sociopsychological, some with epistemological barriers; others have to do with tacit assumptions about race, class, and culture, or with the structural myopia of the text- and document-oriented science; and some have to do with the priggishness of Western scholarly tradition which refuses to deal with material which is simply too juicy and sensual for Puritan stomachs. (The world famous *Motif-Index of Folk Literature* does not contain any offensive material. Judging on the basis of later and less Victorian collections or indices quite a substantial part of black folklore is overtly or covertly sexual). But even those scholars who have shed their Puritan restraint and reconstructed their inner eye run into a problem: the data are difficult to decode. They require what anthropologist Clifford Geertz called 'thick description.'[17] Black culture is double-edged, indirect and ambivalent and will not yield meaningful answers to the positivist who is preoccupied with surface phenomena. Unfortunately too many scholars of black life knew what they expected to see and believed in what they thought they saw. This approach is bound to fail in the study of something as 'deceptive' as folk culture and as 'invisible' as black culture.

THE POLITICAL SCENE[18]

The structure of acceptable political positions had to change before a shift in the interpretation and assessment of American culture in general and black American culture in particular was made possible. For a long time it was not politically wise to stress any cultural difference between Afro-Americans and Americans. One could not study African retentions without supporting Southern senators who argued for segregation on the grounds of cultural difference. It was not wise in the fifties to appear 'un-American' or 'deviant.' Scholarship was happily ethnocentric and few challenged the 'It-couldn't-happen-here' ideology. The Civil Rights movement, Vietnam, the assassination of John and Robert Kennedy and of Martin Luther King, Urban Renewal à la Watts and Detroit, shattered the dominant self-image of many Americans. The tacit hierarchical definition of culture came under severe questioning by the American youth culture. Proportionate to the decline of the dominant macho-ideology the other cultural alternatives and traditions in America — most of whom had not been victorious — rose into visibility: Blacks, Native Americans, Chicanos, Appalachians, and Women. Bob Dylan, Joan Baez, Janis Joplin, the Stones sang (and translated) the music of these groups. Third world cultures were studied with greater attention after Vietnam. At colleges and universities all over the United States Folklore and Anthropology departments experienced a boom. It was this major sea-change in the general American structure of feeling, in the 'univers du discours', and in the structure of the political public sphere which made the renaissance of black culture possible and which rescued it from the benign neglect of earlier decades.

THE REDEFINITION OF CULTURE

The political change goes hand in hand with a change in the attitude towards culture. Behind most of the ongoing social research lurked a concept of culture which was hierarchical and which saw Western culture in terms of an evolutionary, providential odyssey. Northrop Frye and Leslie Fiedler in literature, Levi-Strauss and Stanley Diamond in anthropology, Fernand Braudel in history (and many others) have begun to understand culture as the resource of all people, not as the privilege of a few. If all cultures which had gone into the making of America were now treated as equal then one deep-seated national image — that of the melting pot of nations — had to be reconsidered. The history of blacks in America has too often been treated as a progress report in acculturation. (It would be useful to look at the metaphors which scholars have used as titles of their books: odyssey, journey, rise etc.). Even popular black journals such as the *Chicago Defender* or *Ebony* would faithfully record the degree of Americanization of black people. By the sixties and seventies American mainstream culture had become so black itself that the real article no longer seemed quite so deviant. In 1970 Ellison wrote that American culture (both high- and lowbrow) is built on black folklore, that it is in fact 'jazz-shaped'.[19] Who would doubt this after listening to George Gershwin and Leonard Bernstein, to Elvis Presley and Janis Joplin?

LITERATE IMPERIALISM AND ORAL CULTURES
Literate cultures are constitutionally unable to fully understand oral traditions. Cecil Sharp, British folklorist, wrote in 1907:

> One of the most amazing and puzzling things about the English folk song is the way in which it has hitherto escaped the notice of the educated people resident in the country districts. When I have had the good fortune to collect some especially fine songs in a village, I have often called upon the Vicar to tell him of my success. My story has usually been received, at first, with polite incredulity, and, afterwards, when I have displayed the contents of my notebook, with amazement. Naturally, the Vicar finds it difficult to realize that the old men and women of his parish, whom he has known and seen day by day for many a long year, but whom he has never suspected of any musical leanings, should all the while have possessed, secretly treasured in their old heads, songs of such remarkable interest and loveliness.[20]

Our comprehension of culture is geared to literate structures of communication and to literate strategies of encoding: to texts and scores. The long invisibility of black culture had to do with the fact that most scholars were used to dealing with documents, with texts and with facts, not with interactions, performances and improvisations. Where neither texts nor documents could be found darkness or ignorance was assumed to prevail. Oral cultures, as Cecil Sharp notes, are 'secretly treasured'. Their reality is not found in a static text (consider how much time is spent in our tradition on the search for the original or pure text), but ongoing performance. Our scholarly culture is built on 'explication de textes' and on hermeneutics. The typical 'tracking devices' of historians, says Lawrence Levine, run along the tracks of documents, treaties, letters and registers. Books are the final resting place of our culture, and hermeneutics is the art of resurrection. When we apply our hermeneutic ingenuity to the textual evidence of minstrelsy or to the score of a jazz performance we miss much of what makes it artistic and successful. Black sermons when printed seem repetitive and at best quaint. Black blues are bland and obscene. Black spirituals lose their spirit when chained to the alphabet. On the other hand one should note what Louis Armstrong or Billie Holiday did with a saccharine Tin Pan Alley text or score. In other words, kinetic and oral cultures need tracking devices and analytical tools appropriate to their dramatic and ritualistic nature. For a long time black culture was seen — if seen at all — from the perch, and analyzed with the tools, of a white literate tradition. However, the limitations of exclusive literacy have not gone unnoticed by the literary avant-garde. In modernist literature there is a pervasive doubt in the power of the printed word or in language as we have come to use it (cf. Hofmannsthal, Musil, Faulkner, Joyce, Beckett, Kafka). Fluxus, Happening, Concrete Poetry are token rebellions against literate imperialism. At the same time a major change has occurred in popular culture. The revolution of the media: film, radio and television, introduced cultural channels which were more open and less hostile to dramatistic black oral tradition. These electronic media, though not strictly speaking oral, were available to the older oral performers who became the heroes of the new subculture. Though blues singers could not read or write they skilfully handled microphones and amplifiers. One should note here that the open anti-intellectualism of the counterculture of the sixties was directed against the culture of books, not against the 'plugged-in' culture of television, film or radio. In short, large parts of black oral tradition were invisible to the white dominant culture because oral items could not be 'received' on the traditional cultural channel of print without losing their appeal and artistry.

DIVISION OF LABOR AND DIVISION OF KNOWLEDGE

There is an increasing division of labor in academic disciplines and an increasing disjunction of interests. The parochialization of intellectual horizons is particularly detrimental to cultural studies. Though ample literary, linguistic and anthropological research was available to contradict many popular assumptions about blacks and black culture, many social scientists simply ignored the scholarship of other disciplines. Black poets and novelists told us much about black culture, but historians rarely read them. Amateur folklorists and music lovers demonstrated the immense artistry of black popular culture, but they remained mavericks. Classical composers and musicians (many Europeans among them) pointed out the richness of black musical tradition long before professional American musicologists took jazz seriously. One could multiply this list. The new crop of folklorists who 'dabbled' in history, linguistics and sociology, the anthropologists who were also folklorists of sorts, and the social historians who actually read black literature took a hard look at their 'tracking devices'. There has been a movement away from parochial specialization and a growing sophistication in methods.

We have only just begun to tap the immense riches of black oral tradition. Copious materials lie unanalyzed in the vaults of the Smithsonian, the Library of Congress and in collections of folklore all over the United States. Levine, Gutman, Toll, Genovese, Abrahams, Hymes, Labov, Huggins and Dundes have broken new ground in the study of black oral tradition. Their books are characterized by that sense of exhilaration which sets in when scholars find much where they expected little. And there is much more.

The tenacious nature of the Black Studies controversy over the past decades should serve as a warning that the past significance of black culture tends to be overshadowed by its powerful present meaning. Often is seems that the adversaries in these cultural battles need each other as an alibi for their own categorical positions. But it would not do to level this welter of contradictions into a middle or balanced view, for the battle of interpretations is itself a significant part of the history of black culture. In fact conflict seems to have been the one consistent aspect of it. This book proposes that the conflict-ridden nature and ambivalent interpretability of black culture is the structural imprint left on its grammar by a long history of race and class contradictions. It proceeds on the assumption that neither poets nor social analysts can afford to step outside this grammar of conflicts, but will have to understand black culture in terms of its own complex history and code. Thus the book will identify some of the structuring principles which have inspired certain of its main features. Far from being comprehensive this book will not even try to do justice to the entire corpus of black culture. Instead it will focus on some of the controversies over black culture, taking them as a vantage point to review both the nature of the conflict and the reason for it.

NOTES

1.   Stanley Elkins, *Slavery: A Problem in American Institutional and Intellectual Life* (Chicago, 1959). Robert W. Fogel and Stanley L. Engerman, *Time on the Cross: The Economics of American Negro Slavery* (Boston, 1974).

2.   This introduction makes direct or indirect references to the work of the following scholars: Roger Abrahams, *Deep Down in the Jungle . . . Negro Narrative Folklore from the Streets of Philadelphia*, rev. ed. (Chicago, 1970). Bruce Jackson, *'Get Your Ass In The Water And Swim Like Me' Narrative Poetry from Black Oral Tradition* (Cambridge, Mass., 1974). Bruce Jackson, *Wake Up Dead Man* (Cambridge, Mass., 1972). A. Paredes/R. Bauman, eds., *Toward New Perspectives in Folklore* (Austin, 1972).
     Norman Whitten/John Szwed, eds., *Afro-American Anthropology* (New York, 1970). Peter Wood, *Black Majority: Negroes in Colonial South Carolina from 1670 through the Stono Rebellion* (N.Y., 1974). Eugene Genovese, *Roll, Jordan Roll: The World the Slaves Made* (N.Y., 1974). Herbert Gutman, *The Black Family in Slavery and Freedom* (N.Y., 1976). William Labov, *Language in the Inner City. Studies in the Black English Vernacular* (Philadelphia, 1972). Dell Hymes, ed., *Re-Inventing Anthropology* (N.Y., 1974). Charles Keil, *Urban Blues* (Chicago, 1966). William L. Montell, *The Saga of Coe Ridge: A Study in Oral History* (Knoxville, 1970). Robert Toll, *Blacking Up: The Minstrel Show in Nineteenth Century America* (New York, 1974). Lawrence Levine, *Black Culture and Black Consciousness. Afro-American Folk Thought from Slavery to Freedom* (N.Y., 1977). Nathan Huggins, *Black Odyssey* (N.Y.,

1977). Much of what these social scientists have to say may be gathered from the works of black artists who articulated similar positions quite a bit earlier: W. E. B. DuBois, Langston Hughes, Richard Wright, Ralph Ellison, James Baldwin and many others.

3. The hermeneutical wind which now sweeps through the descriptive and nomological sciences has also affected the thinking of American literary and cultural historians, whose background assumptions often congeal into ragbag metaphors. Terms such as 'innocence,' 'adamic,' 'mythic,' or, more recently, 'absurdity,' 'apocalypse,' and 'culture of paradox' tend to reduce complex phenomena to a common denominator which tells us more about the mood of the critic than about the subject matter. Proclaiming their immunity to historical change and therefore their priority over the details of this world, these terms belittle the historical uniqueness of the subject matter they set out to explain. They will call to order only those contingencies of reality which willingly yield to the metaphor. The behavioral sciences were taken to task by Georges Devereux, *From Anxiety to Method in the Behavioral Sciences*. (The Hague, 1967).

4. Quoted by Keil, *Urban Blues*, p. 40. The terms 'mainline' or 'mainstream culture' as well as 'popular and high culture' are at best general orientations, not precise designations of objectively definable aggregates. The term 'mainstream' in this essay defines that body of American culture from which blacks were excluded or chose to withdraw. Mainstream or high culture does not possess a clear social structure, at best a professional or occupational structure which in turn exists in a social system. Too often the complex mediation between cultural, social, and economic systems is reduced to a type of Pavlovian mimesis which short-circuits culture and economics. For a short and cogent definition consult Raymond Williams, 'On High and Popular Culture,' *The New Republic*, November 23, 1974. Cf. footnote 2, above. See also Hermann Bausinger, 'Subkultur und Sprachen,' in *Schriften des Instituts für deutsche Sprache*, No. 13, *Sprache und Gesellschaft, Jahrbuch 1970* (Düsseldorf, 1971).

5. The idea of 'providential' or 'redemptive' history is traced by Sacvan Bercovitch, *The Puritan Origins of the American Self* (New Haven, 1975).

6. Fernand Braudel, *Capitalism and Material Life 1400-1800* (New York, 1973). Historians are presently active in correcting this neglect: cf. Tamara Hareven, ed., *Anonymous Americans* (Englewood Cliffs, 1971); Stephan Thernstrom, *The Other Bostonians* (Cambridge, 1973); Herbert Gutman and Gregory Kealy, eds., *Many Pasts: Readings in American Social History 1600 — The Present*, 2 vols. (Englewood Cliffs, 1973). For an interesting attempt to reconstruct black history from oral sources: William Lynwood Montell, *The Saga of Coe Ridge: A Study in Oral History* (Knoxville, 1970). Ernest Lee Tuveson in contrast traces the ideology of a *Redeemer Nation: The Idea of America's Millenial Role* (Chicago, 1968).

7. 'Geschichtsphilosophische Thesen', *Illuminationen* (Frankfurt, 1955). 'The Aging of America', *The American Historical Review* 82, 3 (June, 1977), p. 590: 'The South as loser sustained historic encounters with defeat, failure, poverty, and guilt that embarrassed its later efforts to

embrace the national myth of invincibility, success, opulence, and innocence. . . There were other losers, other Americans with a collective experience at fundamental variance with national myths. They included some of the oldest elements of the population, the enslaved and persecuted black people preeminently and other humiliated minorities of color, along with the rest of the impoverished.' Woodward states somewhat apodictically: 'But our own humiliated minorities have never been able to teach us what they learned at our own hands.' It seems to me that much of the new left scholarship, some of it indebted to his own work, quite clearly contradicts him. One should add that critical views of America were voiced by American literary artists of the nineteenth century: Hawthorne, Melville, Thoreau, Twain. If we stretch the word they may also qualify as 'losers' in their own day.

8.   E. Franklin Frazier, 'Tradition and Patterns of Negro Family Life in the United States,' in: E. B. Reuter, ed., *Race and Culture Contracts* (New York, 1934), p. 194; Gunnar Myrdal, *An American Dilemma* (New York, 1944), p. 928; Nathan Glazer and Daniel P. Moynihan, *Beyond the Melting Pot* (Cambridge, 1963), p. 53. For more criticism see Szwed, 'American Anthropological Dilemma,' in Dell Hymes (ed.), *Reinventing Anthropology*, p. 155–63.

9.   Ralph Ellison, *Shadow and Act* (New York, Signet book, p. 130). Ellison's work is an excellent introduction to black oral tradition for those unable to shed their literate habits. (cf. Chapter V).

10. Notably the Black Muslims and Ron Karenga. The latter in Addison Gayle, jr., ed., *The Black Aesthetic* (New York, 1971).

11. 'Slave Songs and Slave Consciousness', in Tamara Hareven (ed.), *Anonymous Americans* (Englewood Cliffs, 1971).

12. *The Black Family*.

13. Melville Herskovits, *The Myth of the Negro Past* (N.Y., 1941). A brief discussion of the Frazier-Herskovits debate is available in the introduction to *Afro-American Anthropology* by Whitten and Szwed.

14. *Shadow and Act*, p. 301. This review was rejected in 1944 by the *Antioch Review*.

15. The invisibility of minority cultures, one should add, is not a specifically American phenomenon. See note 20.

16. Black writers, Ralph Ellison among them, have focused on the tension between black self-image (achieved self) and white stereotype (ascribed self). In fact black literature reacted to and often rejected the stereotypes of scholarship. It made little difference whether scholars were racists, Social Darwinists, abolitionists, conservative Romantics, progressives or liberals, they rarely came close to the self-image of blacks. Ironically some of the racists and conservative Romantics came closer to the ironic black self-image than many of the neo-abolitionists and liberals of the sixties.

17. Clifford Geertz, 'Thick Description: Toward an Interpretive Theory of Culture,' *The Interpretation of Cultures* (New York, 1973).

18. cf. Robert Kelly, 'Ideology and Political Culture from Jefferson to Nixon,' *The American Historical Review* 82, 3 (June, 1977), p. 531–82, especially p. 554–5.

19. Time Essay, *Time*, April 6, 1970, p. 54–5.
20. *English Folk Song. Some Conclusions*, 4th Edn. (Wakefield, 1972).

II DOUBLE CONSCIOUSNESS: THE MARGINAL PERSPECTIVE IN LANGUAGE, ORAL CULTURE, FOLKLORE, RELIGION

W. E. B. DuBois was the first Afro-American to write about the self-contradictory nature of Afro-American existence and consciousness. In his pioneering work *The Souls of Black Folk* (1903), he called attention to the generative split which gives form to black culture and confuses the interpretations of it. He called it 'double consciousness,' a term at once large and ambiguous enough to encompass a complex social, cultural, and psychological phenomenon:

> After the Egyptian and Indian, the Greek and Roman, the Teuton and Mongolian, the Negro is a sort of seventh son, born with a veil, and gifted with second-sight in this American world — a world which yields him no true self-consciousness, but only lets him see himself through the revelation of the other world. It is a peculiar sensation, this double-consciousness, this sense of always looking at one's self through the eyes of others, of measuring one's soul by the tape of a world that looks on in amused contempt and pity. One ever feels this twoness — an American, a Negro; two souls, two thoughts, two unreconciled strivings; two warring ideals in one dark body, whose dogged strength alone keeps it from being torn asunder.[1]

DuBois's imaginative metaphor has become a belabored common denominator for recent Black Studies theory. It has staled for us by too much repetition and has lost its explanatory power by rampant hypostatization. However, the phenomenon has persisted and has been re-christened by various disciplines, both synchronic and diachronic.[2] Therefore it would be useful to explore its full meaning (surely intended by DuBois) by specifying the synchronic phenomena it covers (linguistic codes, symbolic universe, cognitive structures, interaction rituals, and roles), all of them exhibiting surprising inertia, and by tracing their genesis from, and resistance to, a fast-changing social arena. Where purely historical or purely structural analyses would drift into speculative derivations or settle for question-begging analogies, a combination of the two may not lead to safer answers, but may help to sharpen the questions.[3] In a world of specialists the mixing of methods which this approach calls for is often met with apprehension if not with open hostility. However, if the price of theoretical modesty and methodological purity is submerged prejudice, the results are questionable. Particularly in Black Studies, prejudice-ridden as it is, a close cooperation between the anthropological, socio-historical, and literary-linguistic disciplines is necessary. It is hardly surprising that a number of social historians begin to treat the products of folklore and of the oral tradition as 'documents' encoded by a cultural grammar, and more than one student of black history or society has gone to literature as a more reliable record than statistical facts, which the sociological 'dogma of immaculate perception' mistakenly assumes to be real.[4] 'Prefabricated Negroes are sketched on sheets of paper and superimposed upon the Negro community;' writes Ralph Ellison in *Shadow and Act* (which has become a code manual for the decoding of black cultural data), 'then when someone thrusts his head through the page and yells, "Watch out there, Jack, there's people living under here," they are shocked and indignant.'[5] For Ellison the symbolic action of literature and folklore is part of a larger system of shared meanings. Its grammar, though ultimately dependent on the social arena, has a strong internal organization and is relatively resilient and independent. The intersubjective coherence and the slow developmental rhythm of this grammar must be understood before either the individual forms of that culture or their place and use in society will begin to make sense. This is particularly true of a culture which has been defined and shaped by partial or total exclusion from the main society, an exclusion perpetuated on the basis of race, class, and poverty.

WHITE SOCIETY AND BLACK CULTURE: RACE, CLASS, AND POVERTY

The most frequent source of confusion, which has inspired a good deal of mudslinging across race and class lines, is to assume a direct mimetic and reactive correlation between culture and society, or to exaggerate their respective effects on the socialization of the individual. British labor historian E. P. Thompson warns us that 'we should not assume any automatic, or overdirect, correspondence between the dynamics of economic growth and the dynamics of social or cultural life.' E. R. Dodds has shown convincingly that, despite social upheaval, the cultural forms of Greece had a remarkable *vis inertiae*. He would agree with historian Herbert Gutman, that 'even in periods of radical economic and social change powerful cultural continuities and adaptations continue to shape the historical behavior of diverse working class populations.'[6] Cultural codes such as interaction rituals, language, and kinship behavior are not easily shed or pushed aside. Fed by subconscious sources, they acquire a strong inner coherence and have their own developmental logic, which is markedly different from that of the economic scene. Both Herbert Gutman and Sidney Mintz approvingly quote Eric Wolf's designation of culture as a 'resource' and society as the 'arena' in which it is put to use:

> . . . the distinction is between sets of historically available alternatives or forms on the one hand, and the societal circumstances or settings within which these forms may be employed, on the other. . . Without the dimension of human action, of choices made and pursued — of maneuver — culture could be thought to be a lifeless collection of habits, superstitions, and artifacts. Instead we see that culture is *used*; and that any analysis of its use immediately brings into view the arrangements of persons in social groups, for whom cultural forms confirm, reinforce, maintain, change, or deny particular arrangements of status, power, and identity.[7]

As the term 'cultural revolution' implies, culture may be out of phase with society, a situation which calls for a constant process of adjustment and which expands the 'dimension of human action.' Zygmunt Bauman remarks:

> There is an incessant struggle for the restoration of the coincidence of culture and social structure, which is missing, and actually cannot be attained, in a class society, and this struggle serves to release huge amounts of social energy.[8]

The imbalance between white society and black culture has resulted in what Ellison called 'creative tensions'. Creativity arises from the 'cross-purposes of whites and blacks,' but the attendant tensions do not seem to burden whites.[9] Many black autobiographies stress the importance of that stage in secondary socialization when the black individual becomes aware of the racial division which maintains these tensions *at his cost*. This biographical shock is followed by another lesson: that the 'huge amounts of social energy,' which this imbalance produces, will be silenced or disciplined by the black group since it would have been, and, as Huey Newton writes in his autobiography, still is 'revolutionary suicide' to act upon that energy. Therefore the black individual has been taught to internalize these tensions and conflicts or to turn them into cultural energy within the group or against the out-group, a process which over a long period of time has sedimented in self-protective, adaptive, compensatory and militant cultural behavior.

Myrdal, Frazier, and Elkins did not find any 'culture' among blacks and proceeded to interpret subcultural forms as social wounds, i.e. as mimesis of, or Pavlovian reaction to, an oppressive social scene.[10] Implied is a crude stimulus-response aesthetic, which excludes the notion of culture as a 'resource.' This aesthetic forgets that the symbolic universe of a people is itself a productive force which is able to generate a behavioral charter for managing and overcoming social repression. Moreover, the intersubjective context of shared meanings constitutes a coherent play world which provides cognitive and emotive alternatives to an oppressive social arena: culture may be identity-therapy, but is always also an end in itself. Last but not least the symbolic universe of a people protects its 'dream history' and generates 'strategies of dream realization.'[11]

Admittedly the external social circumstances changed considerably — from Africa to plantation slavery, to sharecropping, to the ghettos of the industrialized North — and the cultural resources of blacks, be they material or symbolic, adapted to, or slipped into, existing slots of the host society. However, the symbolic universe has its own momentum.[12] Its *vis inertiae* increases as we move from the conscious into the unconscious, from linguistic and cognitive levels to sensory levels and role and motor behavior. Though the social organization and hierarchy of the African groups which arrived in America was destroyed and the powerful authorities who maintained and preserved cultural behavior (shamans, medicine men, chiefs) were divested of their power, there was enough in-group cohesion to salvage a good deal of African culture: (1) least on the purely linguistic level (syntax), (2) more in kinship behavior (naming practices, burial, marriage), (3) considerably in the cognitive realm (beliefs, voodoo, superstitions, tales etc.), and (4) most on the level of motor behavior (music, dance, rhythm).[13] Basic similarities between cultures made it easy for some of these African forms to settle into existing American cultural structures. Such palimpsests are particularly evident in religion and music: while they share sufficient surface similarities with white culture and thus may be understood in the context of a larger American grammar (which blacks helped to create), they are part of an internal black frame of reference as well.[14] On the other hand, much of what today is called typically black is due to class or poverty factors.[15] Economic marginality and lack of access to capital resources, artificially maintained over a long period of time, have resulted in the so-called matrifocality of black families, in role behavior such as Samboism, in work behavior which Thorstein Veblen characterized as 'conscious withdrawal of efficiency,' and in traditions of 'hustling', i.e. of ego-centered personal net-works for short-range material gains.[16]

In short, adaptation to economic and social factors caused certain cultural forms to arise which differ considerably from those of the mainstream culture. The 'bicultural ambivalence' or 'double consciousness' they mirror is, however, quite similar to that of other working-class populations and not attributable to African retentions.

Another important background assumption of social scientists and cultural historians has been that acculturation in America was a one-way journey from Africa to America, from primitivism to civilization, from mule to Cadillac. Sidney Mintz argues that the 'cultural life of such countries as Brazil and the United States is heavily "africanized," no matter what the physical appearance of those who reveal this culture stream in their behavior.'[17] And Ralph Ellison speculates, tongue in cheek, 'What America Would Be Like Without Blacks,' a question which upsets the dubious assumption that after all America civilized the African.

> Materially, psychologically, and culturally, part of the nation's heritage is Negro American, and whatever it becomes will be shaped in part by the Negro's presence. Which is fortunate, for today it is the black American who puts pressure upon the nation to live up to its ideals. It is he who gives creative tension to our struggle for justice and for the elimination of those factors, social and psychological, which make for slums and shaky suburban communities. It is he who insists that we purify the American language by demanding that there be a closer correlation between the meaning of words and reality, between ideal and conduct, our assertions and our actions. Without the black American, something irrepressibly hopeful and creative would go out of the American spirit, and the nation might well succumb to the moral slobbism that has ever threatened its existence from within.[18]

Ellison's cautiously optimistic appraisal of black culture as an inspiring or creative element of tension and as criticism of the total culture again raises the question of the Afro-American's role in society. In contradistinction to whites, Ellison says elsewhere, blacks have to bear 'the uneasy burden and occasional joy of a complex double vision, a fluid, ambivalent response to men and events which represents, at its finest, a profoundly civilized adjustment to the cost of being human in this modern world.'[19] The question remains whether this appraisal of black double consciousness applies to all members or only to the 'finest' who were equipped in their youth with a healthy sense of entitlement.

DOUBLE CONSCIOUSNESS AND SOCIALIZED AMBIVALENCE

What DuBois called 'double consciousness' and Ellison 'double vision' refers to an identity conflict and to a schizoid phenomenon evident in all human interaction and communication. Its cause may be the stigma of race, color, class, or physical disability.[20] Its anthropological basis has encouraged many literary and cultural critics to exaggerate the existential character of this phenomenon of black life. Indeed, some recent historians have fashioned double consciousness into an American trade mark. According to their thesis, everyone, white or black, was socialized into a pervasive national ambivalence, due to the 'biformity' or 'split nature' of the American 'national style.'[21] This integrationist gesture, which forces a variety of socio-cultural conflicts into an all-American norm and which domesticates current anxieties by americanizing their genesis, belittles the 'wounds' of black socialization and embezzles the 'bow' of black cultural resources. Black double consciousness is more than an existential constant; it has both a deeper historical and anthropological dimension, the first defined by slavery and segregation along a color line, the second by African cultural retentions.

Melville Herskovits proposed in a discussion of Haitian culture that the Afro-American acculturation process should not be seen as an amalgam of two traditions, but as 'two sets of counterposed values or behavioral alternatives,' one African and the other Euro-American. The fourfold choice which is involved — affirmation or rejection of Africa, affirmation or rejection of Euro-America, and its myriad variations — makes for a rather complex socialization process. Herskovits named its behavioral results 'socialized ambivalence': 'it is responsible for the many shifts in allegiance that continually take place as it is for the change in attitude in everyday association.'[22] Despite far-reaching economic or demographic changes this bicultural or schizogenic socialization pattern of blacks has been relatively consistent. The high visibility of blacks has put a brake on that pattern of acculturation and upward mobility normally enjoyed by most other immigrant groups. Whatever educational and occupational improvement did occur tended to give a radical edge to double consciousness; thus the seeming paradox that the most acculturated blacks are often the most militant. A study of the social mobility of minorities in Boston concludes that black upward mobility had its own logic; no matter how far the Afro-American had gone up the social ladder, the comparable white minorities had gone farther, surely a reinforcement and growing radicalization of double consciousness.[23]

In short, double consciousness has to be understood as a result of existential predispositions, reinforced and maintained by cultural and social factors. It refers to the schizogenic split between being and having a body, radicalized by the color stigma: a flourishing industry is devoted to the elimination of the *black body* in order to be *somebody*. The black-is-beautiful campaign should not be taken as a cosmetic fad, but as a revaluation of deeply rooted American mainstream values which implicitly required this self-annihilation. Double consciousness furthermore refers to the awareness of cultural alternatives, kept alive by social exclusion, and it refers to the awareness of a class difference, often kept alive on the basis of color or poverty. There is ample evidence of double consciousness in language and interaction, which is both content and instrument of socialization.

THE HYPHENATE LANGUAGE OF AFRO-AMERICA

Language is basic to any study of culture. On more levels than the merely syntactical, it contains the 'grammar' of cultural behavior. We know from comparative studies of immigrant acculturation that upward mobility set in when the incoming group had mastered not only the occupations but also the language of the host society. This process was normally completed after a minimum of one and a maximum of two or three generations. It is therefore singularly significant that after 400 years of exposure to the mainstream culture blacks continue to speak their own version of English.[24] The controversy between consensus and conflict linguists has pivoted on African retentions or American assimilation. The consensus school could easily demolish the Africanists by pointing out that, whatever residual Africanisms were still extant, the structure and function of black English was geared to the American societal arena, i.e. that it was syntactically and sociologically American. Differences of accent and intonation were explained as rural or poor variants of mainstream English or as retentions of English dialects maintained by the tradition-bound South. In contrast the advocates of black English pointed out that it would not do merely to analyze structure and function of black English; one ought to investigate pockets of African retentions or peculiarly Afro-American evolutions particularly in the cognitive system and in senso-motoric behavior hitherto neglected by linguists. Again we should ask a set of questions matching social history, linguistics, and anthropology. (1) What was (or may have been) the linguistic preparation of those who came over from a variety of African backgrounds? What happened to them in terms of schooling or language socialization? How much of their old culture and language were they allowed to keep, how much did they keep at their own discretion? (2) How strongly did the master-slave interaction affect black English? Did role playing, *double-entendre*, and the dialectic between affirmation and rejection create certain cognitive structures? (3) How much did the pathology of class oppression and poverty contribute to maintain African forms? Did the lack of schooling create specific oral forms of English which are mistakenly called African?

In other words, the blackness of current Afro-American English cannot be explained solely on the basis of structural or formal analogies between seventeenth-century Africa and twentieth-century America, nor should current political interests induce the neo-abolitionist historian to construct questionable derivations through the jungle of creolization and pidginization in order to create a vista for his own assumptions, however noble they may be.

Since we know precious little about early black English, many of the questions cannot be answered. However, it is possible to reconstruct the historical scene or parts of the scene on which the acquisition of language and role behavior took place. The African slaves came from a variety of linguistic and cultural backgrounds. The thorough description of the Amistad captives reveals that quite a large number of slaves was conversant in more than one African language and Gustavus Vasa reports in the narrative of his enslavement that he could understand though not speak several African languages.[25] Surprisingly the Amistad captives were as eager to acquire English as some modern cultural nationalists are to readopt Swahili. However strong the linguistic shock may have been, the African slaves were not unaware of linguistic differences and were not unwilling to acquire English if given the chance. The question is whether they were given a chance or not. Peter Wood has this to say about the ambivalence of white masters toward language instruction:

> Every master whose Negroes knew no English was courting inefficiency and misfortune. But slaves who developed the greatest facility in English were also the most forward leaders in other ways, and whites were quick to emphasize this dangerous relationship. 'The Negroes are generally very bad men,' the Rev. Le Jau was informed, 'chiefly those that are Scholars.' Such observations among whites meant that after the first generation, contrary to accepted dogma, most new Negroes learned the local language not from Englishmen but from other slaves, a factor which reinforced the distinctiveness of the dialect.[26]

Since literacy carried the germs of discontent and revolt, slaves were denied access to the main culture, which, though it did its utmost to instil obedience and faith in the slave, could not withold the emancipatory and revolutionary message of Christianity. Therefore whites would rather give up instruction of blacks altogether. Cultural exclusion meant that blacks had to fall back on the resources of their oral tradition and to work with their own socialization agencies. This race, class and language separation gave them a chance to maintain forms of their African oral culture and to adapt them to American plantation requirements. It encouraged the retention of such pockets of African culture as would improve work morale and at the same time reinforce in-group cohesion and cultural solidarity: field holler, field song, spiritual, folk tale, proverb, kinship lore, etc.

The oral environment of the early colonies required of the

slave to cull from English an oral medium plus gestures, body language, pitch, and rhythm which would bridge the many different African dialects, and at the same time establish a working communication with the master. This turns the tangle of linguistic and interactional syncretisms, commonly called creolization or pidginization, into an insoluble mystery, in semantics more so than in syntax. One thing we may safely assume, namely, that the in-group cohesiveness of blacks speaks for a relatively consistent socialization and that this socialization was not merely mimesis of white behavior or language. But neither the retention of Africanisms nor the acquisition of 'good' English was unaffected by the master-slave interaction. Peter Wood writes:

> Quite apart from any white reluctances [to teach slaves English], the slaves had serious reservations of their own about the acquisition of English. Proficiency could be a means of advancement, but standard English could not, and never would, provide so simple a key to upward mobility for blacks as it did for white newcomers. And if knowledge of 'good' English could occasionally be used to advantage, as in eavesdropping or newspaper reading, 'bad' English was discovered to be an equally effective weapon. To cultivate a dialect few whites could understand and to be able to adopt a stance of incomprehension toward their masters' speech proved effectual elements of resistance.[27]

Wood characterizes the speech behavior of seventeenth-century slaves. By the twentieth century, oppression had bred a wide repertoire of survival strategies, from a feigned identification with the oppressor's values to the role-playing of illiteracy. (Modern black English knows 'shucking', 'jiving', 'joning', 'sounding', 'signifying', 'copping a plea', 'rapping', 'running it down', 'woofing', 'talking shit', 'telling it like it is', as various forms of speech behavior with in-group or out-group function.) Though analogies across long timespans are dangerous, black speech behavior then and now reveals remarkable similarities. Here is a description of how Charlie Parker, on tour in the Southern states during the 1940s, would deal with the problem. Ross Russell, the author of these lines, knew Charlie Parker from a long and troubled business relationship.

> His ability to act out roles dictated by unequal encounters . . . now proved to be of the greatest value — as he saw it, it was the key to

survival. An accomplished mimic, Charlie began to study the regional speech and manners of Negroes trapped in the cotton-and-turpentine economies of Alabama, Mississippi, and Texas. A narrow line separated 'acting out' from 'copping out'. It was possible to allay hostility and soften confrontations by improvising the necessary roles, just as one might improvise a successful jazz solo. With skill and experience it was even possible to act out parts and convert such situations into charades played at the expense of the oppressor.[28]

Charlie Parker consciously acted out that minstrel Sambo-role, which Stanley Elkins mistook as an internalized form of pathology. Russell makes several interesting connections between language, jazz, and improvisation, which will be explored later. What strikes us most forcibly is the similarity of the behavior which Wood found documented in descriptions of seventeenth-century blacks and that of a highly sophisticated twentieth-century urban black jazz musician. The combination of verbal insolence, of linguistic resistance, of 'putting on massa!' and of play, which has gone into the making of this linguistic and behavioral code, is complex. Critics with strong consensus assumptions have stressed the debasement inherent in this behavior, rightly pointing out its 'deviance' from American mainstream behavior. Recently critics, animated by the appreciation of black folklore and music, have argued against a facile dismissal of black linguistic forms and behavioral patterns.[29] The safety and in-group solidarity of these necessarily subservient roles, they claim, protected and shielded a growing sophistication in mastering conflicts using the resources of language and mimicry. Developed in labor and *refined* in play, this behavioral code masked a consciousness which understood both oppressor and oppressed. A blues explains it: 'Got one mind for white folks to see, 'nother for what I know is me.' Thus the 'frozen' and 'infanticized' attitude which the slave displayed in black-white encounters camouflaged a consciousness which had to remain mobile and dynamic. Blacks have been in a constant linguistic and histrionic-interactionist state of alert, from 1619 to this day (a fact which recent studies relate to the high frequency of hypertension and high blood pressure among blacks).[30] The feeling of impending crisis and disaster (cf. Wright's *Bigger Thomas* or Iceberg Slim's remarks in *Pimp*), the need to deal constantly with 'the man,' the constant reminder of a dual status, the persistent categorical division between black and white America; all these created a communicative competence of remarkable versatility, resourcefulness and, one should add, explosiveness.

Russell observes that the line between 'acting out' and 'copping out' is very thin. Indeed, it has often been asked how Sambo or Uncle Tom could preserve their humanity. Again we should pay attention to the 'thickness' of such behavior, and ought not to jump from surface symptoms to psychological or sociological conclusions. At this point of the argument a brief reference to minstrelsy, which is perhaps the most elaborate outgrowth of this interactive dialectic, will suffice (more in the next chapter). While minstrelsy was started as a white ritual (ca. 1830) which by imitating black behavior in a grotesquely exaggerated manner exorcised the burden of white prejudice, it came into its own through the alienation and implicit rejection of that form by black performers, who, intent on gaining recognition (i.e. surviving in the social arena of entertainment), had to cap the exaggerated and degrading antics of white performers by refining their imitation of a grotesque imitation of themselves. Their double-conscious rendition was often lost on white audiences who were fully satisfied to have their secret prejudices confirmed by the subjects of their derision. Supplementing Gottman's phenomenological description (n. 20, above) with a touch of history, we might say that black performer and white audience are here acting out a *historically* conditioned interaction ritual. Whites are caught in the 'pure' entertainment of the front stage performance, paying little or no attention to the backstage conspiracy between performer and black audience. The latter shared the code by which the white man was being put on and at the same time beaten at his own racist hustle.[31] Black English is trained in this double-edged semantics which permits black performers to set a double scene of interaction: one for the oppressor and one for the oppressed with quite opposite cognitive and cathartic functions. We might consider this radicalization of a universal interactionist phenomenon by race and class factors as the central key to the code of black communication. Ellison uses it in his novel *Invisible Man*, where the 'jiu-jitsu of the spirit' in grandfather's advice is the central metaphor of survival. Grandfather is the holder of the cultural wisdom of black oral culture. He tells the protagonist-grandchild to resist the white man by yessing him to death, to parade denial as agreement and truth as lie. In Ellison's short story 'Flying Home,' a similar figure, Jefferson (mark the historical name), tells a typical 'folk lie,' a story which smuggles historical consciousness past white social and cultural censors by parading it as hilarious entertainment. Folk truth must become a comic lie to survive in history, an inversion typical of black cultural forms. (cf. Chapter V)

Ellison has remarked that this overcompensatory cultural and interactionist training gave black English a deeper resourcefulness in terms of style.[32] Style is geared to linguistic performance, i.e. the *acting out* of communicative competence. Performance has both a linguistic and theatrical meaning, it is a dynamic category pointing to the oral realization of language. In oral cultures performance and style are central, while little attention is paid to textual complexity and discursive logic. This problem, hinted at in the first chapter, needs to be explored further.

ORAL VERSUS LITERATE CULTURES[33]

'Literate society,' writes Ben Sidran in *Black Talk*,[34] 'often turns a deaf ear to the implications of an oral culture.' When it does listen the custodians of literate culture tend to misinterpret the forms of oral cultures since they would automatically measure them against the norms set by literacy. The term 'oral tradition' is normally associated with low-class culture. Enlightened literate society might accept its forms as quaint, regional, or pre-literate, but rarely as an expression of what is generally accepted as 'culture.' 'For a social elite,' says Gramsci, 'the features of subordinate groups always display something barbaric and pathological.'[35] This is particularly true if the subordinate group in question depends on the formally flexible dynamics of oral transmission to maintain its cultural treasures. Recent scholarship has tried to approach oral culture without the literate presuppositions of our post-Gutenberg society. The following ideal type differentiation may be presented as a summary of their scholarship.

Oral cultures are functional, tactile, auditory and direct. They stress oral performance and the attendant improvisational skills. The reception of the performance is immediate and patterned on collective rituals. In contrast, literate cultures will depend more on visual aids and on the formal and thematic complexity or *wholeness* of the text. The reception of these texts is individualized and fragmented; it is controlled by conditioned, introverted, often quasi-religious responses. Oral cultures are dramatic, literate cultures epistemic in their focus of attention; the first develops the resources of spontaneity, style, affective performance, and catharsis, the second scrutiny, contemplation, or that Romantic art called 'recollection in tranquillity.' Oral folklore reasserts its social genesis and function in its performance, whereas the relative 'autonomy' of literary texts has been postulated on the basis of the constitutional self-reflexiveness of literary products. Literacy engenders historical norms for the production and reception of culture; the resultant lag between past and present forms or habits of reception has to be made functional (i.e. usable for the present) through constant hermeneutical effort. This has created the need and economic niche for exegetical skills such as literary criticism, the very existence of which belies the autonomy of its subject matter. Literacy also puts a brake on semantic freedom and creativity; semantic ratification and adoption into usage are slow and laborious processes. Innovations, adaptations and neologisms are treated as intruders, and subcultural improprieties run into a wall of purists. By contrast, in oral cultures semantic ratification is immediate and linguistic invention the norm. They are warm hosts to loan words and breeding grounds for neologisms and slang. They favor performance words over content words, i.e. words with affective rather than cognitive wealth. Echoes of this 'oral modality' of black speech are to be found in black poetry even today.

Literacy puts a high premium on the message. The audience of oral cultures, though hardly indifferent to the message of their relatively stable tradition, will value the performer for his ability to *create a mood*. Even in forensic situations, in verbal battles, the ability to control a competitive and ambivalent social encounter and to raise the affective sympathy of the audience are more important than the doctrinal or moral truth of a position. The better performer wins. Due to their dramatistic nature oral cultures have a different sense of past and present; indeed they seem to operate in a perpetual present and incorporate all that is functional for everyday survival in a finite, but ever-present province of customs, beliefs, and rituals, the aggregate of which is identical with the active memory of the group. Present needs are the memory filter; this accounts for the structural amnesia which keeps out bothersome inconsistencies of the past. As a result the symbolic universe of oral cultures never expands greatly beyond the horizon of the present collective. They are finite and sedentary and, one should add, conservative and nationalistic.[36] Their chauvinism is due to a strong adherence to a policy of withholding choice and of stabilizing that balance of controls which has guaranteed survival until now. By way of compensation they will create a sense, however unfree, of togetherness and the means of ritual catharsis. But this togetherness will turn into a trap whenever any one member wants to assert his individuality and advance beyond the horizon of the group. Booker T. Washington called this the 'crab basket effect,' that protective mechanism by which the black group keeps the individual away from the dangers of the white forces outside, dangers controlled by collective rituals, which both blacks and whites thoughtlessly accept.[37]

Literate cultures apart from broadening individual horizons may equally become the victims of their progressiveness. They will branch out in all directions of knowledge until it becomes difficult for any one member to participate fully in his literate-historical tradition. The liberation of the individual from mythical or ritual shackles is matched by the dangers of alienation (both from his tradition and his group) and class stratification. Differing degrees of literacy, which implies access to social mobility, and the power struggle over the distribution and control of literary products contribute to class conflict.

Obviously the oral society sketched above exists only in theory. Oral culture never was totally isolated from the mainstream literate culture of America, nor has her culture always been literate. Literacy which built upon illiteracy continued to tease the oral culture it left behind in a manner so complex that an ideal model is the only backdrop against which the welter of influences and counterinfluences may be disentangled. The ideal type is a special instance of what is probable and possible; its purity brings into focus the differences between model and reality, thus defining both. In no case should the 'oral model' be misunderstood as a moral or pastoral ideal. Indeed, we should expect reality to correct or even negate the model. In comparing black oral culture to our model we see that traditional oral culture, which is conservative when taken for itself, may provide an effective countercultural alternative when it meets with the myths of an alienated literate consciousness.[38] For one thing black oral culture lacks the sense of tradition as 'burden'; therefore its present will not appear as 'attenuation' when compared to a glorious past and a dubious future (Faulkner's world view), nor as 'progress' when compared to the dark past and a bright future. The 'irony' of Southern black history has kept alive a strong sense of *ongoing* reality.[39] Furthermore, the advantage of that conceptual freedom, on which enlightened literacy prides itself, is often matched with a curious disapprobation of emotive and cathartic liberation and a fear of sensuality. In contrast, black oral culture and folklore has been trained for centuries in the art of squeezing a large measure of emotional 'liberty' from the enjoyment of the here and now, thus to make the lack of civil and conceptual liberty tolerable. This talent has not gone unnoticed by the mainstream culture. White America turned this cultural resource of blacks into an obsessive stereotype — blacks have rhythm, enjoy sex, and have fun. Leslie Fiedler noted the sense of cultural envy in white American literature for black forms, but quite unnecessarily reduced it to a homosexual fantasy. Stereotypes are fossilized exorcistic social rituals with a *historical* basis; they are proportionate to the sense of alienation which produced them. An obvious point is the complex of guilt, time, and history. Ishmael, in *Moby Dick*, (a figure in which modern critics love to recognize themselves) suffers from the burden of his puritan upbringing and has the November blues fueled by his discontent with civilization. He envies the primitive who is not obsessed with original sin, with the nightmare of history, and with the inexorable sense of temporal attenuation.

It is evident from the above discussion that a strong concept of original sin cannot take hold in an imagination that has no need to differentiate between past significance and present meaning and that turns all things past into present functionality. The black sense of time grew out of an awareness that the present had to be mastered before one could hope for the future; and 'yestiddy can take care ob itself,' as a black proverb has it. 'CPT' (colored people time), as it is called from a protestant nine-to-five perspective, shows a strong resistance to a work ethic which is the result of the past flogging the present into the promise of a bright future. It is moot to argue how much of this resistance is due to African retentions, to oral culture, or to a 'conscious withdrawal of efficiency' by a pre-industrial people meeting a capitalist work ethic which exclusively serves the oppressor.[40] The lack of original sin and the attendant 'aristocratic' sense of time was noted by Ralph Ellison and Eugene Genovese; the latter suggests that the difference may be one between guilt and shame cultures.[41] Ruth Benedict's paradigm, though it freezes the dialectic between culture and society, brings several puzzling phenomena into focus. Obviously Western culture, particularly its American offshoot, is a guilt-ridden culture, obsessed therefore with a usable (or afraid of a nonusable) past. The sins of our fathers return as our own and burden our present and future. Guilt cultures refine the means of objectifying their past in literature, constantly encouraged by the need to explain the internalization of original sin. As Dodds has shown, Greek culture turned from shame to guilt with the advent of literacy, i.e. when division of labor within the Greek symbolic universe set in after the demise of mythical-oral totality.

The guilt, time, and history complex is lacking in black oral culture. For one thing blacks had nothing to feel guilty for; indeed they knew well that they represented an objectification of the white man's guilt. Instead black oral culture focuses on shame, humiliation, and dignity. As Dodds says, shame culture, particularly when there is a 'deepened awareness of human insecurity and helplessness' in the face of external odds, will counteract anxiety and chaos by maintaining a strong sense of individual dignity, which is the antidote to shame. Slave narratives repeatedly stress the importance of maintaining personal dignity against heavy odds. Dignity was the barrier which had to be broken before a slave would sink into pathological behavior. And it was broken by the whip, by the auction block, and the rack. Respect of personal identity and dignity in conduct and behavior are dominant themes in black oral culture.[42] (There is enough evidence of it today; Aretha Franklin and Otis Redding turned their song 'Respect' into a popular hit, and James Brown's music is one long ode to black self-respect.) Social psychologists make the suggestive observation that socialization into inferiority, which the out-group imposes on blacks on the basis of color, would develop a sense of individual shame proportionate to the success of the negative indoctrination.[43] The weapon of dignity and self-respect fights the foreign definition and negation of self.

Shame cultural behavior is obvious in black culture in proportion to white cultural dominance: hair straighteners and skin bleachers are objectifications of a shame that runs deep into the unconscious. The black–is–beautiful campaign stresses the dignity and beauty of blackness. Dodds writes that shame cultures are obsessed with impurity and have greater need for cathartic rituals than do guilt cultures. Although it is difficult to draw a line between anthropological and socio–historical determinants of such behavior, the richness of social rituals of black America would support the speculations of cultural anthropologists. Herbert Gutman in his book on the *Black Family* makes the suggestion that the exogamic purity of Afro–American kinship patterns has nothing to do with what the slave could have learned or seen in the South. Here the popular theory of cultural mimesis is massively contradicted by recent finding. In other words, the slave did not pattern his family structure and kinship behavior on that of the whites — who were strongly endogamic — but, perhaps, retained a good deal of African behavior, which in turn was reinforced by demands of the slavery system on the one hand and by the strong oral culture and by racial exclusion on the other. With this in mind, certain scenes in black literature, such as Trueblood's impure act and his catharsis through the blues, acquire a deep historical and anthropological dimension.

The relationship between oral and literate cultures is particularly important in terms of their respective social organization. Oral culture and folklore, as we have seen, represent a sedimentation of behavior and ritual, developed as a quasi-instinctive reaction to social forces and refined or expanded in play.[44] However, its forms are not made conscious and its rituals remain more or less automatic. Such behavior, as Booker T. Washington, Ralph Ellison, James Baldwin, Malcolm X and many black poets have noticed, is both protection and trap. The sedentary power of folk ideologies and the strict maintenance of the survival techniques of oral cultures are manifested in punitive measures against those individuals who try to break the rules. However, unless made conscious, these patterns of behavior tend to recreate the pathology of socio-psychological bondage even after the material or political causes of this pathology have been changed or removed.[45] Black oral culture has a multitude of terms for this type of behavior: 'slave habits,' 'Uncle Tom', 'handkerchief head,' and last but not least 'don't act like a nigger,' but even these terms are used within ritualized behavior. Since the roots of this behavior reach deeply into the irrational, it can only be shed under great pains and after enduring near-destructive conflicts. This has been a constant theme of black literature. The function of black artists within their black communities, their social act, is to counteract the repressive force of ritualized behavior by lifting it from thoughtlessness into consciousness, from social habit into aesthetic form, from the oral into the literate mode. Their concern is similar to that of some current anthropological studies, namely 'to put people in control of their personal destinies.'[46] Black art is a form of externalizing the wounds of historically conditioned socialization patterns. These have to be objectified and isolated as art before they can be successfully transcended. (The question remains — transcended by whom.)

At the same time, oral cultures, as Richard Wright has observed in his influential essay 'Blueprint for a Negro Writing,'[47] hold the 'usable past' of literate cultures, often serving as a pastoral or pre-industrial antidote to the poison of industrialization. Oral cultures, when left to their own devices, are preoccupied with the present. When put to use in a literate context they serve the function of a pastoral, golden age. Indeed their materials are lifted from social determination into an idealized 'autonomy' and are translated from social fact or praxis into fictive and therefore self-reflexive transcendence. Literate cultures permit man to enter into a fruitful dialogue between himself and various objectified self-images. As long as social and cultural behavior is thoughtless ritual — as it still is in the ghettos — it cannot be understood, but only acted out. When it becomes art, it *may be* recognized and re-enacted, inviting enlightenment instead of perpetuating bondage. Black American literature, as well as literature in general, has often served this function of debunking social stereotypes and of making known the meaning of ritualized behavior. It stands to reason that not all literate culture automatically liberates. We are at the moment only concerned with the *additional* potential of the literate medium, not with its actual use or misuse. One could write a social history of black stereotypes and demonstrate that their death was coincident with their appropriation by and display in literary or dramatic form (see Chapter III).

BLACK ORAL FOLKLORE: THE INDIRECTION OF RESISTANCE[49]

The reluctance of folklorists, literary critics, and anthropologists to deal with Afro-American culture had a number of reasons. While most of them were political, some had to do with the impure nature of the material. In distant cultures, which were protected by inaccessibility, the researcher could find 'pure' folk and rely on the data he received from friendly natives. Afro-America offered no such data nor such friendly natives. The data were at best syncretisms and the informants were at worst over-friendly. The material and symbolic culture of black America had been in a constant process of adaptation or rejection of white models by the time folklorists and linguists took to the field. Field research, particularly when conducted by whites, was always victim of the ambivalence created by white cultural dominance. Many 'natives' kept 'putting on massa' and 'yessed' him to death with his own background assumptions, which the informant intuited from the question.[50] But even those informants who willingly cooperated were victims of the hegemonial socialization which prevented them from making or wanting to make a true assessment of their class or culture. Traditional folklorists, pursuing the pure folk text with philological methods, were duly frustrated by the chaos of the material, the deviance of the informants and the impossibility to trace clean forms. Since they were not concerned with the social organization of their material they mistook some acculturation data as proof of the basic American nature of the material and went back to their less politically burdened and professionally more rewarding European or primitive fields. The shift in interest from text to performance and from a description of the data to an analysis of their social base and function has reopened the discussion.[51] Black literature played an important role in rescuing folk culture from oblivion. Quite a number of white scholars were alerted or awakened by black artists who opened their eyes to what prejudice had made invisible.[52]

We know little about the actual genesis of these oral forms of black folklore. Again we can reconstruct the historical scene and the interaction which spawned these forms. This approach gains in reliability when we consider that the basic symbolic structure of black subculture has been as stable as its socio-psychological causes, the divisive force of the color line. Oral

Folklore, both rural and urban, though exposed to changing economic and demographic conditions, was employed to combat and control a rather similar set of individual and collective problems. The social progress normally associated with urbanization was halted or even rolled back by ghettoization. The culture of poverty, so typical of the rural South, survived the trip North; in black ghettos today black Southern culture is held in high esteem although the South as a political system is strongly despised. The social control function of rural black lore found an urban continuum in street, turf, and prison culture. The careful socialization of rural blacks into a self-protective pattern of behavior was continued by the more sophisticated and aggressive 'College of the Street,' albeit with more urgency, despair, and fatalism. What are the basic socio-psychological functions of this new but old oral culture? They are: (1) To deal with socialized ambivalence by naming the anxieties produced by the color stigma, poverty, and economic marginality and by hyperbolizing them to the point of rejecting their dehumanizing effects. (2) To overcome and counteract situations of irreconcilable conflict by creating a mood of participatory catharsis; to socialize adolescents into the rituals of the black in-group and to teach them the rituals of survival in black-white encounters; to serve as a fictive frame or scene on which dangerous social situations may be enacted playfully in order to immunize adolescents against those dangers; to provide a platform for the individual who may obtain a sense of pride from a successful performance before the group and who may enjoy a feeling of short-term power and control over an audience; to overcome both the alleged lack of a viable past and a viable future by making the most of instant gratification. (3) To maintain race and class consciousness by embedding its wisdom in spontaneous entertainment or religious ecstasy.[53]

None of these functions exist in isolation; all of them could be analyzed in greater depth and detail. Their respective importance varies according to time, place, and external cause or internal logic of the situation. However, we see that the traditional division of folklore materials into motif-indexes or secular vs. sacred slots tends to pass by the social organization. In function and organization secular and sacred black culture are indeed quite similar, but a moral and institutional division has kept them separate. The amalgamation of both traditions into gospel/soul culture is coincident with the breakdown of institutionalized morals. Even before this breakdown the frequent conversions of blues singers and the ease with which they slipped into their new religious roles, indicates that the same talents were required for holding or controlling the same set of socio-psychological anxieties; blues and spiritual share their basis in black oral culture.[54]

Black folk tales, songs, poems, and proverbs show both the wisdom of sedimented folk experience and their function as survival rituals clearly. Frederick Douglass records in his autobiography (1855) the song of a juba beater and comments: 'The performer improvises as he beats, and sings his merry songs, so ordering the words as to have them fall pat with the movement of his hands.' The poem which Douglass calls 'merry' is in fact about exploitation. It expresses the knowledge, certainly shared by all blacks, that the Afro-American had to create a product through his labor and has received nothing or only a fraction of its value in return.

> We raise de wheat,
> Dey gib us de corn;
> We bake de bread,
> Dey gib us de cruss;
> We sif de meal,
> Dey gib us de huss;
> We peal de meat,
> Dey gib us de skin,
> And dat's de way
> Dey takes us in.
> We skim de pot,
> Dey gib us the liquor,
> And say dat's good enough for nigger.
> Walk over! Walk over!
> Tom butter and de fat;
> Poor nigger you can't get over dat;
> Walk over![55]

Judged with the 'grammar' of the dominant culture one would call the text of this poem 'quaint' or 'charming' as respectable historians have done. But culture lies not only in the text. The fact that a 'merry song' should be based on the 'palpable injustice and fraud of slavery' was noted by Douglass, who attributed it to the endurance of blacks, a stereotype which has survived into William Faulkner's work. Instead we should note the thickness of both code and interaction. We may assume that this song would not have been tolerated by Southern censors were it not for the humor and self-irony. The front stage entertainment, which even white masters loved to indulge in, and the scenic props of linguistic and rhythmic quaintness protect the backstage consciousness. The black persona seems to imply: I know the white man better than he does himself because I have to do his work in order for me — and him — to survive. However, the revolutionary and bitter script is transformed by the *mise-en-scène* and the dramaturgy. The white audience took such staging as evidence of the constitutional happiness of blacks. While the white master would thus find a justification for his 'paternalistic rule,' since obviously black happiness had something to do with it, black singer and audience understood each other on yet another level. The singer, raised in an oral tradition which provided the formula, had learned to draw pleasure from his recognition of injustice, and his audience shared both his talent for improvisation and the complicity of the interaction plot. There is no scream, no harshness, no false posturing (other than that meant to mislead the master's attention) and none of the shrillness of some contemporary political or didactic poetry which wants to dictate our response. Comedy here is an underhanded stratagem which smuggles truth past the master's defenses which are down with laughter. His laughter is quite different from that of blacks who are aware of the success of their stratagem. Twentieth-century whites were shocked to see the very same sentiment surface without the comedy. Nate Shaw, an illiterate black share cropper from Alabama, expresses the black power sentiment of the poem to his interviewer Theodore Rosengarten: 'I was born and raised here and I have sowed my labor into the earth and lived to reap only a part of it, not all that was mine by human right.' And then he adds as an afterthought: 'I stays on if it gives them satisfaction for me to leave, and I stays on because it's mine.'[56] While Douglass' songster was left unmolested, Nate Shaw was imprisoned for his politics. Nate Shaw came out of his prison experience unbroken. What DuBois called 'dogged strength' and what Faulkner existentialized as 'endurance' has a deep cultural dimension. The next poem relates work and Christian ideology:

Our Fader which art in heaben,
White man owe me eleben and pay me seben
D'y kingdom come, d'y will be done,
If I hadn't tuck dat I wouldn't git none.

Here the white Lord's Prayer with its promise of justice is placed alongside black experience. The black persona pays his respect to God, who is the highest representative of a benevolent patriarchal and paternalistic order. The next line, however, shows an awareness that in the Southern variant of paternalism double standards prevail and that God's chain of command is out of order. Religious promise up above, materialist practice down below. Implied is the suspicion that God may be for whites only. The final line captures well that curious dialectic between cognitive and cathartic functions: it expresses the collective determination to survive and the knowledge that this survival has to be paid for with a temporary acquiescence to injustice. This backstage knowledge, with its bitter and long history, is transformed *for the time being* into entertainment and laughter, which fills the front stage.

The trickster tale is known in both Europe and Africa. In the Afro-American context, its universal pattern acquires a very special social base. Pitted in an uneven battle with the white man, the black man has to use all his wits to compensate for his social and physical weakness. The animal tale portrays the quick and guileful rabbit outwitting the powerful bear, fox, lion, or elephant. Brother Rabbit may lose a few times, but he is never totally beaten. Often he has to talk himself out of dangerous situations. In these tales, too, the accent is on short range gain and on getting as much out of the opponent as possible. Brer Rabbit is cynical and greedy, self-indulgent and hard; all fantasies triggered by the lack of options in slavery. Closer to its realistic foil are the Master-John stories. John frequently though not always gets the better of his master; he compensates with ingenuity, inventiveness and cunning what he lacks in book learning and power.[57] If he does not win in material terms, he always wins in cathartic resolution, for he often has the last laugh. Playing dumb and tricking was a pervasive weapon of slavery. Nate Shaw remarks that he 'had to play dumb sometimes . . . maybe a heap of times I knowed just how come they done such-and-such a trick, but I wouldn't say. And I could go to em a heap of times for a favor and get it.'

This required an exact knowledge of how far one could go. 'I knowed not to go too far and let them know what I knowed, because they taken exception of it too quick.' Black ritual and folklore explored both the limits set to behavior and the unlimited potential of catharsis. The latter was proportionate to the pervasive feeling of dread that the former would be overstepped:'They'd give you a good name if you was obedient to em, acted nice when you met em and didn't question em bout what they said they had against you. You begin to cry about your rights and the mistreatin of you and they'd murder you.'[58] Comedy was a means to prevent and defuse potential violence. A master ready to use the whip might lose his determination if he could be made to laugh. Laughter and comedy were instrumentalized as manipulative tools. This explains the backlog of bitterness which resonates in much black humor. The awareness of danger and of the boundaries of safety and violence injected a good deal of ambivalence into the cognitive competence and the connected value system of blacks. A 'good nigger' was subservient, religious, and well-behaved, whereas a 'bad nigger' was one who practised individual sabotage of the system by loafing, lying, and by getting his own back from the white man. It stands to reason that a bad nigger, especially one with bravura and style, enjoyed a certain status among black people, particularly among the least assimilated and least religious of blacks. Black folklore, both rural and urban, is full of defiant types and bad niggers: tricksters, confidence men, cheaters, rebels and bums; and, more recently, hustlers, pimps, avengers, and gangsters.[59] All these figures function in ego-centered networks for the sake of short range personal gain through sabotage, but they are not always successful. Whereas trickster, confidence man and comedian manipulate conflict to their own advantage, the bad man, rebel or avenger uses direct punitive action, often self-destructive. Trickster and bad man coalesce in some urban stories of Brother Rabbit, who enters the scene now gun in hand. Charles Silberman reports that the bad nigger syndrome begins at the age of five or six in the ghettos, at which age male children begin to adjust to the reality of the street (viz. in Baldwin's *Go Tell It on the Mountain* the character 'Roy').[60] Most of these mythical folk heroes were and still are the fantasy product of a fierce folk or class reaction to assimilation, to injustice, and to a work ethic which makes false promises to the black man. In reality these bad niggers rarely escaped being lynched, broken, or put in jail. Says Nate Shaw:

> When I jumped up and fought the laws, that ruint me with the white people in this country. They gived me just as bad a name as they could give me; talked it around that I was quick-tempered, I was quick-tempered. The devil you better get quick-tempered or get some sort of temper when you know you livin in a bad country.[61]

Nate Shaw defended his property from confiscation and was sent to prison for it. The folk imagination turned this pattern of behavior into fictional dreams which exaggerated the daring of bad men and let them get away with suicidal behavior. On the other hand, the folk tale tradition was not given to dreams alone. It also recorded truthfully and closer to the historical foil how many of these heroes eventually met death. Even historical rebels such as Nat Turner and Denmark Vesey were thus mythologized; Nigger Bill in our next poem has to be seen in this thick web of social and historical significance:

> I'se wild Nigger Bill
> From Redpepper Hill.
> I never did wo'k and I never will.
> I'se done killed de Boss.
> I'se knocked down de hoss.
> I eats up raw goose widout apple sauce.
> I'se runaway Bill
> I knows dey mought kill;
> But ole Masse hain't cotch me, an' he never will!

The boast — that Bill not only eats raw goose, but eats it without apple sauce — is a form of self-irony which can be found in all forms of black folklore: 'I'm so bad I'd jump in a lion's cage wearing a pork chop jacket.' — 'I'm drinking TNT, I'm smoking dynamite, I hope some screwball start a fight.'[62] And Sonia Sanchez published a book of poems entitled *We a baddDDD People*. The meaning of bad, conditioned by historical experience and by the transvaluation of values which racism bestowed on it, does not depend on its normal 'white' denotation, but on situation and context, i.e. on its situational and functional connotations within racism. 'Mean,' for instance, signifies 'the finest, good, down to earth, honest, and strong' while retaining also its original sense, and 'mean motherfucker' has such latitude of meaning that it includes both the dangerous person and the admirable hero. The particular meaning which the speaker intends is signalled first by the situation, and then by pitch and emphasis (e.g. Sanchez's attempt at phonetic spelling), both of which cannot be satisfactorily expressed in writing. Street language is drama, not text. This heritage carries over into contemporary poetry (see Chapter VI).

The high premium which black culture places on verbal excellence is evident both in rural and urban settings. Zora Neale Hurston remarks on the high esteem in which folk 'liars' are held, Frank Banks and Portia Smiley report on the verbal intricacies of courtship practices (highly reminiscent of African culture) among rural blacks, and Dollard analyzes the prevalence of verbal rituals of insult in practically all classes of rural and urban blacks.[63] Since the dozens represent an interesting example of speech behavior, particularly in view of shame cultural behavior, it deserves close attention. The dozens is a highly competitive and elaborate game of verbal insults involving the opponent's mother and next of kin.[64] The object is to shame the other party by making allusions to the alleged promiscuity of the mother, to the incompetence of the father, and to the dirty habits of the entire clan. Indeed the dozens focuses its insult on the adverse effects which a racial class system has on kinship structure and behavior: promiscuity, illegitimacy, and on stigmata such as extreme ugliness, blackness, or filth. Given the strong exogamic pattern of black kinship structures, the insinuation of sexual abandon of mother and sister is particularly insulting. But equally frequent are allusions to poverty and ugliness:

> yo so poor even the roaches eat out . . .
> yo mother so ugly she kin open a branch face . . .

These are sample first lines which would have to be capped by an insult more outrageous. Dollard reports a typical exchange on ugliness:

> *Joe*: Nigger, if I was as ugly as you I would kill myself.
> *James*: You ain't so hot yourself. Your hair looks like wire fence.
> *Joe*: Your paw's hair look like a wire fence, nigger.
> *James*: You are my paw.
> *Joe*: If I'm your paw I must have done it to your maw.[65]

From the safe perch of middle-class values all this will seem purely barbaric. But the dozens is not played for any provable content. It is enacted for the sake of the performance and the verbal competition within the peer group. The content of the dozens reflects truisms of black reality or basic anxieties of its members. Externalizing it and fashioning it into a duelling performance, the actors at the same time deflect the anxiety into comedy and command the attention of the audience. The above exchange was followed by cat-calls of the onlookers and such comments as: 'Oh, Oh! He told you about your maw. I would not take that if I was you. Go ahead and tell him something back.' Or, to join the game, an onlooker might insinuate: 'He's talking about YOUR mother so bad he's making ME mad.'[66] The delight of the audience will rise in proportion to the effectiveness of the metaphor; through the expression of delight it picks winners and losers. Dick Gregory relates how he came to appreciate the 'power of a joke' in handling the anxieties caused by life in the ghetto:

'Hey, Gregory.'
'Yeah.'
'Get your ass over here, I want to look at that shirt you're wearing.'
'Well, uh, Herman, I got to . . .'
'What you think of that shirt he's wearing, York?'
'That's no shirt, Herman, that's a tent for a picnic.'
'That your Daddy's shirt, Gregory?'
'Well, uh . . .'
'He ain't got no Daddy, Herman, that's a three-man shirt.'
'Three man shirt?'
'Him 'n' Garland 'n' Presley supposed to wear that shirt together.'
At first . . . I'd get mad and run home and cry when the kids started. And then, I don't know just when, I started to figure it out. They were going to laugh anyway, but if I made the jokes they'd laugh *with* me instead of *at* me. I'd get the kids off my back, on my side. So I'd come off that porch talking about myself.
'Hey, Gregory, get your ass over here. Want you to tell me and Herman how many kids sleep in your bed.'
'Googobs of kids in my bed, man, when I get up to pee in the middle of the night gotta leave a bookmark so I don't lose my place.'
Before they could get going, I'd knock it out first, fast, knock out those jokes so they wouldn't have time to set and climb all over me.
. . .
And then I started to turn the jokes on them.
'Hey Gregory, where's your Daddy these days?'
'Sure glad that mother-fucker's out the house, got a little peace and quiet. Not like your house, York.'

'What you say?'
'Yeah, man, what a free-show I had last night, better than the Muni,
laying in bed with the window open, listening to your Daddy whop
your Mommy. That was your Daddy, York, wasn't it?'

The dozens, as many forms of urban subculture, is a game and
a gamble: you either win or lose. The fatalistic world view
reflects the extreme reduction of options and the blockage of
alternatives. It stands to reason that, as in most games of
chance, the game of life knows far more losers than winners.

These rituals are institutionalized forms of rebellion, but
rebellion turned inward; they function as valves for aggression
caused by a highly competitive social arena which is particularly unstable for blacks. Economic marginality and the
reliance on short-run exploitation of human resources, write
Szwed and Whitten, favor ego-centred networks: one man
making it now.[67] Winning in the dozens is one such short-run
gain, but it is fictionalized and has its teeth pulled. By simulat-
ing dangerous situations, cushioned by ritual repetition, the
collective pre-empts and prevents explosions which may be
fatal in out-group encounters. The dozens says all the bad
things which the white man thinks about blacks, but the white
part is manned by one of the black group. This verbal analogue
to burning ghettos (conversely Martin Luther King calls riot-
ing the 'language of the unheard') has carried over into all
black speech and may be felt in black poetry today, which
accordingly seems jarring, exaggerated, and burdened with
jive to unaccustomed ears. But such exaggeration is by no
means unusual for the American literary scene. A quick look at
the nineteenth-century tradition of American speech behavior
makes clear that both Yankee and backwoodsman were prone
to exaggerations and hyperbole, strongly reflecting their
social anxieties.[68] Both were exposed to extreme capitalist
competition within a society which had neither a stable
exchange nor a predictable market. Verbal skill for the Yankee, mostly at the expense of the opponent, and the linguistic
bravura of the backwoodsman were patterns of survival or
means of controlling anxieties. How much this tradition has
contributed to black toasts, signifying, and the dozens is difficult to determine, but black rhetoric, particularly oratory and
sermons, was not immune to these influences. There is, however, also evidence of a strong African tradition in verbal
sparring, ritual insult games, and stigma taunts. While we may

not determine the respective weight of these influences or tradition, we may conjecture that the persistence of hyperbolic black rhetoric to this day is an indication that the anxieties which it expresses and combats are still real.

Urban folklore takes an unromantic, cynical view of American life; as the need for humorous camouflage disappears the humor evaporates with it. The alternatives are still simple: win or lose. The ritual of urban lore, writes Bruce Jackson,

> suspends for a time one's need to respond to challenge totally. The satisfaction of the games comes not only from giving insult, but taking it, from moving the plane of action to a purely verbal level. In the process of this action certain anxieties are excited and eased; one may explore one's own, and the cathartic effect applies both to audience and speaker.[69]

The combat of the social arena is removed to the street theater where the linguistic resource turns permanent oppression and anxiety into a momentary release in catharsis. If present black poetry and literature fasten on these rituals and forms, they perform the important service of objectifying them into art, thus defusing their fatalistic and self-destructive potential while salvaging the fun. In a literary take-off Stanley Crouch parodies, or rather transforms, a typical toast into a poem. Many toasts such as Shine or Stagolee end with the death of their protagonists. They all end in great style. The defeated hero seems to say: in this game of life I may finally lose out, but whatever you say you have to admit that I know how to exit in style. The poem is entitled 'Pimp's Last Mack: Death REquest. A Folk Song.'

> On the way to the bone orchard, the
> dirt house of all the gone daddies' bones,
> I want to go slump-sided —
> on a dago, tilted over just a little.
> I want 3 short fat greasy ho's in red on one side
> & three creole queens 7 foot tall on the other side
> lowering me in the ground from 7 gold chains.
> But on the way I want my casket dragged by 13 giant snakes
>   painted riot ruby red
> and on top of that gold and silver flip top cigar
> I want a 3-headed purple nigguh baby
> blowing 11 connected bugles full of burning nappy hair
> and smearing the top with his muddy feet

and pissing in the tracks left by my coffin's dragging
and 6 devil's feet behind
I want a crowd of blue-eyed baboons sucking the yellow out
                                             of those lines
my casket be leaving on the way to the bone
orchard, dirt house of all the gone daddies' bones.
WAIT
And in the last of the long road go down
among the epitaphs & trees —
wooden ropes holding the grass down —
I want MY grave note to say in gold AND silver:

To dirt, sin, low life
and fast women of river hips
who baptized him nightly
this young man was no stranger.
And when he sat his black ass down
his butt hole stamped down
        DANGER!

Some contemporary poetry postulates the identity of black literate poetry and oral folklore and mistakes itself for the genuine ritual article of the black oral tradition; however, this type of ideological rhetoric finds enough criticism within black culture which is well trained to gauge both honesty and reality. Next to these combative and forensic forms, which require opponents of equal talent within a combat setting, black culture has developed a powerful individual form which has become one of the most important backbones of white culture as well: the blues.[70]

No one knows where the blues come from. The approximate date of their arrival on the American scene in the now classic form must have coincided with the emergence of jazz, around 1900.[71] Both jazz and blues are true Afro-American forms; both have shown a catholic taste for whatever the resources of Africa, America and Europe had to offer. In form they owe much to the call and response pattern of the African tradition. But call and response had been fashioned into a new Afro-American pattern by the time the blues were created. Their notation, particularly the so-called blue notes, were said to be an African holdover. But blue notes had long ago stabilized as a typical and much earlier amalgamation of European and African forms. What we can say with a certain degree of generalization is that the particular social function of the blues ritual is a typical instance of the Americanization of an African cultural resource. Private, almost lyrical form, but collective reception; collective *formulae*, but individual style. To call the blues purely American is as mistaken as to assign to them a purely African base. They have neither the aesthetic autonomy of European music, nor the social determination of African music.

In Africa, music was a form of universe maintenance or of spiritual social control.[72] Music accompanied the work rhythms, the rituals, wars, and celebrations. The blues surely are not as totally grown into the social fabric as were its African antecedents. On the other hand, in comparison to European folk forms they appear much more socially determined and less arbitrary. The thematic repertoire of the blues singer contains such everyday communal experience as will be recognized by the audience, and, more significantly, will inspire the audience to participate. Thus the blues phrase 'The eagle flies on Friday, Saturday I go out and play,' sung by Lou Rawls in a public performance in Chicago,[73] a *formula* which goes back into the metaphoric tradition of black culture, is greeted by catcalls of recognition. These are *formulae* of communal lore, the 'tested rhetoric' of a community, which have achieved a shared symbolic significance.[74] This formula might be a line, a word, or a story-plot; at any rate it will bear the *imprimatur* of the collective. New inventions, which undoubtedly were and still are made, have to pass this public ratification test before they will be added to the repertoire. The public nature of shared knowledge creates the sense of togetherness the blues singer tries to evoke. White reception has often misinterpreted the blues as resulting *from* a mood; the bluesmen rather want to *create* a mood. They are not, as some of their myopic critics claim, passive, masochistic or full of resignation. There is a latent sense of irony in the blues which invites comparison to the humor of the Eastern Jews under the oppressive Czars: 'If you want to forget all your troubles, put on a shoe that's too tight,' counsels Jewish folk humor. 'Got the blues, but too damn mean to cry,' says the blues and also: 'Ef blues was whisky I'd stay drunk all the time.' Undoubtedly the singing and sharing of the blues is a form of conflict management and a safety valve. This has been the most frequent objection of the militant blacks.[75] However, it is not only a reconciliation to, but also a reminder of, the social situation of blacks. Ellison characterizes it both as acceptance and rejection. Consider the character Trueblood in *Invisible Man*, the black novel which has captured best the spirit, the symbols, and the function of black oral culture in a literate world. Trueblood has violated his daughter in his sleep. In the light of the previous discussion of shame cultures, this is a particularly serious offense committed against one of the kin. (Aristotle remarked that tragedy was most effective when involving the 'loved ones'.) There is a tragic finality about the sin growing in his daughter's womb; the biological irreversibility mirrors the relentless quality of Greek fate. The shame of his deed almost kills him, although he seems curiously intrigued by himself and his objectified action. This is his reaction:

> I thinks and thinks, until I thinks my brain go'n bust, 'bout how I'm guilty and how I ain't guilty. I don't eat nothin' and I don't drink nothin' and caint sleep at night. Finally, one night, way early in the mornin', I looks up and sees the stars and I starts singin'. I don't mean to, I didn't think 'bout it, just start singin'. I don't know what it was, some kinda church song, I guess. All I know is I *ends up* singin' the blues. I sings me some blues that night ain't never sang before, and while I'm singin' them blues I makes up my mind that I ain't nobody but myself and ain't nothin' I can do but let whatever is gonna happen, happen.
>
> (*Invisible Man*, p. 58)

Since he committed this kinship crime in his sleep (driven by the powers of his irrational impulses) he is neither guilty nor innocent. Still he is in a corner, alone with himself and his deed. He takes recourse to the most relentless form of self-knowledge and the extremest form of realism which his culture can muster: the blues. Their catharsis reconciles him to being himself, and to his deed. In this scene, as in the prologue and epilogue of his novel, Ellison stresses the *private* function of the blues, its function as identity management. But the blues need listeners and company. In this novel, the Northern white philanthropist is made to share Trueblood's blues experience and he reacts under the full weight of his Manichean tradition and its echoes of original sin.

> 'You have looked upon chaos and are not destroyed! . . .'
> 'You feel no inner turmoil, no need to cast out the offending eye? . . .'
> 'I'm all right, suh,' Trueblood said uneasily. 'My eyes is all right too. And when I feels po'ly in my gut I takes a little soda and it goes away.'
>
> (*The Invisible Man*, pp. 46–7)

Norton's literate consciousness and his Hawthornian obsession with original sin meet the literal and utterly pragmatic Trueblood. Trueblood has a problem and he solves it in the pragmatic fashion of his culture. While for inner turmoil he takes soda, for survival *now* he takes the blues. The irony is that Trueblood has Mr Norton in a bind: as a puritanical white with endogamic fantasies involving his deceased daughter, his prurient interest is stimulated; at the same time, he shares the guilt of slavery and of Trueblood's degradation with white America. His reaction has a larger symbolic significance: he buys his freedom with a gift of 100 dollars, a symbolic precursor of some current welfare programs.

Ellison's emphasis on individual therapy as one of the chief functions of the blues amounts to a literarization of an oral form. A writer concerned with the individual growth of a hero or character would stress its effect on the individual psyche or its private, lyrical mode; he writes:

> The blues is an impulse to keep the painful details and episodes of a brutal experience alive in one's aching consciousness, to finger its jagged grain, and to transcend it, not by the consolation of philosophy but by squeezing from it a near-tragic, near-comic lyricism. As a form, the blues is an autobiographical chronicle of personal catastrophe expressed lyrically.[76]

This definition leaves out the audience and the particular mood created by the singer *for* the audience. One should expand Ellison's definition and add that of Henry Townsend, bluesman from St Louis:

> You express yourself in a song like that. Now this particular thing reach others because they have experienced the same condition in life so naturally they feel what you are sayin' because it happened to them. It's a sort of thing that you kinda like to hold to yourself, yet you want somebody to know it. . . . Now I've had the feelin' which I have disposed it in a song, but there's some things that have happened to me that I wouldn't dare tell, not to tell — but I would *sing* about them. Because people in general they takes the song as an explanation for *themselves* — they believe this song is expressing *their* feelings instead of the one that singin' it.[77]

We can modify Ellison's definition by saying that the blues are individual *style* presented in an interactive 'performance' using such *formulae* as are based on the experience of the collective. Country blues, though by no means as private and lyrical as

Ellison says, were indeed sung either alone or before smaller groups, among friends, kin, prison mates etc. and the themes were appropriate for the occasion. As the blues moved cityward they adapted to the new locale, to the new audience — at once more anonymous and demanding — and to the media. The exposure to a new market and to an urban audience reduced the private and lyrical nature even more and brought out the collective social control function of the blues and the related soul music. In the rural context the anonymous collective ratified the experience of the individual blues artist; now artist and repertoire men, their fingers on the pulse of the mass audience, direct blues singers toward expressing present anxieties, wants, and dreams.[78] A quick look at more recent urban blues and soul lyrics reveals that much of the unideological truthfulness of the classic blues has gone, and that many lyrics are the tin-pan-alley palliatives of a capitalist dream world, which has little bearing on black reality. But there is also a sharper edge of protest and urgency in the lyrics of Nina Simone, Curtis Mayfield or B. B. King, which have shed the so-called resignative existentialism of the classic blues, but have retained the sense of solidarity. The enormous success of the blues among Euro-Americans has made it vulnerable to minstrelization and economic exploitation, as can be seen in the music and economic strategies of the 'rocking prince valiant types from England.'[79] David Evans has demonstrated in an illuminating essay that the commercial success of blues and soul plagiarists is based on a different relationship between performer and audience. While many white blues and soul performers *learn* one stable version of a song, which they present to a variety of audiences and which the audience learns to expect, the technique of blues composition among black folksingers is geared to the 'moods the singer feels or would like to create. They must also express moods and thoughts to which the audience can relate, or else they will be unsuccessful.'[80] This requires improvization, i.e. strategies of adaptation to a variety of circumstances. The ideological basis of this new urban blues and soul solidarity may at times be questionable, since it exalts studs, pimps, and hustlers as new culture heroes, but it cannot be dismissed as manipulation of the masses by cynical hustlers of negritude. These forms both symbolize and reinforce that social behavior which grew out of the historically-conditioned cultural resources of blacks.[81]

The large-scale imitation of Afro-American social rituals (language, music, dance) by the white counterculture and, somewhat out of phase, by the mainstream culture may be an indication of the alienating turn which Western (white) culture has taken and of the need for less puritanical and more sensual forms of communication.[82]

Double consciousness, irony, ambivalence, equivocality, contradiction — these are the terms of various disciplines applied to a central form-giving conflict in black culture. Its equivocal nature is particularly striking in that social agency which in the Western hemisphere has been the epitome of self-denial and emotional or erotic constraint — the church. Though unquestionably Western in its social organization, the black church has created its own version of Christian culture. Socially and politically it is part of the larger Protestant or Catholic movement, but its culture, its notion of doctrine, its idea of sin, its accent on immediate experience and emotive abandon remove it from the mainstream. The intensity and sensuality of its rituals point to strong links with secular black culture. Although religious blacks often reject the blues as 'devil music' with their emphasis on whoring, drinking, and the good life, both the preacher and blues singer share a certain social role: they are promoters of catharsis, they are leaders of the community, backed by a following with whom they interact on a strikingly erotic level. Indeed, many blues singers or pimps have easily slipped into the role of preacher, and many a preacher has continued his blues life with the tacit approval of his congregation, particularly when his conduct was intended as an insult to the white power structure.[83] Some preachers will admit that their former life as blues singers was an important preparation for preaching, while in blues concerts the audience will react with 'preach it, brother' or 'Amen.' Recently the revivalist techniques of black religion have had a strong impact on civil rights oratory and on secular music.[84] It seems then that the difference between secular and religious culture is defined more by moral choice than by social function or formal resource.

The history of black religious culture in the Americas still needs to be written. Both in historical evolution and geographical distribution such immense differences confront the student of black religion, that no generalization seems possible. Erika Bourgignon rightly refuses to speak of *one* New

World Negro religion. The patterns of adaptation from Brazil to Haiti, to Cuba, and the USA are remarkably different.[85] Within the United States strong differences may be observed as one moves from Louisiana to Virginia, not alone differences between Protestantism and Catholicism, but also between classes and temperaments. Black religious culture comprises the ecstatic rituals of store front churches in Harlem, the fundamentalism of Southern rural Baptism, and the sober dignity of the socially more exclusive forms of Protestantism.

As in secular culture, it would be difficult to disentangle the factors of race, class, and poverty which have gone into black religion. The question of Africanisms is particularly ticklish. However, a tentative interpretation of historical data and certain insights gathered from other cultures permit a few cautious conclusions. It we grant that the period from 1650 to 1800 was most important for the development and adaptation of African cultural resources, such as survived, to the American social scene, and if historians of slave culture tell us that massive Christianization set in around 1800, we may safely assume that black religious life before 1800 maintained a good deal of fragmented African beliefs, rituals, and songs. This assumption gains weight when we hear from anthropologists that retentions are particularly intense in the religious sphere. We may therefore assume that certain patterns of syncretistic religious behavior had already stabilized by 1800 and thus were able to withstand the pressure of acculturation.[86]

Black cultural nationalists make much of the 'spirituality' of black religious culture. This lands us in semantic trouble, since we assign a specific meaning to the term in the context of our dualistic Christian universe.

In oral cultures the animate realm blends with the inanimate in superstition and witchcraft. Certain aspects of black religion make more sense if we assume that African concepts of spirituality have been preserved by black oral culture. In West African culture there was no split between the real and imaginary, the tangible and immaterial, the physical and metaphysical.[87] Its spirituality was in the service of this world. Large parts of this African spiritual universe adapted to the Christian notion of metaphysics and found a welcome home in its rituals, symbols, and doctrines. But it is curious to find that significant parts of what constitutes Western Christianity are missing, certain doctrines were disregarded, and only those parts of the Bible were fully explored which touched the resonant strings of collective memory. On the other hand, certain rituals, symbols and ecstatic forms of worship, which Christianity found hard to digest, were maintained, often furtively. Macumba, Candomblé, and Umbanda in South or Middle America, voodoo, shuffle, and ring shout in North America coexisted or have fused with Christian forms of worship. Janheinz Jahn claims the West African origin of the religious behavior described by James Baldwin in *Go Tell It on the Mountain*. Certainly the notion that God's presence (getting the spirit) depends on the concerted ecstatic effort of the community has parallels in the *participation mystique* of African religions. But it would be rash to conclude on the basis of formal similarities that black American religion is essentially African. The cultural resources of African religion were transplanted and reinterpreted for an American social reality, where they helped to manage survival in this world. As Genovese writes, black religion

> counseled a strategy of patience, of acceptance of what could not be helped, of a dogged effort to keep the black community alive and healthy — a strategy of survival that, like its African prototype, above all said yes to life in this world.[88]

Black religion has been accused of serving the function of a safety valve. Indeed the emphasis of oral culture on the here and now has not been conducive to revolutionary strategies and activities. The emphasis on immediate experience and ecstasy rather than on doctrinal belief has kept alive strategies of externalization which manage conflicts through catharsis rather than combat them through cognitive charters for future action. However 'counter-revolutionary' it may have been, this ability of black religion now exerts a powerful attraction on Western religions:

> Moralism and verbalism and the almost complete absence of ecstatic experience characterized the middle-class Protestant churches. The more intense religiosity of black and lower-class churches remained largely unavailable to the white middle class members of the counter-culture.[89]

The irony is that these ecstatic forms of worship survived because the slave owners of the seventeenth and eighteenth centuries were against religious instruction of blacks. Knowledge and scholarship were dangerous weapons. Christianity affirmed the humanity and worth of all people, including the slave. This notion was fondly embraced by black Christians while the attempt on the part of white owners to instil subservience and meekness in the slave was only partially successful, as extant folk tales, slave narratives, and autobiographies will tell us. Frederick Douglass for one exposed the hypocrisy of religion in slavery. Ministers and religious fanatics were for him the worst masters. Not all blacks shared Douglass' negative view of Christianity. Yet, they accepted religion only selectively and tentatively. It stands to reason that a strategy of rejection and affirmation makes for a religion which appears strangely ambivalent. There are innumerable stories and jokes in which God appears to be white, and his deputies on earth, deacons and preachers, are the butt of many folk tales which treat religion as a thinly disguised hustle. Even the symbols of black religion are ambiguous; the cross for one thing was both the dreadful emblem of the Ku Klux Klan and a source of solace symbolizing the shared suffering of Christ. On the other hand, the church created a strong social bond, it inspired in-group solidarity, and it put greater restraint on the self-destructive energies generated by slavery. It managed the contradictions of black life by teaching patience in the face of insurmountable odds, it functioned as a safety valve for pent-up aggression, and it maintained a consciousness of the injustice of the black situation in America.[90]

Black sacred music was the first cultural achievement which whites were willing to acknowledge, particularly when it stayed close to the Methodist hymn book. From the Fisk Jubilee Singers, who toured Europe in the late nineteenth century, to the chamber spirituals of the Golden Gate Quartet, black sacred music, presumably because it was less shocking than the blues and more indicative of the sentiment that abolitionists sought in blacks, has been lionized by white audiences and therefore adjusted easily to mainstream taste. Despite this constant process of assimilation, which has given rise to a great variety of forms, the folk sources of black sacred music have proven to be surprisingly resilient. Although called 'spirituals,' there is little of that gnostic spirituality which negates the body as the prison house of the soul. Granted, there is Christian stoicism, nostalgia for deliverance and the desire of being saved from a painful present, but the other world looks much like this world plus freedom. Too often 'heaven' is a thin disguise for liberty, the Jordan river looks like the Ohio or Mississippi, and the folk of Israel, enslaved by Egypt, is recognizably black.[91] Again, the concept of sin and the figure of the devil deserve attention. Original sin does not seem to burden blacks; perhaps because it was committed against them by whites. And many a folk tale describes hell in terms of the South with whites as devils. But the devil also appears as a rather warm figure, as a trickster or fun and games man.[92] It is certainly no accident that the religious folk call the blues 'devil music,' for the devil is master of ceremonies in the world of fun. Furthermore why should the black folk dread the prince of darkness whom white Christian imagery portrays as black? After the blacks themselves had been made part of a Manichean color scheme, the injustice of which was evident, they had little use for a Manichean construct in their own religious universe. The contradiction of being unjustly identified with the devil left its mark on folklore and religious culture. Indeed the devil appears in an aura of cameraderie and irony; there is some of the trickster and badman in him which endears him to the folk imagination. Whether this pragmatism of black religion is a result of race and class consciousness or whether it reaches back into Africa is again difficult if not impossible to détermine.[93] As we look at the texts of black religious music we realize that large parts of the Bible are missing, namely those that did not contribute to survival in the South; the biblical analogue made sense to blacks in terms of their social situation. 'Let My People Go,' 'And de Walls Come Tumblin' Down,' 'Dere's No Hidin' Place Down Dere' and 'Steal Away to Jesus' are obviously not naive, nor would blacks fail to be reminded of lynchings when they hear 'They crucified my Lord, and He never said a mumbalin' word.' This does not make all black songs loaded; nor does their world imagery negate its religious character. What interests us is the genesis and social function of these songs. Here the selective interest of the collective creators of these spirituals is evidence enough.

Get on board, little children . . .
The gospel train's a-coming, I hear it just at hand
I hear the car wheels rumbling and rolling through the land
The fare is cheap and all can go,
The rich and poor are there
No second class aboard this train, no difference in the fare.

This gospel song of the twentieth century expresses an old theme in the imagery of today. As in secular culture, improvisation is central to religious life. It's a form of making it new. Dizzy Gillespie, a contemporary jazz musician, drew appreciative shouts from his gospel-trained audience when he adapted another spiritual formula to urban ghetto reality: 'Swing Low Sweet Cadillac.' Had it not been for the early codification of spirituals by collectors such as Allen, Ware, and Garrison[94] and their popularization in print, this improvisational and ecstatic nature of black religion would have remained more obvious. But improvisation and ecstasy have surfaced again in the twentieth-century store front churches of the Northern ghettos and have in turn revitalized jazz, blues and soul. The ecstatic and participatory nature of black liturgy, the call and response pattern of its sermons, the cathartic function of rhythm and shout, handclapping and shuffle, and last but not least, the emphasis on *getting* the spirit rather than praying up to it, have found a welcome reception in present-day American culture. Ray Charles and Aretha Franklin draw on both the spiritual and secular tradition of collective participation. Preachers as well as blues singers exhort their audience 'to make some noise' when the spirit moves them and to generate ecstasy.[95]

NOTES

1. W. E. B. DuBois, *The Souls of Black Folks* (1903; New York, 1953), p. 3. DuBois's neutral use of the term self-consciousness, meaning self-awareness or identity rather than embarrassment, may date from his studies in Germany. See chapters 'Selbstbewuβtsein' and 'Herrschaft und Knechtschaft' of Hegel's *Phänomenologie des Geistes*.
2. Melville Herskovits speaks of 'socialized ambivalence' in *Life in a Haitian Valley* (New York, 1937); Erik Erikson speaks of pseudo-species in 'The Concept of Identity in Race Relations: Notes and Queries,' in *The Negro American*, ed. Talcott Parsons and Kenneth B. Clark (Boston, 1966); Thomas Kochman talks about the constitutional ambiguity of black semantics in 'Toward an Ethnography of Black American Speech Behavior,' in: Whitten/Szwed, *Afro-American Anthropology*; also in Kochman, ed., *Rappin' and Stylin' Out*.
3. On structural and historical variables see the introductions by Sidney Mintz and Norman Whitten and John Szwed in Whitten/Szwed, *Afro-American Anthropology*. Also Thomas Nipperdey, 'Kulturge-

schichte, Sozialgeschichte, historische Anthropologie,' *Vierteljahres-zeitschrift für Sozial- und Wirtschaftsgeschichte*, 55 (1968–9).

4. Bourdieu quotes Nietzsche, *Soziologie der symbolischen Formen*, p. 27. Mintz, Szwed, Whitten, Gutman, Genovese use literary data in their work; many of them rely on Ellison when they need explanatory support.

5. Ralph Ellison, *Shadow and Act* (New York, Signet, 1966), p. 130.

6. E. P. Thompson, *The Making of the English Working Class* (London, 1963), p. 192; E. R. Dodds, *The Greeks and the Irrational* (Berkeley, 1951), pp. 243–4; Herbert G. Gutman, 'Work, Culture, and Society in Industrializing America, 1815–1919,' *American Historical Review*, 78 (1973), 542–3.

7. Mintz, Foreword to: Whitten/Szwed, *Afro-American Anthropology*, p. 10.

8. Zygmunt Bauman, 'Marxism and the Contemporary Theory of Culture,' *Co-existence*, 5 (1968), 171.

9. *Time*, April 6, 1970, pp. 54–5. Larry Neal quotes an editorial of the 1943 *Negro Quarterly*, which he attributes to Ellison: 'The problem is psychological; it will be solved only by a Negro leadership that is aware of the psychological attitudes and incipient forms of action which the black masses reveal in their emotion–charged myths, symbols, and wartime folklore. Only through a skilful and wise manipulation of these *centers of repressed social energy* will Negro resentment, self-pity, and indignation be channelized to cut through temporary issues and become transformed into *positive action*.' 'Ellison's Zoot Suit,' *Black World*, 20 (December 1970), italics mine.

10. The Frazier-Herskovits debate in Whitten/Szwed, *Afro-American Anthropology*; Stanley Elkins, *Slavery: A Problem in American Institutional and Intellectual Life* (Chicago, 1959), has caused a nationwide controversy. See Eugene Genovese, 'Rebelliousness and Docility in the Negro Slave: A Critique of the Elkins Thesis,' *Civil War History*, 13 (1967), 293–314. The most recent exercise in tautology is Robert Fogel and Stanley Engerman's *Time on the Cross*; the authors prove by statistical methods that black Americans were essentially pigmented Horatio Algers.

11. Herbert Marcuse quotes Peter Schneider in *Counter-revolution and Revolt* (Boston, 1972), p. 110. See also Rolf Schwendter, *Theorie der Subkultur* (Köln, 1973), who lists cognitive and cathartic functions of art, p. 241.

12. My notion of the symbolic universe owes to Peter Berger and Thomas Luckmann, *The Social Construction of Reality* (New York, 1966). Braudel, *Capitalism*, makes a distinction between material life and economic life; he forgets to add symbolic life.

13. Syntax: J. L. Dillard, *Black English: Its History and Usage in the United States* (New York, 1972); kinship behavior: Herbert Gutman, *The Black Family*; cognitive realm: Alan Dundes, ed., *Motherwit from the Laughing Barrel: Readings in the Interpretation of Afro-American Folklore* (Englewood Cliffs, 1973); on motor behavior Sidney Mintz has this to say: 'It is reasonable to view these expressions as continuities with the African past, and as some evidence of the success of Afro-Americans in

conserving cultural materials that could not be conserved in other aspects of life. Patterns of socially learned motor behavior are probably not readily destroyed, even by extremely repressive conditions; and the aesthetic and creative possibilities implicit in these traditional patterns and their cognitive accompaniments may have been among those cultural traditions most readily maintained under slavery.' Foreword, p. 5.

14.   Herskovits makes a difference between retentions (the African material remains intact), reinterpretations (the African material slips into existing slots and changes its function), and syncretisms (the African material amalgamates with American material); cf. *The Myth of the Negro Past* (New York, 1941). See Whitten/Szwed, *Afro-American Anthropology*, pp. 25ff. Huey P. Newton makes the observation: 'Different cultures and life styles in America use the same words with different shades of meaning. All belong to one society yet live in different worlds.' *Revolutionary Suicide* (New York, Ballantine, 1974), p. 94. Clyde Kluckhohn, *Mirror for Man* (New York, 1949) expresses a similar idea.

15.   Charles Valentine, *Culture and Poverty: Critique and Counterproposals* (Chicago, 1968).

16.   Typical occupations are hustler, pimp, numbers runner, prostitute, entertainer. Cf. Whitten/Szwed, *Afro-American Anthropology*; Kochman, *Rappin' and Stylin' Out*.

17.   Sidney Mintz, 'Toward an Afro-American History,' *Journal of World History*, 13 (1971), 318.

18.   Time Essay, *Time*, April 6, 1970, pp. 54–5. Ellison calls American culture a 'jazz' culture. In an interview with Alan McPherson, Ellison said 'that we've looked at our relationship to American literature in a rather negative way. That is, we've looked at it in terms of our trying to break into it. Well, damn it . . . *that literature is built off our folklore to a large extent!* . . . I ain't conceding that to *nobody!*' — *Atlantic Monthly*, 226 (December, 1970), reprinted in John Hersey, ed., *Ralph Ellison: A Collection of Critical Essays* (Englewood Cliffs, 1974), p. 54.

19.   *Shadow and Act*, p. 137. At another time Ellison adds a note of caution: '. . . I have a problem of communicating across our various social divisions, whether of race, class, education, region, or religion — and much of this holds true even within my own racial group. It's dangerous to take things for granted.' Interview with John Hersey in Hersey, ed., *Ralph Ellison*, p. 12. LeRoi Jones speculates on the reasons for class divisions within the black community and elaborates 'double consciousness': 'The poor Negro always remembered himself as an ex-slave and used this as the basis of any dealing with the mainstream of American society. The middle class black man bases his whole existence on the hopeless hypothesis that no one is supposed to remember that for almost three centuries there was slavery in America, that the white man was the master and the black man the slave. This knowledge, however, is at the root of the legitimate black culture of this country. It is this knowledge, with its attendant muses of self-division, self-hatred, stoicism, and finally quixotic optimism, that informs the most meaningful of Afro-American music.' *Blues People* (New York, 1963), p. 163.

20. Erving Goffman, *Stigma: Notes on the Management of Spoiled Identity* (Englewood Cliffs, 1963), investigates role, role performance, and role enactment; R. D. Laing's study *The Divided Self* (London, 1959) focuses on the existential factors in double consciousness. Hans Peter Dreitzel, *Die gesellschaftlichen Leiden und das Leiden an der Gesellschaft: Vorstudien zu einer Pathologie des Rollenverhaltens* (Stuttgart, 1972), is the most comprehensive statement of the problem.

21. Michael Kammen, *People of Paradox: An Inquiry Concerning the Origins of American Civilization* (New York, 1972). Nathan Irvin Huggins, *Harlem Renaissance* (New York, 1971), follows a somewhat similar course.

22. Herskovits, *Life in a Haitian Valley*; cf. Sidney Mintz, 'Melville J. Herskovits and Carribean Studies: A Retrospective Tribute,' *Caribbean Studies*, 4 (1964), 46.

23. Stephan Thernstrom, *The Other Bostonians: Poverty and Progress in the American Metropolis, 1800-1970* (Cambridge, 1973). Thernstrom concludes that next to overpowering external odds against upward mobility there was an equally powerful internal resistance in the black population against a business ethic which required the investment and accumulation of capital: 'Blacks in Boston must have been held back either by something in their own culture that limited their desire or capacity to compete in the marketplace, or by discrimination directed against them by others. . . . Could it be that the long and bleak historical experience of Negroes in the United States, an experience of more ruthless subordination than that, say, of the Irish peasantry, produced an enduring black lower class culture that rendered the average Negro objectively less qualified for economic pursuits than the average white?' (pp. 213–4) Thernstrom is asking the wrong question; it should be rephrased: blacks were not 'objectively less qualified' but subjectively less inclined to internalize a work ethic which throughout history had served their oppressor.

24. Dillard, *Black English*; Lorenzo Turner, *Africanism in the Gullah Dialect* (Chicago, 1949); David Dalby, 'The African Element in American English,' in: Thomas Kochman, *Rappin' and Stylin' Out*; Dundes, *Motherwit*; Robert Hall, *Pidgin and Creole Languages* (Ithaca, 1966).

25. John Barber, 'A History of the Amistad Captives,' first published 1840, reprinted in Jules Chametzky and Sidney Kaplan, eds., *Black & White in American Culture* (Amherst, 1969).

26. *Black Majority*, pp. 186–7.

27. Ibid., pp. 187–8.

28. Ross Russell, *Bird Lives! The High Life and Hard Times of Charlie (Yardbird) Parker* (New York, 1973), p. 119, a biography which consistently courts fiction.

29. Prominent among them Ralph Ellison. The 'pejorative school' is strong among certain Marxist groups some of whom use Bernstein's questionable designation of low-class language as 'restricted'; cf. Peter Böhmer et al., eds., *Der Rassenkonflikt in den USA: Sozialisation und Probleme der Emanzipation am Beispiel der Afroamerikaner*, 2 vols. (Frankfurt, 1972) who stress the resignation, apathy, and linguistic incompetence of lower-class populations. Their model of socialization has very little to do with Afro-America and seems strictly focused on West

German reality. Black speech is everything but apathetic, resignative, or 'restricted,' though it is unquestionably different.

A cartoon in the *Chicago Defender* reflects the changing attitude toward the resources of linguistic survival: two black hobos have just escaped arrest by two white policemen. One says to the other: 'Alright, alright! So what if I did sing a couple of stanzas of Dixie and cut a few buck and wing steps back there. It saved the both of us from going to jail for vagrancy. The trouble with you is that you don't know how to differentiate between tomming and progressive maneuvering.' Kochman, *Rappin'*, p. 248.

30.   Doctors William H. Grier and Price M. Cobbs, *The Jesus Bag* (New York, 1971), list an extensive bibliography. On understanding the oppressor Ellison remarks: 'For years, white people went through Grand Central Station having their luggage carried by Ph.D.'s. They couldn't see the Ph.D.'s because their race and class attitudes had trained them to see only the uniforms and the dark faces, but the Ph.D.'s could see them and judged them on any number of levels.' In: Hersey, *Ralph Ellison*, p. 15.

31.   Robert C. Toll, *Blacking Up*: 'Since such indirect and covert jibes [against whites and against slavery] were common in black folk culture but not in white, many blacks in the audience would have been sensitized to hear and enjoy even such surreptitious barbs, while most whites might not even have noticed them.' (p. 246).

'In any case, it is clear that black minstrels themselves did not feel the devotion and subservience to white folks that whites chose to believe they did.' (p. 248).

'To survive, blacks had developed masks and façades that allowed whites to indulge their racial fantasies, while blacks created their own hidden culture within. Thus, the same words and actions could have very different meanings for whites, for the black bourgeoisie, and for members of the black subculture.' (p. 262).

Toll insists that minstrelsy is a 'microcosm of black history,' both concerning its strategy of indirection or its inversion of a racial stereotype, and concerning its powerful hold on the white imagination. (pp. 257ff.). Donald Bogle makes a similar observation in his study of blacks in American films, *Toms, Coons, Mulattoes, Mammies, & Bucks* (New York, 1973).

32.   Ralph Ellison and James Alan McPherson, 'Indivisible Man,' *Atlantic Monthly*, 226 (December 1970), 49: 'Black writers will become influential in terms of style.'

33.   This chapter draws on the following works: Ian Watt and J. Goody, 'The Consequences of Literacy,' in P. P. Giglioli, ed., *Language and Social Context* (London, 1972); Albert Lord, *The Singer of Tales* (Cambridge, 1960); Roger D. Abrahams, 'Personal Power and Social Restraint in the Definition of Folklore,' *Journal of American Folklore*, 84 (1971), 16–30; Richard Baumann, 'Differential Identity and the Social Base of Folklore,' ibid., 31–41; Janheinz Jahn, 'African Oral Literature,' in *Neo-African Literature: A History of Black Writing* (London, 1968); Bruce Jackson, *Get Your Ass in the Water and Swim Like Me: Narrative Poetry from Black Oral Tradition* (Cambridge, 1974); R. Hoggart, *The*

Uses of Literacy (London, 1957). An introduction to current oral litera-ture theory in: Heda Jason, 'A Multidimensional Approach to Oral Literature,' *Current Anthropology*, 10/4 (October 1969), 411–26.

34. New York, 1971.

35. Gramsci, quoted by Gutman, 'Work . . .' pp. 584–5.

36. Frederick Douglass writes that literacy not only gave him a sense of new options in life, it also turned him from a victim of the past and present into a man with a future, 'a future with hope in it.' He was well aware of the self-protective, limited horizon of oral cultures. See Eric Wolf's analysis of peasant culture in *Peasants* (Englewood Cliffs, 1966). Both Booker T. Washington and Markus Garvey drew on the conser-vatism of their grass roots public. Viz. the success of nationalists among blacks.

37. Called 'crab basket effect' or 'lobster basket' this phenomenon has been discussed by a variety of writers: Ralph Ellison, *Shadow and Act*, pp. 96, 100, 101; Anne Moody, *Coming of Age in Mississippi* (New York, 1963); Richard Wright, *Black Boy* (New York, 1945).

38. Ellison uses oral folklore as therapy for his alienated bourgeois heroes. See my analysis of his short story 'Flying Home' in Chapter V.

39. C. Vann Woodward, 'Irony of Southern History,' in *The Burden of Southern History*, rev. edn. (Baton Rouge, 1970) makes the point that American history written from the point of view of the victor is more easily victimized by ideological presumptions than that of the losers. If Southern historiography introduced a sense of irony into American history, then black Southern oral history would add an additional ironic dimension to it.

40. E. P. Thompson, 'Time, Work-Discipline, and Industrial Capitalism,' *Past and Present*, 38 (December 1967). Without falling into Herskovit-sian analogies we may point to philosopher John S. Mbiti's discussion of the concept of time in Africa. He points out that there is hardly any sense of the future, and a sense of the past which is different from that of the literate West. 'Such history and prehistory [i.e. mythical] tend to be telescoped into a very compact, oral tradition, and handed down from generation to generation. If we attempt to fit such tradition into a mathematical time-scale, they would appear to cover only a few cen-turies whereas in reality they stretch much further back; and some of them, being in the form of myths, defy any attempt to describe them on a mathematical time-scale. In any case, oral history has no dates to be remembered. Man looks back from whence he came, and man is certain that nothing will bring his world to a conclusion.' *African Religions and Philosophy* (New York, Doubleday/Anchor, 1970), p. 30. See also Ruth Finnegan's article 'A Note on Oral Tradition and Historical Evidence,' *History and Theory*, 9 (1970), 196, who found no evidence of *historical* poetry in Africa. On the work ethic of blacks see: Eugene Genovese's *Roll, Jordan, Roll: The World the Slaves Made* (New York, 1974), particularly chapters 'Time and Work Rhythms' and 'The Black Work Ethic.' Hudson defines 'hustling' as 'a way of making it without killing yourself on whitey's jobs.' An important aspect of the hustling ethic is the disdain for manual work, particularly for service jobs historically associated with blacks. Julius Hudson, 'The Hustling

Ethic,' in Kochman, *Rappin'*, p. 413. A street poem, 'The Backstreet Hustler,' collected by Julius Hudson (p. 415), runs like this:

A hustler is a very wise person, but yet he is lost
he's a person who refuses to 'eight' (for Charlie)
the white boss. . .
(to eight = to work from nine to five)

41. Genovese, *Roll, Jordan Roll*, pp. 120–3. See also E. R. Dodds, *Greeks*, particularly the chapter 'From Shame-Culture to Guilt-Culture,' pp. 28–63.

42. See Theodore Rosengarten, *All God's Dangers: The Life of Nate Shaw* (New York, 1974). Nate Shaw, an illiterate share cropper from Alabama, relates his life story as a series of attempts to maintain his dignity. Similar sentiments are expressed in Gilbert Osofsky, ed., *Puttin on Ole Massa: The Slave Narratives of Henry Bibb, William Wells Brown, and Solomon Northrup* (New York, 1969). B. B. King on 'respect' in Keil, *Urban Blues*, 106.

43. Goffman, *Stigma*.

44. On sedimentation see Berger and Luckmann, *Social Construction*, and R. Abrahams, 'Personal Power. . .'.

45. Ulf Hannerz, *Soulside* (New York, 1969), looks into the conservative bias of ghetto behavior.

46. Paul Bourdieu, *Soziologie der symbolischen Formen*, p. 39: 'Die anthropologische Wissenschaft verlohnte nicht die Mühe einer einzigen Arbeitsstunde, stellte sie sich nicht die Aufgabe, den Subjekten den Sinn ihres Verhaltens wieder verfügbar zu machen.'

47. Reprinted in Gayle, ed., *Black Aesthetic*.

48. Notably in Baldwin, *Go Tell It on the Mountain*, and Ellison, *Invisible Man*.

49. Sterling Stuckey, 'Through the Prism of Folklore: The Black Ethos in Slavery,' *The Massachusetts Review*, 11/3 (Summer 1968), reprinted in Abraham Chapman, ed., *New Black Voices* (New York, 1972). Lawrence W. Levine, *Black Culture and Black Consciousness*.

The most important source books are: Langston Hughes and Arna Bontemps, eds., *Book of Negro Folklore* (New York, 1958), and Richard Dorson, *American Negro Folktales* (Greenwich, Conn., 1967), who lists an extensive bibliography. On current urban lore see Roger Abrahams, *Deep Down in the Jungle: Negro Narrative Folklore from the Streets of Philadelphia*, rev. edn. (Chicago, 1970) and Jackson, *Get Your Ass in the Water*; Dundes, *Motherwit*; Kochman, *Rappin'*. The comparatist may look at Hermann Bausinger's *Formen der 'Volkspoesie'* (Berlin, 1968).

50. Dundes writes that even Alan Lomax was being put on by his informants, *Motherwit*, p. 469. Roger Abrahams admits that his informants were by no means relaxed with him and that he did not have their full support. 'Foreword' to *Deep Down in the Jungle*, rev. edn.

51. See Paredes and Baumann, Dundes, Abrahams, Jackson.

52. Many admit their debt to Ellison quite openly, e.g. Genovese and Gutman. Ellison says in an interview: 'We are by no means, as is said of the Jews, "people of the Book" — not that I see this matter for regret. For we have a wider freedom of selection. We took much from the ancient Hebrews and we do share, through Christianity, the values

embodied in the literature of much of the world. But our expression has been oral as against "literary".' — 'A Very Stern Discipline: An Interview with Ralph Ellison,' *Harpers*, 234 (March 1967).

53. Cf. Abrahams, 'Personal Power. . . ,' and Keil, *Urban Blues*.

54. Rev. Rubin Lacy started out as a blues singer. He claims that preaching and singing the blues are similar activities. Bruce A. Rosenberg, *The Art of the American Folk Preacher* (New York, 1970), p. 41.

55. *My Bondage and Freedom* (New York, 1969), pp. 252–3.

56. Rosengarten, *Nate Shaw*, back cover.

57. Bruce Dickson Jr., 'The "John and Old Master" Stories and the World of Slavery: A Study in Folktales and History,' *Phylon* (December 1974), 418–29.

58. Rosengarten, *Nate Shaw*, p. 545.

59. H. C. Brearly, 'Ba-ad Nigger,' in: Dundes, *Motherwit*. The Benjamin Franklin work ethic of 'industry and frugality' had been severely discredited by the slave experience. Though black history is full of honest workers, the 'worker' never appears as a heroic figure in black folklore or in black poetry. The folk imagination obviously gives preference to the badman and trickster who does not break his neck for whitey. This may be one more reason why Marxists found it hard to generate working–class solidarity among the black masses. They preferred 'badman' Garvey or Adam C. Powell Jr. See also Stephen Henderson, *Understanding the New Black Poetry: Black Speech & Black Music as Poetic References* (New York, 1972), p. 25.

60. *Crisis in Black and White* (New York, 1964).

61. Rosengarten, *Nate Shaw*, p. 545.

62. Mimi Clar Melnick, 'I Can Peep Through Muddy Water & Spy Dry Land: Boasts in the Blues,' in: Dundes, *Motherwit*; see also Jackson, *Get Your Ass in the Water*, and Abrahams, *Deep Down in the Jungle*.

63. Zora Neal Hurston, *Mules and Men* (Philadelphia, 1935); Banks, Smiley, and Dollard in: Dundes, *Motherwit*.

64. Closely related to the dozens is the toast, a long narrative poem recited on street corners. Its themes are survival in the urban arena, its characters are tricksters or badmen, its plots know the alternative win or lose. See Dennis Wepman, Ronald B. Newman, Murray B. Binderman, 'Toasts: The Black Urban Folk Poetry,' *Journal of American Folklore*, 87 (July-September 1974). See also Jackson, Abrahams, Dundes. Recorded versions: *The Third Rudy Ray Moore Album; The Cockpit, Featuring Petey Wheatstraw — The Devil's Son-In-Law*, Kent Records, 5810 S. Normandie Ave., Los Angeles. For further information consult the record reviews of the *Journal of American Folklore*.

65. Dollard, 'The Dozens: Dialectic of Insult,' in Dundes, *Motherwit*, p. 284.

66. Hannerz, *Soulside*, p. 133. The protagonist of Langston Hughes's novel *Not Without Laughter* (New York, 1963) has to realize that the dozens 'are not really jokes at all, but rather unpleasant realities.' (p. 199). Labov writes: 'Many sounds [= dozens] are 'good' because they are "bad" — because the speaker knows they would arouse disgust and revulsion among those committed to the good standards of middle class society.' — 'Rules for Ritual Insults,' in Kochman, *Rappin'*, p. 289.

Labov points out the difference between ritual and personal insults: 'A personal insult is answered by a denial, excuse, or mitigation, whereas a sound or ritual insult is answered by another sound . . . we must presuppose a well-formed competence on the part of members to distinguish ritual insults from personal insults.' (pp. 298–9). Also: 'Considerable symbolic distance is maintained and serves to insulate the event from other kinds of verbal interaction.' (p. 306).

67. On the cynicism of the ghetto and on its win-or-lose philosophy see Hannerz, Abrahams, Jackson, Szwed and Whitten. Kochman has this to say about the philosophy of the ghetto: 'The purpose for which language is used suggests that the speaker views the social situations into which he moves as essentially agonistic, by which I mean that he sees his environment as consisting of a series of transactions which require that he be continually ready to take advantage of a person or situation or defend himself against being victimized. He has absorbed what Horton has called "street rationality." . . . he hopes to manipulate and control people or situations to give himself a winning edge.' *Rappin'*, pp. 263–4. Dick Gregory, *Nigger: An Autobiography* (New York, 1964), Pocket Book, pp. 40–1. Also L. Hughes, ed., *Book of Negro Humor* (New York, 1966). Also Charles Silberman, *Criminal Violence, Criminal Justice* (New York, 1978).

68. Constance Rourke, *American Humor* (New York, 1931).

69. Jackson, *Get Your Ass in the Water*, p. 39.

70. Paul Oliver, *The Meaning of the Blues* (New York, 1960), contains a bibliography up to 1960. LeRoi Jones, *Blues People* (New York, 1963), though weak on history is full of insights for the present scene. Charles Keil, *Urban Blues* (Chicago, 1966), investigates the blues market. Bruce Jackson, *Wake Up Dead Man: Afro-American Worksongs From Texas Prisons* (Cambridge, 1972), lists discography and bibliography. More articles in Dundes, *Motherwit*, or Whitten, Szwed, *Afro-American Anthropology*. David Evans, 'Technique of Blues Composition among Black Folk-singers,' *Journal of American Folklore*, 87 (July–September, 1974), 240–9.

71. Gunther Schuller, *Early Jazz* (New York, 1968).

72. John S. Mbiti, *African Religions*, p. 87.

73. Capitol Records ST 2459. On it there is also his marvellous version of the 'Street Corner Hustler's Blues'.

74. Abrahams, 'Personal Power. . .'

75. Ron Karenga, 'Black Cultural Nationalism,' in: Gayle, *Black Aesthetic*.

76. Ellison, *Shadow and Act*, p. 90.

77. John Szwed, 'Afro-American Musical Adaptation,' in Whitten/Szwed, *Afro-American Anthropology*, p. 223.

78. See Keil, *Urban Blues*, for a detailed discussion of the relationship of bluesmen, a & r men, and audience. p. 77ff.

79. Ibid., p. 44. — A cartoon in a recent issue of the *New Yorker* shows a successful white rocksinger sipping a drink on the lawn of his ocean-front estate. A luxury yacht is moored nearby. He says to his female companion: 'The Blues have been good to us, Binky!'

80. Evans, 'Technique. . . ,' p. 248.

81. Raymond Williams writes in 'On High and Popular Culture,' *The New*

Republic, Nov. 23, 1974, pp. 13–16: 'There is a kind of culture that has been developed *by* a people or by the majority of a people to express their own meanings and values, over a range from customs to works. There is also a different kind of culture that has been developed *for* a people by an internal or external social group, and embedded in them by a range of processes from repressive imposition to commercial saturation. The distinctions between these two kinds are not simple; influential interaction constantly occurs. The choice of process, in the popularization of an alien culture, depends on variable historical and social conditions but usually includes close attention to the culture that is already popular.'

82. Robert Coles quotes a black nurse on white vs. black culture: 'And look at those white college kids. They are so 'deprived' culturally that they more and more try to talk like us, dress like us, play our music, dance like us. My God, I hear from my sons that there's no limit to the white man's interest in our habits and our values and our ways of doing things! Doesn't that show that we've been busy doing more than feeling sorry for ourselves and complaining that we have nothing? Doesn't that show that we're more than sick, sick, sick? Was it "sick" of us to learn how to survive and keep our thinking straight and learn how to whistle a good tune and pray plenty and smile and swing, rather than sit and cry all day long? I don't want to hear my mother turned into a huge, smothering dictator and my father into some drunken, doped-up philanderer. Who has come and talked to me, or to my brothers, or to thousands and thousands of others like me in Roxbury and Harlem and any other city? Why don't they know about our good side, our tough side, our damn smart side, our clever-as-can-be side?' *The South Goes North*, = vol. III of *Children of Crisis* (Boston, 1971), pp. 206–7.

83. Adam Clayton Powell Jr. was such a 'badman preacher' whose behavior often was felt to be insulting to the white power structure.

84. Richard Dorson recorded evidence of 'the continued techniques from revivalist preaching to civil rights oratory.' *American Folklore and the Historian* (Chicago, 1971), p. 75.

85. Whitten/Szwed, *Afro-American Anthropology*, pp. 35ff.

86. Lydia Parrish and Peter Wood have come to similar conclusions in this question. Herbert Gutman claims that by 1800 Afro-American culture had settled into a relatively stable pattern. Eugene Genovese's monumental work on black religion operates with a locked dialectic between lord and bondsman; it is frozen in time, somewhere around 1840; therefore it cannot tell us much about the historical evolution of Afro-American religious syncretisms. See also Orlando Patterson's review of it in *The New Republic*, Nov. 9, 1974, pp. 37–38.

87. Mbiti, *African Religions*. p. 6 and passim.

88. Genovese, *Roll, Jordan, Roll*, p. 279.

89. Robert Bellah, 'New Religious Consciousness: Rejecting the Past, Designing the Future,' *The New Republic*, Nov. 23, 1974, pp. 33–41.

90. Genovese writes on p. 212: 'Afro-Americans accepted Christianity's celebration of the individual soul and turned it into a weapon of personal and community survival.'

91. Robert Toll's study of minstrelsy arrives at the same conclusions:

'With the singers of slave spirituals, they [black minstrels] sang of an immediate, concrete religion that contrasted greatly to Euro-Americans' otherworldly, abstract religion. Following African patterns, the black folk did not divide the world into antithetical spiritual and secular domains. Their religion and their everyday lives were one. The same 'worldly' language could describe them both.' *Blacking Up*, p. 239. — Miles Mark Fisher, *Negro Slave Songs in the United States* (New York, 1953), makes a strong case for a social interpretation of spirituals. See also John Lovell, Jr., 'The Social Implications of the Negro Spiritual,' in Dundes, *Motherwit*, pp. 452–464. See also Lawrence Levine, 'Slave Songs,' and Sterling Stuckey, 'Through the Prism of Folklore.' I find myself in agreement with Lawrence Levine, who takes Fisher to task for overinterpreting the social implications of black music. However, both Levine and Stuckey argue for a sophisticated exploration of these neglected sources in terms of their social message. My own approach owes to their insights. — On the gnostic and orphic traditions and on the notion of the soul being exiled in the body see Paul Ricoeur, *The Symbolism of Evil* (Boston, 1969), particularly the chapter 'The Archaic Myth: "Soul" and "Body".'

92. Whitten/Szwed, *Afro-American Anthropology*, p. 28. Genovese writes: 'But their apparent indifference to sin, not to be confused with an indifference to injustice or wrongdoing, guaranteed retention of the collective life-affirming quality of the African tradition and thus also became a weapon for personal and community survival. The slave reshaped the Christianity they had embraced; they conquered the religion of those who had conquered them. In their formulation it lacked that terrible inner tension between the sense of guilt and the sense of mission which once provided the ideological dynamism for Western civilization's march to world power. But in return for this loss or revolutionary dynamism, the slaves developed an Afro-American and Christian humanism that affirmed joy in life in the face of every trial.' *Roll, Jordan, Roll*, p. 212.

93. The African devil is such a trickster who competes with God. Cf. Whitten/Szwed, *Afro-American Anthropology*, p. 28. The analogies to Africa are indeed striking. Dathorne writes in his study of African literature that there is no relationship between sex and sin, but a strong identification of sex and pain in African culture — the latter is a shorthand definition of the blues feeling. O. R. Dathorne, *The Black Mind: A History of African Literature* (Minneapolis, 1974).

94. William Francis Allen, Charles Pickard Ware, and Lucy McKim Garrison, *Slave Songs of the United States* (New York, 1867). See Dena Epstein, *Sinful Tunes and Spirituals*.

95. Aretha Franklin, *Live at Fillmore West* (Atlantic), Ray Charles, *Live in Concert* (ABC).

III   MINSTRELSY: IMITATION, PARODY AND TRAVESTY IN BLACK-WHITE INTERACTION RITUALS 1830–1920[1]

> If white and black blend
>   soften and unite
> A thousand ways,
>   is there no black and white?
> Pope, *An Essay on Man*

Throughout history the stigmatized black self has felt the powerful dialectic pull between outside ascription and personal achievement. Depending on how heavily the black problem weighed on the public consciousness the force of outside ascription increased and the chances for personal achievement for blacks dwindled. In short, the black sense of self had to operate with few and limited chances for self realization while being bullied by a disproportionately large number of prefabricated roles. Though this disproportion between strong ascription and limited achievement has remained fairly stable for most blacks, there was a change in the manner in which whites perceived blacks and in which blacks reacted to such stereotyping. An obvious place to study public fantasy at work is the popular stage. Here the role repertoire, the interaction rituals and the iconography of racial stereotypes is fully realized. Unburdened by any serious moral calling and swept by the demotic contempt for propriety the minstrel stage articulated current racial fantasies with an abandon rarely found elsewhere. In many ways the minstrel stage was a comic decompression chamber for minority groups. It offered acculturation, but only at the price of self-denial. Most incoming ethnic groups received a thorough hazing on the popular stage, some more than others, and blacks more and longer than anyone else. The effects of this ongoing process on black people and on black culture have been of lasting consequence. Patterns of minstrelization and deminstrelization may to this day be observed in black-white interactions on stage or in public life. It has penetrated in particular all facets of American popular culture.

By 1900 American popular culture had grown into a poly-ethic hybrid, a vernacular culture quite unlike anything that could be found in either Africa or Europe. On the basis of the previous discussion we may safely assume that the borrowing and exchanging between diverse American groups, of which minstrelsy and jazz are unique results, began at least in the eighteenth century.[2] Unfortunately we have very little dependable evidence, musical or otherwise, to go by. For the nineteenth century documentation is much better. With the rise of minstrelsy, i.e. from 1830 on, a cross-fertilization occurred between Euro-American and Afro-American cultural repertoires with important consequences for all future American popular culture. If there is any substance to Ralph Ellison's claim that American popular culture is 'jazz-shaped' and that it is built on black folklore the evidence would have to be sought in periods when such borrowing and exchanging (whether conscious or unconscious) began.[3] In minstrelsy American vernacular culture began to imitate, incorporate and acknowledge the black idiom.[4]

Blackface minstrelsy is commonly characterized as a symbolic slave code, a set of self-humiliating rules designed by white racists for the disenfranchisement of the black self. The evidence to support this indictment is overwhelming and has given rise to all sorts of neo-abolitionist outrage which has made a sober analysis of minstrelsy difficult. For some time white critics studied minstrelsy with a sense of shame which produced two strategies of evasion: high brow critics dismissed it as puerile (which surely it was), low brow critics belligerently defended it as 'just fun'. Most of the cultural custodians ignored it. But all groups visited the shows in great numbers. Until recently black critics could not afford the study of minstrelsy since they were trying to overcome or forget the social wounds inflicted by the minstrel stereotype. Most of them saw in minstrelsy racism pure and simple. However, we should not judge nineteenth century phenomena with twentieth century attitudes, nor let our Civil Rights sensibility interfere with an understanding of an age less delicate in its racial politics. What would have been a viable alternative for Jacksonian America? How could whites have reacted to the threat of intermixture and acculturation, given the ruling ideology of the day which believed, if not in racial, at least in cultural inequality. Alexis de Tocqueville captured the dilemma of the 1830s.

When I contemplate the condition of the South, I can discover only two modes of action for the white inhabitants of those States: namely, either to emancipate the Negroes and to intermingle with them, or, remaining isolated from them, to keep them in slavery as long as possible.[5]

Minstrelsy anticipated on stage what many Americans deeply feared: the blackening of America. Minstrelsy did in fact create a symbolic language and a comic iconography for 'intermingling' culturally with the African Caliban while at the same time 'isolating' him socially. In blackening his face the white minstrel acculturated voluntarily to his 'comic' vision of blackness, thus anticipating in jest what he feared in earnest. By intermingling with a self-created symbolic Ethiopian he meant to forestall actual assimilation. Yet, however caricatured this vision of blackness may have been it began the translation of black music, black song, and black dance into the mainstream of American popular culture. However, this was a slow process. Initially, it was not the genuine black folklore which appeared on the minstrel stage, but the white man's version of it. But then a feedback pattern emerged and black folklore entered the stage surreptitiously under cover of a white-imposed stereotype.

Many observers of American life in the 1830s have commented on the discrepancy between the American masterplan of an ideal social order and the reality of slavery. The rationality of ideology had to be reconciled to the irrationality of political praxis. Blacks were living proof of that contradiction. One American method of solving social contradictions, as de Tocqueville, Martineau and Trollope have noted, was to ignore them. A second method was to rationalize them, and a third buried them under comedy. Until well into the nineteenth century black slaves had not been viewed as people with a cultural or moral identity, except in isolated cases. During the early decades of the century blacks began to assert their identity, supported by the growing abolitionist debate. Soon various rationalizations of the status quo were forwarded by pro-slavery politicians, but these did not hide the fact that suddenly America was saddled with a moral and epistemological dilemma. Winthrop Jordan writes:

Within every white American who stood confronted by the Negro, there had arisen a perpetual duel between his higher and lower natures. His cultural conscience, his Christianity, his humanitarianism, his ideology of liberty and equality demanded that he regard and treat the Negro as his brother and his countryman, as his equal. At the same moment, however, many of his most profound urges, especially his yearning to maintain the identity of his folk, his passion for domination, his sheer avarice and his sexual desire, impelled him toward conceiving and treating the Negro as inferior to himself, as an American leper.[6]

Minstrelsy reflected this dilemma. It forced one of the tragic figures of American history to accept a comic role on the American public stage. Yet, this process is strangely double-edged. For comedy, though it 'converts downward' or 'dwarfs its object' (Kenneth Burke), is based on a frame of acceptance. Comedy is the mode most appropriate for acculturation since its typical plot model ends with a ritual of social inclusion. When comedy turns to satire, burlesque and grotesque — and there is this movement in minstrelsy — the frame shifts from acceptance to rejection. In minstrelsy the line between acceptance and rejection was very thin. On the one hand, the American common man, who supported these shows, admitted against much enlightened opinion that there was indeed something of interest in blacks and black culture. On the other hand, for reasons of racial and social self-preservation, he could not afford to be serious about his recognition. Therefore he coated it in comedy, humor, satire, or grotesque, depending on his fear of or attraction to blacks. The comic dramaturgy did two things: the blackface minstrel could assert his superiority by making blacks the butt of his comedy, and the humor disclaimed any serious racial or social intention, it was just fun. Yet it was the first recognition of blacks as people with bodies and voices *worthy* of imitation.

Is minstrelsy a singular and unique phenomenon of nineteenth century American society? Most histories treat it as a discrete American feature with an exact periodization and a tangible objective corpus. Surely the objective data of minstrelsy are uniquely American and much work needs to be done to merely inventory the hard material evidence.[7] However, under the surface of minstrelsy there is a 'soft' anthropological substratum, a deep symbolic structure as it were, which makes it an ideal vehicle to study cultural interaction (or melting) between groups under conditions of hegemony or exploitation. On its most abstract level minstrelsy is a symbolic interaction ritual which arises when different classes (rich and poor, urban and rural), different races (black and white), and different castes (ingroup vs. outgroup) have to deal with each other. That minstrelsy is not a parochial American phenomenon is borne out by its tremendous success in colonializing Europe, a success which in Britain lasted into the sixties, sustained by moribund fantasies of empire. What makes minstrelsy work is the race, class, and caste polarity: black and white, primitive and civilized, rich and poor, rural and urban. Jacksonian America was characterized by the emergence of these contradictions:[8] White America, and the South in particular, feared the twin threat of intermixture and insurrection. In America at large political conflict arose over the basic organization of time, space, and life styles which one may loosely call urban and rural. Jacksonian rhetoric articulated populist grievances about the distribution of wealth. The twin dangers of urbanization and industrialization threatened to 'eviscerate' the ideal, free American yeoman, artisan or artist who looms large behind the American dream. Many of these conflicts found articulation in, or gave structure to, minstrelsy: the black-white and urban-rural conflict was explicitly dramatized in the choreography of minstrelsy, where the white interlocutor (master) interacted with the black urban Zip Coon and the black rural Tambo or Bones. The pre-industrial pastoral plantation world of minstrelsy appealed to the laboring poor for a variety of reasons which will be examined below.

In the above binary sets (their ideal-type nature should be taken into account) there is a dominant group and an oppressed group. There is the group that 'wants in' and the dominant group which determines the price of admission. Though there was hardly any danger that white America would lose control of the nation, Jacksonian America was not altogether convinced that it would be able to weather just any conflict. The American Prospero had to look for ways to control the African Caliban by white magic, a magic which would get him out of the double bind of material need against ideological self-image. On the one hand many Americans would just as soon ship all blacks back to Africa, on the other hand — as Miranda puts it so well in *The Tempest* — 'we cannot miss him. He does make our fire, fetch in our wood, and serves in offices that profit us.' In order to maintain the 'titre' of white supremacy, someone had to take care of 'les choses.' The abolitionist discussion threatened to loosen the bonds of slavery and with it the care of 'les choses'. A new type of social control was called for since the contract between white and black, hitherto defined by the visible and material contract of slavery, no longer seemed to hold and had to be substituted by more devious immaterial types of contract. De Tocqueville saw this process in American society at large: 'Thus it is in the United States that the prejudice which repels the Negroes seems to increase in proportion as they are emancipated, and inequality is sanctioned by the *manners* while it is effaced from the *laws* of the country.'[9] Minstrelsy was one such symbolic substitute for material and economic bondage, a new contractual symbolism designed to take over from the whip and the lash. Those first white minstrels literally *incorporated* the role and circumscribed the symbolic space which they wanted blacks to occupy. They assumed the face (mask, persona, role, identity), the bodies and dresses of the unmanageable group and showed them who they 'really were'. And yet, no caricature succeeds when it is purely fantastic. In order to be effective it has to remain within the bounds of probability. Legend has it that one white minstrel bought the entire outfit of a black pushcart vendor, learned his walk, his talk and sales pitch. Beside the caricature there must have been some appreciation, appreciation of the manner in which blacks handled the rather difficult matter of being Americans in blackface.

Appreciation and caricature were already at work on the side of the Africans when they improvised and 'minstrelized' themselves into Americans. On the other side of the color line the process of imitation had started much earlier. Did not the black Africans have to assimilate and incorporate Euro-America? Did not the process of imitation and counter-imitation, of borrowing and exchanging begin before 1830? How did these black Africans deal with time, space, and bodies over which they were denied control but within which they had to survive?

The African slaves had come from a variety of cultural backgrounds and spoke a variety of languages. For these diverse groups the American language, though clearly associated with the oppressor, provided the only common denominator, the only *lingua franca* they had. Most African groups showed a remarkable cultural appetite, freely borrowed from other cultures, and therefore learned English gladly. (It is somewhat ironical that the black Cultural Nationalists should have adopted the nineteenth century Aryan obsession with racial or cultural purity as their battle cry. Purity is not an African ideal nor of much anthropological significance.) Ever since the beginning of the slave trade these incoming black groups created out of what they had brought and what they found a new pidgin culture, recasting and adapting it sufficiently to their own needs and carving out areas which they reserved for themselves. In short, black language, black music, black dance were by 1800 neither purely African nor purely derivative Anglo-Saxon, but already a pidginized, creolized, travestied 'incorporation' of America by blacks. There was also transcultural common ground: not all white culture was alien or unfamiliar to the Africans. It may be assumed that they recognized certain aspects of white culture and compared it to aspects of their own: white song, dance, laughter, sorrow, religion and stories were made up of what anthropologists call 'interaction universals', a behavioral language common to all cultures. Black Africans playfully acquired these forms, or, if they found them strange, caricatured them. White dance, the Schottische or the quadrille, must have appeared singularly stiff to juba dancing blacks and they 'condescendingly' imitated what they saw in the big house. Harriet Martineau, British visitor in Jacksonian America, writes: 'The Americans possess an advantage in regard to the teaching of manners which they do not yet appreciate. They have before their eyes, in the manners of the coloured race, a perpetual caricature of their own follies; a mirror of conventionalism from which they can never escape.'[10]

When around 1830 and 1840 a group of white entertainers began to blacken their faces and imitate black Americans they thought they were imitating African or Ethiopian behavior, at least this is what their playbills announced. What they were trying to imitate, however, was already a new black American hybrid culture whose double edge they failed to appeciate, i.e. their imitation was far from accurate. In fact, the first minstrel shows had precious little to do with Africa, almost nothing with the new Afro-American culture, and took most of its inspiration from Euro-American vernacular sources. But then these white minstrels were new at their difficult business of imitation; they had to train their eyes and limbs. As time went by they learned and added to their repertoire, both in form and content. However travestied their act was, something of the new hybrid culture seeped through. In 1858 Phil Rice published a book of banjo music:

> There were thinly disguised Irish reels, hornpipes and English country dances, but there were others, with strange modal harmonies, and a sharply rhythmic dissonance. . . . Either they were slave songs or Rice was familiar enough with slave music to be able to arrange the melodies in a style similar of slave music. One of his first exercises was the famous 'Juba', the minstrel solo dance that was supposed to have been taken from the plantations.[11]

Something non-white, as Samuel Charters notes, was added at this point to American popular culture, and a collective taste and demand grew for *just that difference*. Further along in the century, after the Civil War, black entertainers saw that minstrelsy was one of the few lucrative careers open to them as performing artists and they began to break into this market improvising their repertoires of song and dance along the desires and demands of an ever-changing audience. By this time minstrelsy had changed from what Twain called its 'pristine purity.' It had become vaudeville with minstrel acts thrown in. The minstrel comedian, however, was and remained a fixture of these shows. Those black artists who broke into this circuit faced a difficult task: they had to work from within prefabricated roles and were up against a public which expected certain types of performance from them. At the same time they had to maintain their integrity and humanity. By post Civil War times minstrelsy had become burdened by a new fear of blacks. Many Americans, North and South, tended to blame blacks for the evils of reconstruction politics and this attitude effected a shift in minstrelsy from comedy to the grotesque. Programs and caricatures, acts and iconography became more vicious and insulting. The paternalistic and condescending humor of early minstrelsy gave way to a mixture of aggression and antebellum sentimentality. Black artists who wanted to enter the minstrel stage at this late a date had to be especially good, especially comic, and especially 'deviant' and double-conscious. They had to outdo the white caricature of alleged African behavior, which was, in fact, a black incorporation of American culture. Several layers of travesty and parody, of imitation and counter-imitation went into their act providing ample room for ambiguity and paradox. No wonder Carl Van Vechten missed the point of William and Walker's performance.[12]

What explains the rise of minstrelsy in 1830 and what explains the viciousness of minstrelsy after 1880?

Minstrelsy was most popular when the black group seemed most threatening. In 1831 the Nat Turner rebellion jolted the abolitionist discussion. The nation became painfully aware of free blacks, whose role, as de Tocqueville remarked, was becoming rather questionable: 'the presence of a free Negro vaguely agitates the minds of his less fortunate brethren and conveys to them a dim notion of their rights.' After the Civil War the threat became more severe. One Northern journalist, James Pike, experienced South Carolina as a *Prostrate State*, the title hinting at some deep sexual threat.[13] Minstrelsy more than before focused on the social, political and cultural pretension of free blacks. By presenting them as children, animals or fools their cultural pretensions were ridiculed, the legitimacy of their political and social demands was questioned and the symbolic dominance of whites was reaffirmed. Even enlightened Americans indulged in minstrelsy. They could do so with an easy conscience since it was just fun. Mark Twain is a case in point. He made a curiously ambivalent use of minstrelsy in Huckleberry Finn and he claimed in his autobiography: 'But if I could have the nigger show back again in its pristine purity and perfection I should have but little further use for opera.'[14] Even if we make allowances for Twain's studied anti-intellectualism his response to minstrelsy was uncritically enthusiastic. For Twain minstrelsy formed part of a Golden Age of childhood where the African primitive could meet with the native child, Huck Finn and Nigger Jim. Twain's flight into jest was symptomatic of the nation. In minstrelsy America buried a deep fear under laughter.

There is more to minstrelsy than unconscious racism or Social Darwinism. It is both of these and more. Mrs. Trollope observed that black manservants were often not treated as individuals with an identity or a sense of shame, but rather as domestic animals before whom Southern ladies would freely undress or speak up.[15] But by the 1830s blacks were moving into public view, and minstrelsy was a symbolic recognition of this fact. Yet, however human blacks were admitted to be they were not accepted as cultural or social equals. The abolitionist discussion, however, split on the moral issue of slavery, did not question that there was a fundamental physical and cultural difference. And, if social differences could not be found, they had to be invented. Already by 1790 free blacks had been described as lazy and shiftless, though there was little historical basis to the accusation. The emergence of this stereotype at this particular time was a symbolic expression of the fear which *free* blacks, not slaves, instilled in Americans. Apologists of slavery, Jefferson among them, saw slaves as children with the attendant immature but safe emotions. Jefferson in 1814: 'What is a child? Completely selfish. His object is to gratify himself.' After emancipation the stereotype shifts from safe to unsafe, acceptable to inacceptable, and blacks are increasingly depicted as uncontrollable animals with emotions that need to be disciplined. Accordingly the mode changes from humor (which includes) to satire and grotesque (which rejects). The changing cast of minstrel shows reflected the various conflicting impulses of this political discussion. The early shows featured plantation types such as 'Banjo' and 'Bones', banjo-picking, heel-kicking blacks. During the sixties minstrel shows concentrated on the uncontrollable, spine-chilling primitivism, the animalism of blacks. In both cases the minstrel shows articulated the fear of 'difference' by exaggerating it and by fixing or domesticating the difference in a stereotype. After recognition and exaggeration the ritual comes to rest in stereotypes: a series of rigid and fixed social and cultural roles which are deeply ingrained in the American consciousness. After 1890 these roles had become so familiar that few people realized the insult. And since few whites realized the degradation of blacks in minstrelsy, blacks found it difficult to blame white America for it. The stereotypes were accepted by many blacks with a stoic resignation. This stance of resignative wisdom is found in black folk culture. It is the superior knowledge of all oppressed classes, the knowledge which turned Diderot's servant Jacques into a fatalist. Thus the minstrel stereotypes became public property and entered advertising (Uncle Ben's Rice, Aunt Jemimah's Pancake Mix), film (Stepin' Fetchit', *Birth of a Nation*), song (coon songs), poetry (Dunbar), jokes, and, last but not least contemporary television programs (*Good Times, The Jeffersons, The Flip Wilson Show*.)

There is something visceral and deeply irrational about minstrelsy. The popular stage, by virtue of its roots in a popular structure of feeling, displays its chief function as social ritual more openly than high theater. Mark Twain had this social function in mind when he introduced Bret Harte's sketch on the 'Heathen Chinee' with the following words:

> The Chinaman is getting to be a pretty frequent figure in the US, and is going to be a great political problem and we thought it well for you to see him on the stage before you had to deal with that problem.[16]

Harte's portrait of the stage-Chinese was not meant to do them justice. The reason for presenting him on stage — in the display window of theater — was not to understand Chinese culture, but to help his American audience to deal with 'that problem'. The presentation was seen as a function of white 'acculturation'. Therefore it had to be a Chinaman the public could tolerate. Normally any public will only deal with the alien on condition that he accept a lower definition of self. Erving Goffman tells us that our role concept aims at a higher social and emotional level than what we know ourselves to be.[17] The presence of the alien facilitates this maneuvre since we can achieve a higher role concept quite easily by ascribing a lower role to the alien outsider. Minstrelsy was the staging of *alien* culture as *lower* culture. Caricature and stereotype are the appropriate strategies. In caricature the teeth of black culture were pulled and as stereotype it would at all times be safely recognizable by all. The folk saying 'You've seen one, you've seen them all' is the formula for handling the unwelcome alien. Its main function is to stabilize the role concept of the domin- ant group and to keep the alien in line. The stabilizing function of stereotype comes into view when individuals of the stereotyped group, whatever the alleged stigma may be, act out of the socially assigned character. W. C. Handy writes that it was dangerous for him when he toured the South to appear out of his minstrel role.[18] He tried not to walk alone, not to wear his regular middle class clothes publicly or outside his tent. Whenever his minstrel troupe entered or left a Southern town, they would go in full formation as a band, strike up 'Dixie' and be safe from persecution. Minstrelsy fits into the larger pattern of Sambo role-magic in the South. Even blacks who never saw a minstrel show were familiar with its reper- toire and used it to manage conflict situations. If blacks left the safety of the proscribed mask they were experienced by whites as uppity and dangerous, liable to do almost anything. However, the better blacks learned to play the role, the more whites feared the real thoughts of blacks which fear urged them to tighten the role corset even further and insist that it be worn religiously.

Hegemony, symbolic or political, operates on a complex set of tacit contractual arrangements. Though minstrelsy was staged by the dominant group for the purpose of symbolic dominance and for the maintenance of white cultural integrity, it could not operate without involving the oppressed group as well. The symbolic pidgin of minstrelsy was first staged in a fantastic, anthropological no-man's land which existed in the imagination of the threatened white group. However, the mockery and travesty were not entirely hostile; they were also an indirect tribute and a crude courtship, the type of courtship Mark Twain immortalized in his story of the relationship between Huck Finn and Nigger Jim which develops to the point that Huck Finn 'humiliates himself before a nigger.' However much the dominant group may reject the threat of the incoming blacks by caricaturing them, it cannot help but acknowledge them and thus get closer to them. By blackening their faces the early minstrel artists struck out for new ground. They left their Puritan-Aryan bodies — which no longer could accommodate their desires — and went on an anthropological exploration into uncharted regions, regions tabooed by their own cultural heritage. The oldest definition of mimesis is the incarnation of the threatening powers in a dance. In the very act of mimesis, however, the dancer is contaminated by or becomes identical with the dance, i.e. with the force he is trying to contain. Black people could not miss that they were 'not only the object of abomination, but also the object of admiration and envy'[19] when they read articles such as the one published in *Knickerbocker Magazine* in 1845. Though the article assumes the pseudoserious rhetoric of minstrelsy, the author half-believes what he parodies:

> Who are our true rulers? The Negro poets, to be sure. Do they not set the fashion, and give laws to the public taste? Let one of them, in the swamps of Carolina, compose a new song, and it no sooner reaches the ear of a white amateur, than it is written down, amended (that is, almost spoilt), printed, and then put upon a course of rapid dissemination, to cease only with the utmost bounds of Anglo-Saxondom,

perhaps with the old world. Meanwhile the poor author digs away
with his hoe, utterly ignorant of his greatness.[20]

What this author presents tongue in cheek, Stephen Foster
admits quite openly. He learned from black workers singing
on the wharfs of Pittsburgh.[21] Although his songs rest firmly
in the stereotype there is a new non-European element in
them. As a European I confess that we experienced Foster's
songs as authentically *non*-European; in fact, we assumed
them to be black. Despite the saccharine vapidity of popular
taste some of the genuine blood, sweat and tears of black music
entered the American mainstream and affected it profoundly.

In short, in minstrelsy American popular culture opened
itself to the massive influence and influx of black American
culture, however travestied the first items may have been.
Without the social corset of minstrelsy certain traditions of
black oral tradition which were smuggled into America via
that stage and which we value today for their intrinsic beauty,
would not have survived the restrictive cultural climate of
nineteenth century America. By keeping blacks barred from
middle class literate culture America forced them back upon
the resources of their folk tradition. Blacks had to develop
their artistry and style in areas *below* cultural standards and
within the circumscription of the minstrel role. While white
America was forcing itself to be 'civilized', black America and
the minstrel stage were unburdened by cultural standards,
most of them imported from Europe. Today we realize the
benefits of such enforced illiterary since the world at large
benefits so much from its cultural results, but we should
always keep in mind the price that was paid in social and
political disenfranchisement. We need not speculate what
would have happened if blacks in America had been permitted
to enter the middle class in 1800 or 1840 when Louis Armstrong tells us that by 1920 many of his Northern black middle
class brethren had to be reeducated in Southern folklore. This
is no cheap apology for slavery or minstrelsy. It merely calls
attention to the fact that black culture thrived in an enforced
cultural enclave of a pre-industrial life style, in the primitive
reservation set aside by the Brave New World, a reservation
which today seems a haven to the culturally alienated. The
lower class folk in Western society, and blacks among them,
have served the dominant classes in two ways: first in setting
up the material basis of high civilization, second in healing the

injuries of that civilization by maintaining alternative life styles and cultures. This explains the strange fact that dominant groups often adopt for their past-time the culture of the people they keep in chains. The historical renaissances of folk cultures (cf. German Romanticism) which occur at regular intervals in Western society openly acknowledge the repression of body and soul which our Western definition of civilization and its capitalist production ethic requires.[22] More than any other oppressed group blacks have served this function in the United States; black culture served as a reminder of the denial of self which Western Civilization extorts from its most successful members.

It remains something of a mystery for many critics that minstrelsy was not only a tremendous success among white male middle and working class audiences, but also quite popular with black performers and black audiences. It would be terribly simple to accuse blacks of being in collusion with their oppressor or to dismiss the phenomenon as identification with the aggressor. It is illuminating to study the motives of black and white audiences side by side. First the white groups.

During the period when minstrelsy and other forms of popular entertainment flourished, American working class audiences suffered the pains of adjustment from a rural to an urban, from an agrarian to a technological society. To save the nation certain facets of the puritan work ethic and of Victorian propriety were marshalled as countermeasures against the disintegration of the 'ideal America'. Toward the end of the century (when incoming immigrants were experienced as 'hordes' by James and Wister), there was a wide-spread cry for a tightening of the reigns of civilization which was felt to be in jeopardy. In this climate of social unrest and Victorian moral rearmament the folk audience found joy in precisely that primitive hedonism which was supposed to be a threat and danger to the Anglo-Saxon moral fibre. Mark Twain reports that his church going aunt strongly disapproved of minstrelsy. Only by promising her that she would see a group of African missionaries did he manage to get her into the minstrel show. Though outraged at first by those 'stage niggers' his pious aunt soon caught the spirit and cackled along with the rest.

For many white audiences the black African was the creature of a pre-industrial life style with a pre-industrial appetite. He was a true primitive, anarchic in his innocent carnality and orality, a cross between animal and child — two rather stable fantasies of white males. Minstrelsy quite openly concentrated on black food, black music and black talk. This was just the fantasy to delight alienated, industrialized, urban America. Supported by the appreciative howls of his audience the individual performer would don the mask and go in search of a pre-civilized innocence, an innocence the 1830 audience was about to lose. By 1890 this sense of loss was total and was drowned in vapid sentimentality. By this time American culture had been feminized, to use Ann Douglas' words.[23] Though there was already a substratum of femininity in the stereotype of blacks (cf. Nigger Jim nursing Tom and mothering Huck Finn), it fully emerged in the sentimental minstrel figure. One very famous minstrel artist specialized in female impersonations. Under cover of these polymorphous minstrel masks American white males could explore the irrational and tabooed areas of their own selves. They could enter an *Afrique de l'esprit*, cut loose in a symbolic colony, go native, enjoy (female) sensuality:

> — wait, wait a minute there, yes it's Karl Marx, that sly old racist skipping away with his teeth together and his eyebrows up trying to make believe it's nothing but Cheap Labor and Overseas Markets. . . .
> O no, colonies are much, much more. Colonies are the outhouses of the European soul, where a fellow can let his pants down and relax, enjoy the smell of his own shit. . . . Christian Europe was always death, Karl, death and repression. Out and down in the colonies, life can be indulged, life and sensuality in all its forms, with no harm done to the Metropolis, nothing to soil those cathedrals, white marble statues, noble thoughts.[24]

Minstrelsy permitted the return to an earlier stage of the civilizing process. Phylogenetically the mask was the visa to animalistic pre-civilization. Ontogenetically it permitted the return to infantile orality. Animal and child merged in the totally hedonistic irrational minstrel creature on stage. By assigning 'forbidden' physical passion to the inferior race and by impersonating this very passion on stage the minstrel could have his cake and eat it: he asserted his mental/genetic superiority and indulged in pleasures forbidden by his own culture. (It is revealing that our culture associates 'physical passion' with low culture.)

What made minstrelsy work among the working poor was

not only the racism but also the implied protest against the puritan work ethic, against the rising threshold of a Victorian guilt culture and against the rigors of protestant rational individualism and its attendant alienation. Mark Twain's preference of minstrel shows over opera illustrates that it served as a folk rejection of Eastern cultural pretense. America in the nineteenth century was afflicted by a pervasive self-doubt in cultural matters which was fanned by visitors such as Basil Hall, Frances Trollope or Dickens. It is telling that these visitors gleefully recorded black and white cultural behavior which sophisticated America would have preferred to flush into invisibility. In minstrelsy Americans could be as uncivilized, barbaric and irrational as they pleased and then pass the buck to blacks. American popular culture could cultivate the very vices that Europeans had singled out as distinctively low American and then exorcize them on the black scapegoat.

The search for the primitive goes hand in hand with the search for the pastoral which is, however, a middle or upper class self-indulgence. By glorifying the golden age of the antebellum plantation South and by telling their audiences that the South was where blacks really wanted to be these Northern minstrels fulfilled two functions: first they offered a palliative for the bad conscience of Southern whites. For minstrelsy was an ex-post-facto rationalization of slavery. W. J. Cash quotes an imaginary Ur-Southerner, apologist of reconstruction politics:

> The lash? A lie, Sir; it had never existed. The only bonds were those of tender understanding, trust, and loyalty. And to prove it, here about us in this very hour of new freedom and bitter strife are hundreds of worn-out Uncle Toms and black mammies still clinging stubbornly to the old masters who can no longer feed them, ten thousand Jim Crows still kicking their heels and whooping for the smile of a white man. Such is the Negro, sir, when he is not corrupted by meddling fools. Hate him? My good friend, we love him dearly — and we alone, for we alone know him.[25]

Secondly, they expressed a certain abolitionist, but nonetheless anti-black sentiment, pervasive in the North. Many abolitionists pontificated about the evils of slavery from the safe perch of an all-white neighborhood, but preferred blacks to remain where they were. The post-Civil War North experienced incoming blacks as a burden and a threat. Stephen Foster's pastoralism of 'Old Folks at Home' and 'Massa's in

the Cold, Cold Ground', though seemingly innocent, expressed a subconscious desire to see blacks 'way down upon the
Swanee river' and not in Pittsburgh. The combined efforts of
primitivism and pastoralism demarcated the true place of niggers in a free society: swimming in innocent carnality in an
illiterate, rural South ringing with song and presided over by
(hopefully) benevolent masters. Even Mrs. Stowe did little to
eradicate this stereotype. The sentiment is by no means dead.
Many 'genuine' lovers of jazz and blues in white America and
Europe labor under this colonial heritage. Sometimes racism
or Social Darwinism surface as pastoral purism. The fanatic
quality of the fights between aficionados over genuine New
Orleans jazz or blues should alert us to the dangerous
psychopathological implications of pastoral purism. For many
of them blues are not genuine if the singer does not qualify in
most of the following points: He should be illiterate, of inde-
terminate age, preferably ugly, recently dragged from his
plough and mule into a makeshift studio, unwilling to make
any money off his music and, most importantly, unwilling to
leave the South. Some of this pastoralism emerged in the
Dixieland revival of the forties. Each wave of nostalgia, it
seems, is fueled by the pastoral yen with all its dubious connotations. It was at work in the writing of Panassié, Mezzrow,
Blesh and many others.

Minstrelsy is proof that negrophilia and negrophobia are
not at all contradictory. Minstrelsy is negrophobia staged as
negrophilia, or vice versa, depending on the respective weight
of the fear or attraction. Pastoralism is an excellent vehicle for
contradictory passions for it wears the same Janus face. Pastoralism arises from a genuine want and desire. Suffering from
overcivilization the dominant, urban group turns to its
agrarian, rural subculture. By saying to the rural poor and
oppressed 'Stay where you are, you've got it so much better'
pastoralism soothes the bad conscience of the oppressor and
makes the oppressed feel better. The exhortation 'Don't
become like us, we're so alienated up here' makes sure that
things stay that way. This is the invisible pragmatic-political
side of the 'genuine' pastoral urge.

Underneath all these contradictory motives there was
indeed genuine interest in black culture. However, though the
interest was genuine both the market and the ruling epis-
temology of color were controlled by tacit racism. Quite

naturally the academic interest fastened on the 'legitimate' aspect of the black experience: religion and spirituals. The Fisk Jubilee singers were a great success with white audiences and this interest was by no means salutary, for the white expectancy led to a whitening of the repertoire. The urban working class, less refined and rigid, found satisfaction in the baser sentiments expressed in minstrelsy. After all it expressed many underdog sentiments, underdog slurs, and class injuries which must have been familiar to them. Underdogs love to laugh about underdogs, and not necessarily in a vicious fashion. Clearly the working class public loved and cherished certain songs about being lonely, ugly, outcast and downtrodden. They also agreed with the hedonism and love of life expressed in minstrelsy. They supported the disdain of capitalist employer norms. Certainly the expression of sorrow met with open hearts. There is a report of Massachusetts mill workers in tears over a plantation melody sung by a black minstrel in a public bar.[26] Underneath Bert William's travestied version of 'Nobody' there is a genuine tragicomic emotion, a *tristesse* which is the substratum of most black culture and which must have made this culture attractive to the laboring poor. This is the double consciousness in black culture, the indirectness of a culture of adversity, the I'm-laughing-to-keep-from-crying sentiment which may be found in other working class folklore.

If white interest in minstrelsy may be characterized by a subconscious desire to reaffirm white cultural dominance, by a search for the primitive and pre-industrial life-style, and by some genuine class solidarity on the level of feeling, what would explain the great popularity of minstrelsy among black audiences all over the country, even to this day? David Grimstead writes that 'conspicuously more Irish went to see the Irish portrayed and more blacks to watch T. D. Rice 'Jump Jim Crow' than regularly attended the theatre'.[27] Clearly the theory that the Sambo black contributed to his own debasement is too simple. Patterns of behavior come into view which unite the black experience to those of other oppressed groups in the world.

The first and foremost attraction of minstrelsy was economic. Black artists after the Civil War found that most avenues of upward mobility were gradually being closed on them. Therefore they moved into the only lucrative routine

open to them. Initially these black performers had to blacken
their faces in order to be 'themselves'. This is an open acknowledgement of the fact that the public did not want to see real
blacks, but Jim Crow, Zip Coon, Banjo and Bones. Thomas
Low Nichols tells us in his autobiography *Forty Years of American Life 1820-1861* (1964) that P. T. Barnum once advertised
for a blackface minstrel, but only found a real black boy who
could, however, sing and dance uncommonly well. Barnum
fitted him out with a wig, blackened his face 'as to pass for a
make-believe one, because the New Yorkers who applauded
what they supposed was a white boy in blackened face and
wooly wig, would have driven the real Negro from the stage
and mobbed his exhibitor.' (p. 70). When later in the century
the minstrel stage did admit blacks the audience insisted on the
mask as a token of submission. Many young blacks submitted
to the tyranny of expectation since minstrelsy permitted survival and economic success on a white market. Bert Williams
had wanted to become a classical actor, but where would he
have found an audience, when certain groups in Boston and
New York weren't accepting white American talent yet? In
this doubly restrictive climate minstrelsy provided some sort
of freedom and black artists carved out a new art form in this
area of repressive tolerance: Afro-American popular entertainment. Gradually these black minstrels managed to change
both form and content of the white-inspired minstrel show to
their advantage by minimizing the dehumanizing aspects and
maximizing the artistic and human potential.

A second attraction lay in competition and gamesmanship.
Black American culture is what Toynbee called a 'warrior
culture', a culture of competition, rich in games, ritual insults,
and verbal one-upmanship. The blackface minstrel was in
competition with white blackface minstrels and also with his
white audience. He had to out-minstrel his white competitors
and out-maneuvre his audience. To wit, the object in this
game of competition was 'to be himself' seen through the filter
of a triple caricature *and* to beat the white man at his racist
game. Due to his training in a rich oral tradition the average
black minstrel found it easy to put down his white rivals, even
though with a bitter taste in his mouth. Many black minstrels
transcended the stereotype through artistic hyperbole. They
exaggerated the minstrel characteristics in a manner so grotesque and absurd that the performance entered the realm of

surrealism (a tradition which has gone right into the making of
Ishmael Reed). The racist slur was outdone by the sheer artistry and nonsense of the performance. Kersand's billiard balls
and William's 'Nobody' come to mind, but also Louis Armstrong's scat vocals. These black artists not only reinterpreted
the stereotype, but they implicitly told their white imper-
sonators and audiences 'You don't know how bad we really
are. Let me play awhile and show you.'[28] Thus they accepted
the counterfeit image of themselves with a poker face; claiming insider knowledge and monopolizing the *mise en scène* of
this double counterfeit they asserted their artistic superiority.
This type of shame management through hyperbolic selfpre-
sentation is not peculiar to America; it is at work in many
ethnic jokes and explains phenomena such as the Jewish anti-
Jewish joke, the Polish anti-Polish joke and much dialect
comedy.[29] The grandfather in Ellison's novel, who is old
enough to be of minstrel vintage, advises his grandson to
apply a 'jiu jitsu of the spirit, a denial and rejection through
agreement' and to yes the white man to death. Black minstrelsy was the jiu jitsu not of the spirit but of song and dance.
Rudi Blesh writes:

> The canny Negro . . . turned his version of the burnt-cork divertis-
> sement into a subtle but devastating caricature of the white Über-
> mensch, employing the blackface like an African ceremonial mask,
> and through the whole thing insinuated his way onto the white
> stage.[30]

The black minstrels were competing for two audiences, sometimes for mixed audiences. This called for subtle maneuvres
and doubleconscious strategies. Their comedy operated on
several levels, and a pattern emerged which is well known in
the world of jazz: the backstage conspiracy. While superfi-
cially confirming the racial stereotype of whites on the front
stage these minstrels let their black audiences in on the backstage secrets. Jazz musicians are familiar with the problem of
having to satisfy mixed audiences. While they have to please
their *economic* gin-guzzling patrons who often know nothing
of jazz and keep asking for the equivalent of minstrel numbers
they try to communicate on a different level with their *musical*
friends. The division of audiences is openly acknowledged in
concert programs, with its set number of crowd pleasers. Even
Preservation Hall has its drunken fools: A sign reads: 'Request

one dollar; "When The Saints Go Marching In" five dollars.'

A third reason for the popularity of minstrelsy among blacks after the Civil War was that artists could for the first time cultivate areas of their own culture and enter into a relationship with their own people in the national limelight. White audiences continued to ask for the symbolic pound of flesh, but when black artists were alone with black audiences minstrelsy was turned into the first institutionalized cultural stage on which blacks could enjoy *aspects* of their own life and culture with impunity. Moreover there was a professional factor: The minstrel stage gave black artists a chance to gain legitimate skills in full view. W. C. Handy writes:

> It goes without saying that minstrels were a disreputable lot in the eyes of a large section of upper-crust Negroes . . . but it was also true that all the best talent of that generation came down the same drain. The composers, the singers, the musicians, the speakers, the stage performers — the minstrel show got them all.[31]

They could thus maintain their own tradition and at the same time absorb various popular musical traditions of Europe. This is quite revolutionary since blacks were not suffered to acquire skills beyond a crude professionalism in most other walks of life. Many black jazz musicians learned their trade in minstrelsy. They were left alone because minstrel music was not legitimate and not in competition with the concert hall. Minstrel musicians were not only suffered but *expected* by their white audiences to play their music and instruments illegitimately, off key and dirty. This was particularly true of the rougher sort of minstrels. As in most cultural pursuits there was class division and distinction in minstrelsy. Charles Edward Smith writes:

> There were two types of minstrels, one more roughhouse than the other; the rougher type of minstrel was the first to employ jazz musicians very widely. It was the whistle stop, cross-roads minstrel that gave work to such people as Butterbeans and Susie, Ma Rainey etc. W. C. Handy worked with a minstrel company that prided itself on its musicianship, Mahara's minstrels.[32]

But these better class minstrels did not play 'legitimate' music beyond the patience and tolerance of their black audiences for very long. Many times a backwater audience had a chance to educate their middle class black brethren. They were instrumental in leading black artists, who took pride in their 'white' literate skills, back into illiterate blues and jazz. As was noted before at the end of the nineteenth century many Northern blacks were cut off from the oral musical style. W. C. Handy describes his conversion to the grass roots:

> My own enlightenment came in Cleveland, Mississippi. I was leading the orchestra in a dance program when someone sent up an odd request. Would we play some of 'our native music', the note asked. This baffled me. The men in this group could not 'fake' and 'sell it' like minstrel men. They were all musicians who bowed strictly to the authority of printed notes. So we played for our anonymous fans an old time Southern melody. . . . A few moments later a second request came up. Would we object if a local colored band played a few dances. . . . The music they made was pretty well in keeping with their looks. They struck up one of those over-and-over strains that seem to have no very clear beginning and certainly no ending at all. The strumming attained a disturbing monotony, but on and on it went, a kind of stuff that has long been associated with cane rows and levee camps. . . . I commenced to wonder if anybody besides small town rounders and their running mates would go for it. The answer was not long in coming. A rain of silver dollars began to fall around the outlandish, stomping feet. The dancers went wild. Dollars, quarters, halves, the shower grew heavier and continued so long I strained my neck to get a better look. There before the boys lay more money than my nine musicians were being paid for the entire engagement. Then I saw the beauty of primitive music. . . . That night a composer was born, an American composer. . . .'[33]

Handy would later be billed as the 'Father of the Blues' though he adopted the blues when it was already a full grown child and Handy a man. The historical irony is that minstrelsy which was designed to 'keep niggers in their place' opened for many blacks a new avenue of social mobility: musical entertainment. It confounds the irony that the illegitimate musical skills into which black minstrels were pushed by the demands of their audiences for vulgar grass roots fun would be one basis of the only American music which European legitimate composers found worthwhile: jazz. This is an instance of what is often called the irony (or cunning) of history.

After looking at minstrelsy as an ongoing symbolic interaction whose deep structure continues to determine patterns of cultural borrowing, exchanging and marketing in the US, we should look at the cultural results, the objective 'sedimentations' and the more subjective patterns of behavior which this initial interaction left behind. There were several key stages each of them with a peculiar cultural corpus. First and foremost we can isolate in the minstrel repertoire the Euro-American cultural tradition which in some areas of America continues unaffected by any outside or black influence. Then we have a new adaptive culture arising from black Africans adjusting to America: Juba, banjo, certain religious traditions which survived the acculturative pressure in enclaves such as the Georgia Islands. The third stage was white minstrel culture which left behind a body of popular songs, skits, dances and stereotyped 'roles'. Though firmly rooted in Euro-American musical and dance tradition these white minstrels affected both white and black America: first and foremost they revolutionized the white structure of feeling by creating a taste for black culture in their audience and secondly they opened the market for black minstrels. The black minstrels had a crucial function for American popular culture: they perfected, enlarged and popularized all previous repertoires and mixtures or hybrids thereof. The traveling minstrel shows were training centers for a large number of black artists. Out of their combined efforts emerged certain forms of popular culture: burlesque, stand-up comedy, ragtime and cakewalk, blues, surrealist nonsense, coon songs and black minstrel tunes. It was this culture which provided the subsoil and market of the emerging jazz music. Black jazz musicians going North to Chicago would then inspire a new group of white translators of black culture: Carmichael, Condon, Beiderbecke, Gershwin, Whiteman and many others became the new minstrels who, *Ladies Home Journal* and the Church notwithstanding, would 'corrupt' American popular taste.

Next to the objective corpus of music and popular culture which came out of these exchanges and productive misunderstandings there is a less tangible *behavioral* heritage as well. The minstrel show refined the talent of improvisation. Most obviously both minstrelsy and early jazz, in contrast to our text-and score-oriented culture, are part of the oral tradition. They are dramatistic, face-to-face forms of improvised culture in which anything goes as long as the audience is entertained. Both minstrelsy and early jazz catered to and belonged to working class tastes, though the educated Americans loved to indulge in it as well. In order to maintain rapport with an ever-changing range of black and white audiences minstrels had to remain in an 'interactionist state of alert.'[34] They had to master the art of quick improvisation. It seems that one of the most important single heritages of minstrelsy is the versatility in the presentation of face, voice, and body on stage in music and dance. Gunther Schuller notes that one important contribution of blacks to American music was the handling of voice.[35] I would enlarge this to the handling of the body, including the voice, i.e. the handling of the entire body as instrument and the handling of instruments as extensions of voice and body. Three different people of radically different political ideologies seem to agree that there is something non-European in American bodily behavior. Ralph Ellison, a black novelist, Sidney Mintz, a white American anthropologist, and C. G. Jung, Swiss psychologist, have suggested that black culture has affected all American culture outside of genetic intermixture. Jung, who visited America in 1909, wrote an article about 'Your Negroid and Indian Behavior' and lists religious behavior, dance, music and sports as instances where the black influence is strongest.[36]

Minstrelsy got its start as the imitation of a dance step: Jim Crow. This dance involved the entire body. Ironically the name of this dance would become the folk term for racism, equally a bodily rejection. Early jazz, as Handy and others have noted, struck listeners so forcibly because it called for the entire body. Many converts to jazz tell us that the initial effect of jazz was total. For many it was not just a music, it was a new body feeling and a new world view. The new gospel of jazz preached against Victorian restraint, against the denial of the body for the sake of a production ethic, and asked its disciples to swing. Minstrelsy may be said to have maintained in the midst of a culture of alienation an affirmative attitude toward the body, literally on the backs of Afro-America. Peter Carroll and David Noble speak of the 'general evisceration of the human body in industrial society'.[37] The puritan work ethic would discipline all bodily activity, be it oral, anal or genital. In proportion to the evisceration of the White Anglo-Saxon Protestant body the oral, anal and genital exaggerations and antics of minstrels grew in importance as cultural compensation. Black minstrels recognized this need of white America and by satisfying it openly were secretly able to fulfil cultural needs of their own. They danced to a different tune and a different need and whenever possible restored black culture to its true functions. Today we would not waste much thought on the presentation of the self by popular singers or dancers. It has become a normal routine of popular entertainers to cut a few buck and wing steps and dance, surely, has been liberated into a free for all. But jazz dance and tap dance clearly are a non-Western presentation of the human body which was salvaged in minstrelsy and professionalized in jazz. Again the uneasy question arises would such dance have survived the cultural ice age of nineteenth century America except in the 'lunatic reservation' of minstrelsy. If we approach this question negatively we may begin to see the crucial importance of minstrelsy: What would American and European culture be like without this tradition of enforced subcultural hedonism? Surely both in high culture and in white Anglo-Saxon folklore the body is suppressed, expressive behavior is corseted in stylized gestures, and ecstasy of any kind is tabooed.

The handling of body as voice would affect the repertoire of songs and the handling of melodies. Early jazz musicians leaned heavily on the melodic tradition of minstrelsy which had by 1900 fused with the black folk tradition. Eileen Southern characterizes the feedback:

> Black folk sang the minstrels songs just as did the whites. There was a curious kind of interaction. The minstrel songs, originally inspired by genuine slave songs, were altered and adapted by white minstrels to the taste of white America in the 19th century and then were taken back again by black folk for further adaptation to Negro musical taste. Thus the songs passed back into the folk tradition from which they had come.[38]

Many minstrel numbers have survived to this day, one being 'Bill Bailey Won't You Please Come Home.' Coon songs, ragtime numbers and marches were part of the minstrel repertoire. Budding musicians would not only learn to play music straight, but given the right audience would rag tunes. Minstrelsy was the vernacular American disrespect for the Western musical tradition and for classical propriety. The New Orleans marching bands played music indistinguishable from that of the minstrel marching bands. 'Was it ragtime. No, no, it was nothing but marches they were playing — brass marches — parade music,' says veteran Picon speaking of the 1890s in New Orleans. Certain aspects of the black religious tradition (hymns, sermons, spirituals) were trivialized in minstrelsy.

They surfaced as innocent jazz numbers such as 'Didn't He Ramble' or in Armstrong's 'Lonesome Road' of 1931, a parody of a black sermon exhorting the faithful to give plentifully. According to bassist Joe Lindsay, Armstrong adlibbed this number. Such hokum numbers were part of the repertoire of the early jazz orchestras and should be judged with some leniency considering the racy public discourse of the times, which was less sensitized to racial disparagement.

This is the deep irony of American popular culture: by confining the black man in a culture stereotype of primitivism and hedonism, the white man inadvertently permitted the black man to salvage large parts of a pre-industrial, anti-Victorian and anti-Puritan working class culture which went into the making of twentieth century American popular culture. This perhaps is what Ellison has in mind when he claims that large parts of American culture are built on black folklore.[44] Today the American musical vernacular with its recognizably black inflection has become the inspiration for most of the international youth culture including that of the East. It serves disenchanted youth all over the world as counterculture: as therapy from social wounds inflicted by Western progress. 'The plaintive and derisive songs of an oppressed people have become the background of the whole society's pleasures and distraction,' writes British anthropologist Geoffrey Gorer in 1953 with a sense of wonder. Fifty years earlier W. E. B. DuBois, then probably the most acculturated black in the United States and well versed in the legitimate culture of the West, wrote prophetically that one day black music would be the key tradition of American musical culture.[45] What, I wonder, would he have made of Elvis Presley or the Rolling Stones?

NOTES

1. A slightly different version has appeared in *The Massachusetts Review* vol. 20, no. 3 (Fall 1979).

2. In an important essay Sidney Mintz remarks: 'Traits and elements of culture bear no pedigrees. . . . Culture diffuses by borrowing and interchange, by learning and imitation — not genetically, but socially. As a result, the immense contribution of African cultures to the contemporary civilizations of the Americas is less noticed, and sometimes

underestimated.' 'Toward an Afro-American History,' *Journal of World History* 13 (1971), 317–31. Historians are beginning to reconstruct the history of 17th and 18th century America on the basis of rather scant evidence. Peter Wood, *Black Majority: Negroes in Colonial South Carolina from 1670 Through the Stono Rebellion* (New York, 1974). William D. Piersen, *Afro-American Culture in 18th Century New England*. Ph.D. Diss. Univ. of Indiana 1975. Dena Epstein, *Sinful Tunes and Spirituals. Black Folk Music to the Civil War* (Urbana, Ill., 1977) thoroughly discredits the school of thought which sees in black culture a pathological version of white culture.

3. *Time*, April 6, 1970, p. 54–5. Ellison is emphatic about this in all his recent interviews, cf. *Massachusetts Review* vol. XVIII/3.

4. There are several ground-breaking studies of minstrelsy: Hans Nathan, *Dan Emmet and the Rise of Early Negro Minstrelsy* (Norman, Okla., 1962). My interpretation of minstrelsy owes much to Robert Toll, *Blacking Up. The Minstrel Show in Nineteenth Century America* (New York, 1974) and to the last chapter in Nathan Huggins' *Harlem Renaissance* (New York, 1971).

    In his discussion with Stanley Edgar Hyman on the place of black folklore in American culture, Ralph Ellison makes a number of pertinent remarks about the social function on minstrelsy and the diametrically opposed reactions to it by whites or blacks. 'Change the Joke and Slip the Yoke', *Shadow and Act*, 48ff.

5. *Democracy in America*, vol. 1 (New York, 1945), p. 394.

6. *The White Man's Burden* (New York, 1974), p. 225. The White Man's Burden or, in Myrdal's words, his 'dilemma' was successfully repressed, flushed into invisibility, relegated to the unconscious whence it reemerged as fantasy. Ellison, who has repeatedly pointed out that much of American culture is based on black folklore, feels ambivalent about the fact that the Negro emerges in white American culture as a figure of such fantasy and that much black culture is adopted by whites for the wrong reasons. On the one hand he writes: 'This unwillingness to resolve the conflict in keeping with his democratic ideals has compelled the white American, figuratively, to force the Negro down into the deeper level of his consciousness, into the inner world, where reason and madness mingle with hope and memory and endlessly give birth to nightmare and to dream; down into the province of the psychiatrist and the artist, from whence spring the lunatic's fancy and the work of art.' On the other hand he castigates just that sort of projection and, implicitly, its cultural results: 'one of the most insidious crimes occurring in this democracy is that of designating another, politically weaker, less socially acceptable, people as the receptacle for one's own fears of and retreats from, reality.' Would he, the Renaissance man from Oklahoma, deny anyone his retreat from reality? *Shadow and Act*, 99–100; 124.

7. George Rehin, 'The Darker Image: American Negro Minstrelsy through the Historian's Lens,' *American Studies* 9, 3pp. 365–73. The Walter Harding Collection of American popular songs which is accessible in the Bodleian (Oxford) contains a great number of minstrel tunes. Mr Harding compiled his own list of 'Songs written about

Negroes — Coon Songs — Negro Dialect — Plantation Jubilee — Ethiopian Melodies before 1918' which I was fortunate to discover in one of the boxes. Harding lists titles, authors and composers.

8. Alexander Saxton, 'Blackface Minstrelsy and Jacksonian Ideology,' *American Quarterly*, 27 (1975), 3–28.

9. P. 374 (italics mine). Diderot in *Jacques le fataliste* provides the classic contract between master and slave. Being in control of 'les choses' the servant is able to blackmail the master into paternalism or benevolence. See Genovese's *Roll Jordan Roll* (New York 1974), a book which develops this dialectic.

10. *Society in America*, ed. by Seymour Martin Lipset (Gloucester, Mass., 1969), p. 288. For a similar observation see Richard P. Madden, *A Twelvemonth's Residence in the West Indies* (Philadelphia, 1835), p. 107.

11. Samuel Charters, *The Country Blues* (New York, 1959/75), pp. 26–7. See also G. Schuller, *Early Jazz* (New York, 1968), p. 36.

12. *In the Garrett* (New York, 1919). Van Vechten comments on Williams and Walker: 'How the darkies danced and sang and cavorted! Real nigger stuff. . . . They're delightful niggers, those inexhaustible Ethiopians, those husky, lanky blacks!' pp. 312f.

13. James Shepherd Pike, a Northern newspaperman and Republican, visited South Carolina in 1873 and wrote a dramatic condemnation of its Republican, black government. Pike is a typical representative of Northern ambivalence toward the Negro. Though he hated slavery he considered blacks as naturally inferior. His description of a session in the South Carolina legislature may be read as an inspiration for a minstrel act; *The Prostrate State. South Carolina under Negro Government* (New York, 1874), 18:

> 'The intellectual level [of the house] is that of a bevy of fresh converts at a negro camp meeting. Of course this kind of talk can be extended indefinitely. It is the doggerel of debate, and not beyond the reach of the lowest parts. Then the negro is imitative in the extreme. He can copy like a parrot or a monkey, and he is always ready for a trial of his skill. He believes he can do anything, and never loses a chance to try, and is just as ready to be laughed at for his failure as applauded for his success. He is more vivacious than the white, and, being more volatile and good-natured, he is correspondingly more irrepressible. His misuse of language in his imitations is at times ludicrous beyond measure. He notoriously loves a joke or an anecdote, and will burst into a broad guffaw on the smallest provocation. He breaks out into an incoherent harangue on the floor just as easily, and being without practice, discipline, or experience . . . he will go on repeating himself, dancing, as it were to the music of his own voice, forever.' D. W. Griffith's minstrelized rendition of the Carolina legislature in *Birth of a Nation* is based on Pike.

14. Chapter 12, *Autobiography*.

15. Frances Trollope, *Domestic Manners of the Americans* (London, 1832, 1927), p. 212. It is reported that Voltaire's lady friend used to undress before her servant whom she did not recognize as a man. This type of negligence or invisibility is not only a matter of race but of class

difference. Eduard Fuchs. *Illustrierte Sittengeschichte vom Mittelalter bis zur Gegenwart.* Bd. 2, München 1910, 7–99.

16. quoted in Toll, p. 169.

17. *The Presentation of Self in Everyday Life* (London, 1959, 1972).

18. *Father of the Blues.*

19. Bernard Wolfe, 'Ecstatic in Blackface. The Negro as Song-and-Dance Man (1947–48)', reprinted in Mezz Mezzrow and Bernard Wolfe, *Really the Blues* (New York, 1946, 1972). Rudolf zur Lippe, *Am eigenen Leibe. Zur Ökonomie des Lebens* (Syndikat 1978).

20. J. Kinnard, 'Who are Our National Poets?' *Knickerbocker Magazine* 26 (1845), repr. in Bruce Jackson (ed.), *The Negro and his Folklore in Nineteenth Century Periodicals* (Austin, 1967). Some blacks did achieve a measure of recognition before the Civil War. In New Orleans one black singer, named Old Corn Meal, was generally accepted by the public as a great talent in 1840. His repertoire included minstrel songs but apparently his performance transcended the stereotype inherent in these songs. In talent he outstripped his white competitors. See Henry A. Kmen, 'Old Corn Meal: A Forgotten Urban Negro Folksinger,' *Journal of American Folklore*, 75 (1962), 29–34.

21. cf. Eileen Southern, *The Music of Black Americans. A History* (New York, 1971), p. 103. This is a curious book, Southern's history is heavily biased in favor of legitimate music. Her comprehension of jazz is rather limited. Alexander Saxton, in 'Blackface Minstrelsy and Jacksonian Ideology' points out the anti-bourgeois, rebellious, antinomian substratum of minstrelsy.

22. cf. Herbert Gutman, *Work Culture and Society* (New York, 1976).

23. Ann Douglas, *The Feminization of American Culture* (New York, 1977) describes the coalition between two disenfranchised groups, women and the clergy, who became custodians of culture and determined the bounds of the permissible. This accounts for the sentimentalizing of American popular repertoires, including that of minstrelsy. By 1870 females as well as blacks had become the object of male 'impersonation'. She writes in a packed sentence: 'Many nineteenth century Americans in the Northeast acted every day as if they believed that economic expansion, urbanization and industrialization represented the greatest good. It is to their credit that they indirectly acknowledged that the pursuit of these "masculine" goals meant damaging, perhaps losing, another good, one they increasingly included under the "feminine" ideal. Yet the fact remains that their regret was calculated not to interfere with their actions. . . . The sentimentalization of theological and secular culture was an inevitable part of the self-evasion of society both committed to laissez faire industrial expansion and disturbed by its consequences.' p. 12.

24. Thomas Pynchon, *Gravity's Rainbow* (Viking 1973), p. 317.

25. *The Mind of the South* (Vintage pb. 1941), p. 131. The chief promoters and innovators of minstrelsy (Rice, Christy, Emmet, Foster) were Northerners who catered in particular to the histrionic tastes of the urban masses. Though Northerners and often Democrats they still supported the antebellum self-image of the South. Alexander Saxton explores the conflicting motives of minstrelsy and Jacksonian ideol-

ogy: op. cit. See also Alan W. C. Green, ' "Jim Crow", "Zip Coon": The Northern Origins of Negro Minstrelsy,' *The Massachusetts Review* 11 (1970). Green underestimates the give and take between black and white.

26. quoted by Gutman, op. cit.
27. 'Melodrama as Echo of the Historically Voiceless', Tamara Hareven (ed.), *Anonymous Americans* (Englewood Cliffs, 1971), p. 91.
28. This dialectic is explored by Nathan Huggins, *Harlem Renaissance*, pp. 244–302.
29. On shame management: Goffman, *Stigma. Notes on the Management of Spoiled Identity* (Englewood Cliffs, 1963).
30. Rudi Blesh, *They All Played Ragtime* (New York, 1950, rev. edn. 1971), pp. 84–5.
31. W. C. Handy, p. 36.
32. 'New Orleans and Traditions in Jazz,' in Nat Hentoff and Albert McCarthy, *Jazz* (New York 1959/75), 31.
33. Handy, pp. 80, 81.
34. See pp. 29f. of this book.
35. *Early Jazz* (New York, 1968).
36. in *Forum* LXXXIII/4 (New York, 1930), pp. 193–199.
37. *The Free and the Unfree. A New History of the United States.* (New York, 1977), p. 154.
38. Southern, p. 104. See also Newman White, 'The White Man in the Woodpile', *American Speech* IV, 1929, 210.
39. Ernest Bornemann draws the analogy between Russian culture and American culture. Russian official culture is built on the folklore of Russian serfs; American culture is built on the folklore of the slaves: 'The Roots of Jazz', in Hentoff and McCarthy, op. cit.
40. *The Souls of Black Folk* (1903).

IV SOCIAL MOBILITY AND CULTURAL STIGMA: THE CASE OF CHICAGO JAZZ

F. Scott Fitzgerald called the twenties the Jazz Age, a ragbag metaphor which he chose for its connotations of alienation and erotic abandon. When at one of Gatsby's parties Vladimir Tostoff's *Jazz History of the World* is played, 'girls were swooning backward playfully into men's arms, even into groups, knowing that someone would arrest their falls.' In Europe Hermann Hesse welcomed the primitive vitality of this new American import. The hero of *Steppenwolf* describes it as a 'whiff of raw meat'. Though his bourgeois self finds it repellent it nonetheless excites him. The raw violence of jazz regenerates and revitalizes his dormant 'drives' and its 'naive, but honest sensousness' exerts a 'powerful charm'.[1] These stereotypes of jazz, and by implication of jazz musicians, stand firmly in the minstrel tradition. They are primarily a bourgeois white fantasy, a mixture of rejection and affirmation of the primitive triggered by the discontent with civilization. Fitzgerald's misnomer which tried to capture the fragmented and alienated sensibility of the lost generation had more to do with a particular life style of the damned and the beautiful than with music. But it is telling that he should try to locate the spirit of the age in its newest fad, jazz, a musical idiom eagerly adopted by the rebellious young and deplored by the establishment. But jazz, this 'noble savage' of Western culture, survived both the eager embrace of the young whites and the hysterical rejection by the cultural custodians. Today the study or practice of jazz no longer call for an apology. It is the only original American contribution to world music; a musical *lingua franca* which has outgrown the scars of its youth and which has broken through the constricting corset of stereotype.[2] Yet patterns of minstrelization and deminstrelization have dogged jazz to this day.

One may begin to explain jazz as the product of socio-economic forces which in their coincidence are uniquely American: the breakdown of a slave culture and the large-scale migration of rural black and white laborers to the North, the contact and mixture of ethnic groups and cultures, urbanization and industrialization, the rise of film and radio.[3] Yet, the rise of jazz has defied a purely socio-economic explanation. Given the market pressures and social stigmata it is surprising that it survived at all. It has at all times in its short history managed to escape its social and transcend its economic determinants. Soon after its emergence it acquired the characteristics of a new art form with its own grammar which articulated at its best a new structure of feeling and helped a variety of groups in America to deal with a fast-changing social scene.

Jazz is both product of social conditions and an autonomous art form with its own developmental logic; it is both *commodity* and *art*. This contradiction is mirrored in its history and its musical grammar and has given rise to what Max Margulies called the 'duality of bygone jazz'.[4] Jazz shares the fate common to all emerging art forms: on the one hand it depended on and was shaped by market pressures, on the other hand it tried to resist and negate these very pressures by developing its inner-artistic potential. By another turn of the screw every musical innovation was threatened by commercialization. Yet, it would be simplistic to accuse jazz of being in collusion with the cultural industry (Adorno). Admittedly jazz was easily prostituted, but at all times there were artists who successfully combatted commercialization. By now it should be evident that jazz has widened our range of musical expressiveness and has profoundly changed our notion of dance.[5]

Jazz stands at the confluence of *rural* and *urban, oral* and *literate* cultures. Its musical roots reach deep into the nineteenth century, not only into genuine folk traditions, but also into travesty, burlesque and parody of black and white traditions. Jazz cannot be divorced from its 'impure' origins; it is foolish to claim it sprang from 'pure' sources which then were soiled and travestied. It is equally foolish to bill it a folklore or an oral tradition, for it was never exclusively so. Though its musical inspiration owes much to local black or white oral traditions, it emerged as a new *literate* musical idiom *in the cities*.[6] Next to film it was the most important new mass cultural phenomenon of the urban scene. Needless to say that urbanization and the dynamics of mass production and distribution affected its content, form and function.

Jazz grew out of a long history of dialectic exchange between blacks and whites under conditions of hegemony and exploitation. It was first of all the entertainment of the laboring poor in New Orleans and, like many other subcultural forms, it was initially associated with sex, crime and depravity. But it rose from the gutter and gained social respectability, though often at the price of artistic compromise. The growing 'legitimation' of jazz, however, implied a growing acknowledgement of the black vernacular culture and of black musicians. Thus custodians of legitimate culture who argued against jazz and for musical standards, were in fact defending the racial and social status quo. Playing 'legit' implied social status and literacy.[7] Literacy and legitimacy were for a long time demarcated by the color line, but even after many blacks broke into literacy this did not mean social mobility. The so-called jazz age is an ideal period in which to study social and cultural interaction between black and white musicians and audiences of different class backgrounds. All groups reacted to this new phenomenon from within their specific class or ethnic context. For the first time white musicians who enjoyed a class advantage over blacks openly acknowledged black artistic superiority. Though this did not immediately improve the social status of black musicians, it did set the stage for future changes by bolstering black self-respect.

Jazz developed within a larger cultural scene, modernism, which in turn was embedded in far-reaching developments of capitalism. Jazz was initially called 'novelty music', a fitting musical accompaniment to the 'new' capitalism with its shift from a production to a consumption ethic. Though there is nothing intrinsic to jazz which would preach a consumption ethic, the minstrel stereotype of incontinence and abandon carried over into jazz and was made to work toward that end by the entertainment business.[8]

In most Jazz Histories Chicago has received short shrift. Jazz was popularized and commercialized, watered down and whitened, say the purist and radical critics.[9] But these very pressures and processes make it an interesting case study which brings into focus the role of black music in American culture. Chicago played indeed a major role in the *whitening* of black vernacular culture and in commercializing it. But it equally continued the process of *blackening* white taste which had begun in minstrelsy.[10] Our own listening habits were conditioned by this long-range osmosis; every commercial or popular musical program on radio and TV carries some of that musical hustle in it. Our popular traditions in song and dance would be unthinkable without the borrowing and exchanging between black and white groups which began in minstrelsy and had its first peak in Chicago during the twenties and thirties.

THE BEGINNINGS

Jazz is older than New Orleans, but it was there that most of the shaping and honing of a musical style known as New Orleans jazz took place. New Orleans was a bustling town at the turn of the century.[11] First there was a mixing of cultures unparalleled in the rest of the United States: Spanish, French, Creole, Black American, White American cultures met and meshed. New Orleans was both sea port and the chief river port that serviced the Mississippi. It had a red light district, Storyville, an area of social licence, a reservation of easy-going morals, set aside by wise city fathers in 1897, where some of the most important early jazz artists, such as Jelly Roll Morton found employment (and a name) and where the subsequent popular association of jazz and immorality originated.[12]

Two elements accelerated the growth of jazz in New Orleans: the breakdown and subsequent urbanization of the old slave culture and the social fall of the free creoles of color. Creoles, who were caught right on the color line, became the mediators between white legitimate music and black folk music. They taught blacks how to play written music and in turn learned how to 'rag' tunes, i.e. improvise.[13] New Orleans was rich in music, and even before the Secretaries of the Navy and of War closed Storyville after four soldiers were killed in a brawl, there had been a steady exodus of musicians who followed the traditional routes of vaudeville artists and minstrel shows and the routes of migrating negroes.[14] Chicago was a natural place to go for a variety of reasons. First, ever since reconstruction days, but increasingly so during the war years, there had been a steady migration of cheap black labor into the Northern cities encouraged by the dream of mobility. In terms of fantasy, mobility and emancipation were synonymous; blues and spiritual were full of mobility imagery, imagery that told of escape, ascent, flight, of trains and quick departures: pack up my things and go, stealing away to Jesus, crossing the river Jordan. Going up the river was the obverse of being sold down the river, and 'up' meant Chicago. In terms of music Chicago was not far from that famous riverboat route North. Boats belonging to the famous Streckfuss brothers of New Orleans would ply the river daily, each of them with a band. By 1917 Chicago was already known as a fast hustling town: 'The City on the Make', 'Hustler to the World', 'Shameless City' are some of the contemporary epithets. Most of all there was money and there were jobs for musicians. There was a large black audience nostalgic for Southern music and a large white audience, ready for something new. Chicago, less caste-ridden than New Orleans, was at once more urban, sophisticated, and liberal with its money. Last but not least, there was the protection of organized crime who supported this music as long as the musicians played their game and did not interfere with the racket.[15] And the law, if it did not participate in the racket, looked the other way.

Without doubt jazz would be unthinkable without the presence of the Afro-American on the American continent. On the other hand jazz is certainly not purely African, or purely Afro-American. It is a music that developed in the center of an assimilation and amalgamation of folk song, work song, wake and funeral music, marches, the dance tradition including the jig, reel, and juba, and the religious tradition. All these traditions had by and during the nineteenth-century fallen under the sway of an irreverent populist leveling influence, had in fact become new American hybrids.[16] New Orleans was not the only place where such mixing occurred, but its heady musical atmosphere and its rather sophisticated and catholic musical taste encouraged competition and innovation.

The leadership of New Orleans musicians was acknowledged by most other musicians of the day. In fact, when New Orleans musicians came to New York or Chicago, Northern blacks who had lived there for some time had to learn oral music all over again, particularly the blues. They, the Northern blacks, had shed their Southern ways and were well within the tradition of white popular music. W. C. Handy who was from a Northern middle class home describes his first encounter with the blues: 'It was the weirdest music I had ever heard . . . I hasten to confess that I took up with low folk forms hesitantly.'[17] But he did when he found out how popular this type of music was with all black audiences. And Louis Armstrong tells us in his autobiography that he was expecting musical wonders from his colleagues in Chicago, but found that he could outplay anyone, particularly in terms of 'improvising', though he had to admit that many Northerners could read music better.

There are black cultural nationalists and militant musicians who imply that whites stole black music and marketed it for their own gain. Whites indeed controlled the means of production and marketing and also dominated the channels of distribution: film, radio, publishing. Moreover blacks depended on the white market and on white taste and therefore were forced to prostitute their music.[18] There is much truth to this indictment, particularly considering the careers of Armstrong and Ellington, but things aren't that simple. There are some major contradictions and ambiguities which need to be considered. First, Jazz began as a subcultural music, as a primitive folklore, with a strictly local appeal. It was the product of a particular social class in the rural South, the laboring poor. The dreams, hopes and aspirations which blacks had invested in that ritualized journey North affected jazz deeply. Going North meant social ascent, literacy, and emancipation. Musicians going North hoped to widen their repertoire, improve their musical skills and appeal to a larger public. Thus they would pay attention to the norms and expectations of this wider market and play up or down to musical standards which were not necessarily theirs. Since the so-called 'low' forms of 'illiterate' jazz met with a great deal of resistance from middle class critics some musicians tended to soften their style and adjust to so-called 'legitimate' forms of playing. Often the decision was purely economic. The choice for black New Orleans musicians was between being poor, subcultural and genuine (Freddie Keppard, Bunk Johnson, etc.) or being an 'adjustor', a 'traitor' to his own tradition, but successful. Both Armstrong and Ellington were often accused of selling out to white demands, when they adopted a lot of Tin-Pan-Alley material in their repertoires. One might argue, however, that their achievement was greater, for they fought to transform and revitalize the popular repertoire and in doing so raised the general level of taste. Whatever they played they managed to keep a degree of musical authenticity and sincerity by using strategies of irony and indirection. Throughout the nineteenth century black musicians and dancers had learned to deal with the constricting stage stereotype of the happy song and dance man. They had to accept the market appeal of their art and had to bow to the tyranny of expectation. By audience demand musicians such as Armstrong and Ellington included 'minstrelized' material in their repertoires. Ellington managed to create surprising orchestral jazz within the stereotype of 'jungle music' which was played nightly to white audiences in the Cotton Club in Harlem, a club which only reluctantly admitted blacks.[19] Second, any popularization of music means a turning away from folk sincerity and country culture. This is the pattern of all culture in mass societies, or of all culture that moves from a pre-industrial country to an industrialized city. New Orleans was still country when compared to Chicago. The urbanization of jazz meant its 'corruption' only for those who believe that culture is pure when it is poor and regional. Third, many black musicians from New Orleans were for the first time exposed to general American middle class culture when they arrived in Chicago. Chicago provided a freedom of a sort they had never before enjoyed. They may have been miserable, lonesome, alienated and homesick, but few went back South. And yet, culturally the South always connoted 'home'. Jelly Roll Morton used to divide America into 'Dixie and Civilization'. Despite all the misery of urban life, in terms of personal freedom Chicago was heaven compared to the South. It did not take long for a new local pride to emerge which is expressed in Lou Rawls' record *Live in Chicago*: 'you're dirty and you're filthy, but yo're my home.'[20]

Then there is the importance of film — this was an entirely new dream world, a dream perspective, both radically new and radically seductive. Blacks during centuries of slavery had not acquired a puritan work ethic and after freedom had little time to do so. Thus work is called 'a slave' to this day; for blacks the historical mortgage of slavery weighs heavily on all labor.[21] Blacks soon found that working for Mr. Charlie down South or up North were two sides of the same coin, exchanging chattel slavery for wage slavery. Thus they became an easy prey for conspicuous consumption which was promoted by the Hollywood dream factory. Armstrong and Ellington, for example, always showed a remarkable interest in and fascination for the lush sweet and luxurious style of film music composers. Armstrong would praise Guy Lombardo, and Ellington adored the music of Paul Whiteman and André Kostelanetz neither of whom ever wrote a note that would compare to Ellington's or Armstrong's music. Perhaps, as Ellison once suggested tongue-in-cheek, blacks acquired an 'expensive' and 'aristocratic' taste after emancipation since their only model of culture was the aristocratic plantation master.

There is a pervasive feeling even among non-militant blacks that whites ripped off black jazz. The rejoinder that all culture lives by borrowing and exchanging and that cultures have no built-in copyright may be equally valid, but is unsatisfactory as an answer. Nobody, not even militant blacks I assume, could blame people for adopting other cultural ways if their own can no longer meet their needs. The rip-off does not lie in individual instances of borrowing but in the total hegemonial situation in which all black culture and black-white amalgams are produced and marketed. Clearly whites enjoyed more options in choosing their music or careers than blacks. It was the blockage of all but the jazz avenue which made blacks feel proprietary about the music and its market. However, the process of assimilation and adoption across the musical 'color line' occurred so early in jazz that practically from the beginning of its emergence as a distinct music the repertoires and musical idioms of black and white musicians overlapped in more than one area. And yet, black musicians felt rightly resentful, when white musicians of lesser talent competed successfully for their jobs. The hegemonial market tended to perpetually downgrade black talent for social, not artistic reasons.

In the early days of the century there were many half-whites, creoles and whites in New Orleans — or poor whites in the entire South — for whom the music of blacks was not so strange since it merged and meshed at many points with their own indigenous folklore. Bill Ferris writes that many blacks played white music and many whites played black music until it becomes somewhat tedious to argue what is white and black.[22] Most music in the South was first of all 'poor people's music' which had crossed ethnic barriers with great ease and in doing so had borrowed from many traditions. The idea of originality or purity seems hardly applicable to a music that many races listened and contributed to. The difference between white and black contributions may be easier to understand if we consider the primarily oral background of black and the primarily literate background of white players. White and creole players came from relatively better social strata and had often enjoyed a classical training in music. They approached jazz from composition, as did Jelly Roll Morton, rather than from improvisation. Fire and innovation, handling of instrument and voice were on the side of oral tradition, control and organization, discipline and harmony on the side of literacy. Many whites from New Orleans adopted the oral black style, and did so with feeling and appreciation, even if they lacked the 'oral' ear. Many blacks strove for literacy in music and learned to read music *after* they had mastered their instrument.[23] The difference in sequence of literacy and/or mastery affected the improvisational talent deeply.

The situation becomes immediately more confusing as great numbers of black and white Southern musicians moved to Chicago where this type of 'poor people's folk music' was not indigenous. It was not altogether unknown, since there had been itinerant musicians before the great exodus to Chigaco. The new music fell on welcome ears: first there were white musicians in Chicago, youngsters, all in their twenties. The most important figure was without doubt Bix Beiderbecke; then there were Benny Goodman, Frank Teschemacher, Jimmy McPartland and others. They found in jazz a means to combat social anomie. Jazz for them was what today would be called counterculture, therapy for the depressive socialization of second generation immigrants. Jazz filled a vacuum for the jazz age flappers, and it spit right in the face of a fossilized middle class culture. These 'serious young white musicians' as LeRoi Jones writes, 'were quick to pick up more or less authentic jazz accents'.[24] Many of these young whites in Chicago found a new lease on life in jazz. They were themselves ethnics who had suffered from caste stigmata: Jews, Russians, Italians, Germans, even Armenians. They appreciated the undercurrent of sorrow and welcomed the hedonism. Many of them were caught between a moribund European ethnic culture, represented by their grandparents, and a cold Victorian middle class American culture, into which they were pushed by their parents. They fled into a musical genre and life style which promised them two things: greater libidinal freedom and instant Americanization. Indeed Mezz Mezzrow, Hoagy Carmichael, Eddie Condon and many others became the new minstrels of the twenties, this time not caricaturing black music and dance but propagating it like a new religion. Invariably they described their first encounter with jazz in metaphors of religious conversion. It was a 'total vision of life' they had found. Mezzrow's book *Really The Blues* is a chronicle of the circumstances which led to the discovery of black culture by a generation of white American ethnics. His book tells us why this music appealed to a young Jew and it helps to explain why many of the promoters of black music were Jews. It is interesting to note that for many young whites the pleasure of this new music far outweighed the social stigma attached to being a jazz musician. Clearly the self-image of being a rebel also played an important role. Hoagy Carmichael, the author of many jazz evergreens, writes that he was 'drugged' by the first experience of jazz.[25] And indeed they were plugged into a total world view, a total cultural idiom, at once more carefree and uninhibited than what they were used to. These white musicians on the strength of their enthusiasm added to the black idiom, changed it to their needs, gave it an aggressive rhythm and beat. Bix Beiderbecke and Frank Teschemacher are good examples. Both were totally committed, both died young, burnt out.[26]

Then there were the mere translators and adaptors. These whites saw that New Orleans music was a lucrative racket and they played this music with verve and dedication. What they needed was a solid technique, not imagination. They never really grew and matured, but stayed in a fixed formula. Their dream was to come as closely as possible to the masters in their own music: thus Eddie Condon still plays pretty much the same music today that he learned in the twenties.[27]

Then there were the commercializers and popularizers, such as Paul Whiteman and Lopez who often presented themselves as the saviors and the true avantgarde of jazz.[28] Their aim was not only to make a lot of money, but also to bring middle class respectability and legitimacy to jazz. Whiteman did this by introducing all sorts of classical gimmicks and band novelties which led to his being called 'The King of Jazz'. Benny Goodman debated in his youth whether he should stay in the classics or go into jazz. He had a choice because he was white. He chose jazz because there was more money in it.[29] Later he was to become the 'King of Swing'. Many black musicians had no such choice. Whites could *choose* jazz, but blacks were typecast on jazz.

The first genuine white innovators in Chicago died young

and poor, the second group, the imitators, remained nicely padded in money, the third, the commercializers and self-styled saviors of jazz made a fortune.

THE AESTHETIC, SOCIAL, AND MORAL STATUS OF JAZZ IN THE EARLY 20th CENTURY

Among blacks from the working class, for the Southside people, for the Southern blacks who had come up North in search of freedom and money, jazz and blues were an expression of their life style. It was their reality. Jazz and blues formed the center of their culture. Still they were constantly reminded that it was a subculture, a race culture, an inferior culture. These social stigmata notwithstanding they supported this music wholeheartedly. One reason for the support of a music of Southern and pre-industrial origin was that it provided an antidote to the injuries of race and class, to the rigors of a new urban work ethic and life style.

For the black middle class this same jazz was a badge of inferiority. If they were to be accepted according to the norms of the dominant culture they had to shed these crude cultural habits. Thus there was a fierce rejection of jazz even among the militant political black groups. The black political movements like the NAACP or the black Chicago Newspaper *The Chicago Defender* fell far behind the advanced positions of W. E. B. DuBois who had championed black music as early as 1903 in his book *The Souls of Black Folk. The Chicago Defender*, which was an heir to many of DuBois' political positions, publicly praised blacks who deserted the black musical style and played music like Paul Whiteman.[30] To us Whiteman's music sounds saccharine and vapid, but during the twenties it represented middle class taste in jazz. Thus the cultural and political pages of *The Chicago Defender* were curiously at odds: Political advancement at the price of cultural denial. They, the *Defender* people, were willing to pay the price of admission to the general cultural mainstream. They would give up jazz à la Armstrong and accept jazz à la Whiteman for the sake of social mobility. Though the *Defender* was very critical of *political* or *social* white dominance, they willingly accepted *cultural* white dominance. They fought the white plantation master, but they accepted him as a cultural master. Nonetheless even middle class blacks enjoyed the blues when they were out of public view. Perry Bradford writes:

It was confusing to see some of those 'Hate Blues' hypocrites, who were preaching and brain-washing before the public how much they detested the blues, yet whenever the same so-called sophisticated intellectuals and top musicians would hear some low-down blues sung and played at a House-Rent Party or some hole in the wall speakeasy, they'd let their hair down, act their age, be themselves, and go to town belly-rubbing and shouting, 'Play 'em daddy — if it's all night long'.[31]

On the other hand there was a curious admiration even among the greatest of jazz musicians for the world of 'legiti- mate', middle class music. The admiration, however, was more for the *world* of the middle class than for the *music*. Blacks were attracted by the lush, plush life style and the attendant social promises of such music. Armstrong and Ellington praised the music of Whiteman and Kostelanetz, although they never managed — even in their worst moments — to sound quite as bad. For those middle class intellectuals and poets who were part of the selfconscious revolution called Harlem Renaissance jazz presented a dilemma. On the one hand, there was 'a loud, sudden, but understandably strained, appreciation for things black' (LeRoi Jones), on the other hand they didn't want to be caught by their white patrons advocat- ing the music of sin and animalism. Thus their patronage of jazz was at best lukewarm.

For the custodians of culture, the groups in control of media, the middle class press, the traditional musical establ- ishment (much of it German), the left groups, the *Ladies Home Journal*, the Hays Office, and the Church, jazz was dirty and low. It was whorehouse music which belonged in 'dens of iniquity' and should stay out of public view. Today we experi- ence Dixieland or New Orleans as good time music which all ages enjoy, particularly children. During the twenties that same music was considered erotic and animalistic. It was a badge of a low cultural life style and a symptom of a social pathology — the after-effects of slavery and bondage. Moreover, the conservative forces realized with a sense of alarm that this music was catching. It was a contagious disease, a disease comparable to masturbation in its effects on the nervous system and the moral fibre. 'Jazz is putting sin into syncopation' or 'Jazz is pointing the way of Greece and Rome' were alarming titles of newspaper articles. Music critics con- sidered it unmusical and, much worse, unoriginal. They looked at it from a classical background and found that it was 'gesunkenes Kulturgut', a corrupted, debased and infantile music largely based on yesterday's classical music.[32]

Among the white upper class, the artistic avantgarde, the jet set and in-groups jazz and blues were a form of 'camp'. They were an expression of an unspoiled, erotic, 'uncivilized' lifestyle which could be enjoyed without having to accept their creators as social equals. Furthermore, the cultural and social aristocracy has always had a built-in contempt for the values of the bourgeoisie. They could give voice to their antibourgeois attitudes by openly consorting with the lumpenproletariat. These rich people would go slumming in Harlem or the Southside. They would monopolize certain clubs in black ghettos, such as the Cotton Club in Harlem, which would not admit blacks. This alienated upper class could go and visit their own primitive selves as it were.

Among youngsters, adolescents, rebels and flappers jazz found its younger champions. If the *Ladies Home Journal* was against it, it had to be good. Jazz was the forbidden fruit. The Church was against it, then there must be fun in it. We tend to forget that emotionally the First World War was a far greater shock than the Second. In Berlin, Paris, and New York youth was given over to burning the candle at both ends. Fitzgerald was the representative writer who captured the frenetic and often suicidal interest of the young in fast life, fast cars, fast sex and fast death. Surely they misunderstood jazz, but for them it represented all these things. As opposed to blacks for whom jazz was the center of their life-style, for these flappers jazz was counter-culture, a criticism of middle-class life styles and accepted values, an expression of the 'Unbehagen an der Kultur'. It was this group of people who provided the audience for those second liner white musicians who were for the most part from middle class ethnic backgrounds. These young musicians, often underage, would sit at the bandstand of Louis Armstrong and pick up every note of this new exciting music. They often had access to literate education and some had received instruction in classical music. Thus they were ahead of the black creative artists in terms of technique and reading skill — Benny Goodman being a good example. They therefore used and applied a different technique of learning to play jazz: whereas the black musicians could not always depend on mnemonic devices (sheet music) to learn to play, but had to rely on their ears, their sense of rhythm and their improvisation skills — the white second liner could copy the music, use the crutch of sheet music and develop his skill and technique much faster. By and large one can tell whether a black or a white musician is playing: often the white musicians have a better classical technique, a less resonant tone and play faster, whereas the black musicians play a more 'oral' and 'vocal' style. One thing is striking: very few white Dixieland bands played the blues. They preferred to play 'hot'.[33]

In the professional music world jazz musicians were recognized as talented, but they were not given the social benefits that would match their musical reputation. It is curious to note that many black jazz musicians of the first generation had an inferiority complex. They always made a distinction between what they called 'legitimate' music and their own music. Within the smaller musical entertainment world there was a strange hierarchy at work: though the jazz musician ranked far above the dance musician in terms of creativity, he rarely ranked above him in social status. The barrier was literacy and color. Jazz musicians were often 'illiterates' by the standards of the established musicians union. And many black musicians simply could not play in 'legitimate' places and were forced back into 'illegitimacy'. I am using these terms with caution because the terms legitimate and illegitimate are problematical in the context of jazz. But the jazz musicians themselves were using these terms, which goes to show how far they had internalized the norms of a dominant culture. Very often jazz musicians knew that they were more creative than their legitimate brethren, they saw that the so-called legitimate musicians copied and stole their music. Nonetheless they still felt or were made to feel inferior to them. This explains why so many of them took great pains to learn how to read sheet music, a process which accelerated the subsequent 'whitening' of the jazz style in the thirties.

Yet, acknowledgement of black jazz came from quarters which none of the American high cultural custodians could have expected. The best European composers of the day championed jazz and pointed out its unique character: Stravinsky, Ravel, Milhaud, Dvorak enjoyed jazz and quoted from it in their own work.[34]

The question of illegitimacy brings us to the world of crime and big business. Jazz was good business. It could be used in preaching a consumption ethic, the hedonism of 'live now die later', or 'buy now and pay later'. An illegitimate music, moreover, went along well with an illegitimate business. To market liquor a music was required which was intoxicating. Indeed many of the moralists likened the effect of drink to jazz, one just as bad for the moral fibre as the other. Thus jazz musicians became the unwilling agents in the transformation of American society from a production ethic to a consumption ethic. This was exactly what big business and advertising were set to bring about. Daniel Bell captures the double bind of a production ethic Capitalism propagating a consumption-ethic hedonism to fan the market:

> On the one hand, the business corporation wants an individual to work hard, pursue a career, accept delayed gratification — to be, in the crude sense, an organisation man. And yet, in its products and its advertisements, the corporation promotes pleasure, instant joy, relaxing and letting go.[35]

Al Capone's mob represents an extreme case of this capitalist double consciousness. On the one hand his organization was run like a combination of family and army with a rigid discipline and long working hours, on the other hand the mob peddled the means of instant gratification: alcohol, jazz, drugs. Jazz musicians often enjoyed the personal protection of gangsters, and Scarface himself was in love with jazz. But the musicians were only safe as long as they were 'disciplined' i.e. did not interfere with ongoing business. Many who didn't acquiesce to Al Capone's demands found themselves dead or without a job.

SOCIAL, MORAL, AND AESTHETIC PRESSURES ON JAZZ AND JAZZ MUSICIANS TOWARD ACCULTURATION 1925–1935

One factor uniting minstrelsy and early jazz was their social status. No matter how many whites learned to play jazz, for the larger American audience the music connoted 'blackness' and therefore 'low culture plus exciting life style'. Early jazz clearly remained within the social framework of minstrelsy. Like minstrelsy it affirmed the current white man's stereotype of blacks. When viewed in this light the craving of many jazz musicians for a legitimate social status seems understandable. Early ragtime or jazz musicians, however low their social status, knew that musically speaking they were transcending minstrelsy. Scott Joplin, for one, knew the worth of his music and Eubie Blake emphatically asserts the cultural importance of ragtime for American popular music. But as jazz carried the stigma of being an illiterate and illegitimate culture the artistry of early jazz musicians failed to gain them a higher social status or wider recognition. The trouble was that there was no direct route from illegitimacy to artistic legitimacy in early jazz. Many minstrel artists and early jazz artists who wanted to break through the racial and social stereotype faced the same problem. To avoid the stereotype they fully promoted and accepted the Tin Pan Alley view of American middle class bliss. Thus they exchanged the low cultural earthiness of minstrelsy and jazz for the vapid sweetness of a homogenized culture. This happened to Cole and Johnson, to Armstrong and Ellington. During the twenties there was no other 'legitimate' place to go from low cultural jazz than to middle class conformity. The price of admission to the halls of classical music was the 'whitening' of jazz. Black musicians began to react to market pressures to clean up and whiten their music. They saw the success of Paul Whiteman and tried half-heartedly to go the road of 'classification'. A certain type of patron, say the businessman on the loose and out to have some fun, wanted their stereotypes of rough, raw, sexual music met. For them jazz musicians ranked with other riff-raff and they would only be entertained if things stayed that way. This was the double bind: the social acceptance of jazz could only be achieved by returning to that very puritan constraint which minstrelsy and early jazz had rebelled against.

White musicians and second-liners whitened black music and translated it into a white structure of feeling. As British rock groups tried to do in the sixties, they whitened blues to suit European tastes. There is a deep ambivalence in this: on the one hand, they literally stole other people's music, but on the other hand, they helped to establish a new dominant musical taste from which the creators would also profit. B. B. King puts it succinctly when he says that though the Stones 'ripped off' black music he would not have become as famous as he did without this help from his white friends.

> The change started when the Rolling Stones and other English groups started to playin' blues and bringing them back to America what I call re-importin' the blues. . . . They had a little bit of a different sound,

simply by them being white and English, but they were playing them with soul in the way they could feel it, and enough so that I could feel it, though maybe not as deeply as some of the people I know, because most of them are kids, and when I say that, I mean young people. So then they started goin' into the underground and hippie places and everybody started to listenin'. And so a lot of the white kids — American kids — started to doing research on the blues. And they found that what the Rolling Stones and a lot of the English groups are doin' has been brought from the black people here in America. So then they started listenin' and trying to get over. To me, some of these people are beginnin' to feel a part of it. Naturally, they can't feel it as we do, because we've *lived* it. . . . They are openin' the door for people that really know the blues, that has been carryin' the message for some time. . . .[36]

White musicians with grander designs suffocated jazz by sweetening it. Paul Whiteman, generally acknowledged as the 'King of Jazz', took all the life out of jazz, all the dirt and reality, streamlined it and brought it to Hollywood. He indeed took the sin out of syncopation. Only then was jazz admitted to the concert hall.

Those musicians, white or black, who did not adjust to the demands of the market failed miserably. The once famous King Oliver died in dire poverty. Mezz Mezzrow, the white Jewish boy who crossed the color line and, except for the pigment of his skin, became black, never made it as a 'black' purist. Jelly Roll Morton never got the fame he deserved. Freddie Keppard was all but forgotten because he refused to have his music recorded for fear that white folk would steal it from him. Much earlier Scott Joplin had to be buried in a pauper's grave along with three or four unknown paupers. Where are the statues that would honor these people?

In brief, the supposedly upward mobility of jazz which took place in the twenties was achieved at a great price. Jazz did indeed move from the whorehouse to the concert hall, from illegitimacy to legitimacy, from invisibility to visibility, from the speakeasy to the Plaza Hotel, from sexuality to an ideology of middle class love, from reality to a Hollywood dream factory, from an oral-hot to a slick-cold style.

Social advancement was paid for with aesthetic attenuation. Those who would not compromise were sacrificed on the altar of purity. Those who did adjust to the market could, if they had the creative talent, take on and change the dominant taste or else they would merely blend into mediocrity.

THE BLACK UNDERGROUND

Despite these profound changes which occurred in the realm of American mass popular entertainment, certain musical styles such as blues and boogie-woogie showed a remarkable resilience. There was a specific market which catered to an entirely black audience: race records. People would queue up in the ghetto for a new release by Bessie Smith, but black record stores would rarely store or sell the music of Paul Whiteman. Many black artists were able to operate on both markets. They would cater to whitened American jazz tastes, but would also continue playing their own music. Quite a number of musicians would not prostitute their music and gave up playing professionally, took jobs and surfaced again when America could assess their true merit.[37] Many Blues and Jazz musicians of the twenties had their renaissance in the forties and fifties, when white listening habits had graduated to a greater appreciation of black music.

Despite commercialization, which affected the repertoire of black musicians such as Louis Armstrong, Duke Ellington and Bessie Smith, a basically black-oriented music continued to be played. Kansas City emerged as the place which would inspire the musical revolution of the forties.[38] While Benny Goodman was entertaining white America with a slick and highly sophisticated type of white swing, black orchestras such as those of Benny Moten, Count Basie and Chick Webb were playing to black audiences. Out of these traditions emerged the style which would surface as Bebop, a sad misnomer. (But then all jazz styles are misnamed: jazz (= intercourse), ragtime (= lumpen-music), blues (= sad music which it isn't), boogie-woogie (= intercourse).)

THE LARGER CULTURAL CHANGES

Jazz was part of a collective change in the American structure of feeling from a prohibitive attitude to a more permissive attitude, from a production ethic to a consumption ethic. In 1933 the repeal of the Volstead act ended prohibition. By the end of the decade the medium of radio had so popularized and commercialized musical taste that oral, Southern jazz and blues had moved from a sporadic ephemeral regional culture to mass entertainment. One consequence was a changing relationship between performer and audience. Whereas the pre-radio interaction had been face to face and improvised, the medium of radio introduced new demands in terms of time, speed, effectiveness and impact. The length of a simple shellac record forced jazz musicians into more complex structures: they had to pack all they had to say into three minutes, had to arrange solos and coordinate timing in a manner not necessary before. Moreover they had no bodily interaction with their audience; thus their music had to be especially catching and convincing. This also added some of that frenetic activity so typical of the earliest recordings.

Certainly the most profound change was that the music moved from a subcultural entertainment to music as big business. Jazz was discovered to be eminently marketable. The changes that business interest in jazz effected would require another book.

NOTES

1. In *The Great Gatsby* (N.Y.: Charles Scribner, 1925, 53) p. 39. See also 'Echoes of the Jazz Age', *The Crack-Up* (N.Y. New Directions, 1945): 'The word jazz in its progress toward respectability has meant first sex, then dancing, then music. It is associated with a state of nervous stimulation, not unlike that of big cities behind the lines of war.' 'For a while boot-leg Negro records with their phallic euphemism made everything suggestive. . . .' Paula S. Fass, *The Damned and the Beautiful. American Youth in the 1920's* (New York, Oxford U. Press, 1977). The book is specifically about college youth. They, not the working class, gave the cliched metaphor of the Jazz Age its meaning. Hermann Hesse, *Der Steppenwolf* (Frankfurt, Suhrkamp, 1927/79).
2. The most competent treatment of early jazz prior to Chicago is Gunther Schuller, *Early Jazz. Its Roots and Musical Development* (N.Y.: Oxford U. Press, 1969). Schuller takes no note of Alfons Dauer, *Der Jazz. Seine Ursprünge und Entwicklung* (Kassel: Röth, 1958), who is excellent on African origins of jazz.
3. One of the best social studies of jazz is still Francis Newton (alias Eric Hobsbawn), *The Jazz Scene* (London, Penguin, 1959).
4. 'The Duality of Bygone Jazz', *The Massachusetts Review* II, 3 (Spring 1961). Margulies is a professional musician and cofounder of Blue Note Records, thus knows the market and its pressures well.
5. A book which is written from a militant black point of view and which stands out as unique is Leroi Jones, *Blues People: The Negro Experience in White America and the Music that Developed From It* (N.Y., William Morrow, 1963). Jones is particularly good on the social pressures within which a black musician had to operate. He tends to downplay the importance of white musicians or traditions in the making of black music. A book equally unique, but less well known is Marshall and Jean Stearn's *Jazz Dance. The Story of American Vernacular Dance. A*

History of Dancing to Jazz, From its African Origins to the Present (New York, Schirmer Paperback, 1964/1979).

6. Dan Morgenstern, 'Jazz as an Urban Music', in George McCue (ed.), *Music in American Society, From Puritan Hymn to Synthesizer* (New Brunswick, Transaction, 1977), 133–43.

7. On the legitimation of culture see P. Bourdieu, *Soziologie der symbolischen Formen* (Frankfurt: Suhrkamp, 1970).

8. Daniel Bell expands this argument in *The Cultural Contradictions of Capitalism* (N.Y., Basic Books, 1976). On the literary side Malcolm Cowley describes the ethic of the Jazz Age in *Exile's Return* (1934, 1951). One of the central texts of modernism T.S. Eliot's *The Waste Land* makes reference to the new music, and in his poem 'Under the Bamboo Tree' Eliot obviously quotes the Johnson/Coles hit tune of 1902.

9. The best sources for the study of Chicago jazz are Chadwick Hansen, 'Social Influence on Jazz Style: Chicago 1920–1930' in A. Dundes (ed.), *Motherwit in the Laughing Barrel* (Englewood Cliffs, Prentice Hall, 1973); Neil Leonhard, *Jazz and the White Americans* (Chicago, University of Chicago, 1964) and Nat Shapiro and Nat Hentoff, *Hear Me Talkin' To Ya. The Story of Jazz As Told By the Men Who Made It* (N.Y., Dover, 1955, 1966). Richard Hadlock, *Jazz Masters of the Twenties* (N.Y., Colliers, 1965).

10. A useful book on popular music by an insider: Alec Wilder, *American Popular Song. The Great Innovators 1900–1950* (N.Y., Oxford University Press, 1972). Wilder follows James T. Maher in crediting black folk music with being the chief inspiration of American popular music: 'the impact of Negro syncopation is the major force in the Americanization of our popular music' p. 12.

11. A remarkable document, not so much for its veracity as for its story-telling, is Jelly Roll Morton's autobiography compiled by Alan Lomax, *Mister Jelly Roll. The Fortunes of Jelly Roll Morton. New Orleans Creole and 'Inventor of Jazz'* (University of Cal., 1950). Gunther Schuller, op. cit., interviews one of the early non-New Orleans musicians, George Morrison. Pops Foster, who played with Oliver and Armstrong, is a remarkably shrewd judge of the New Orleans scene: *The Autobiography of Pops Foster. New Orleans Jazzman* (as told to Tom Stoddard) (Berkeley, University of California, 1971). Foster is of interest; for unlike his fellow jazzmen he did not go to Chicago, but West. Standard is of course Louis Armstrong, *My Life in New Orleans* (N.Y., Signet, 1954). William Schafer, *Brass Bands & New Orleans Jazz* (Baton Rouge, Louisiana State University Press, 1977) and Rudi Blesh & Harriet Janis, *They All Played Ragtime* (N.Y., Oak Publication, 1971) cover transitional years, 1880–1910.

12. First hand accounts in Nat Shapiro and Nat Hentoff, *Hear Me Talkin' to Ya. The Story of Jazz As Told By the Men Who Made It* (Dover, 1955). Compiled from many individual interviews.

13. Creoles excelled particularly on the clarinet and the piano, both higher class instruments requiring more technique than the bugle or cornet. Creoles were Alphonse Picou, Jelly Roll Morton, Sidney Bechet, George Baquet, Armand Piron, Manuel Perez, John Robichaux. See

Danny Barker in *Hear Me Talkin' To Ya* on caste and color in New Orleans, p. 50.

14.   Danny Barker 'All the minstrel shows, like the Rabbit Foot Minstrel and Silas Green and the Georgia Minstrels, used New Orleans musicians year in and year out. You would see a cat disappear, you would wonder where he was, and finally somebody would say that he'd left for one of the shows, that they had sent for him', *Hear Me Talkin' To Ya*, p. 67.

15.   Marty Marsala in *Hear Me Talking' To Ya*: 'And at one place we worked, Capone would come in with about seven or eight guys. They closed the door as soon as he came in. Nobody could come in or out. Then he gets a couple of hundred dollar bills changed and passes them around to the entertainers and waiters. His bodyguard did the passing. We got five or ten bucks just for playing his favorite numbers, sentimental things.' p. 130, and Jimmy McPartland describes how the mob took over the entertainment business, p. 129.

16.   On early cultural contacts between black and white: Dena Epstein, *Sinful Tunes and Spirituals. Black Folk Music to the Civil War*. (Urbana, University of Illinois Press, 1977). This is the most comprehensive study of early black music.

17.   Ironically W. C. Handy would later be billed as *The Father of the Blues* (N.Y., Macmillan, 1941). David Horn comments wryly 'Blues commentators prefer to think of Handy (1873–1958) as an uncle, a godfather, or even a musically-inclined obstetrician in the blues family tree, rather than as the father'. *The Literature of American Music and Folk Music Collections* (Metuchen, Scarecrow Press, 1977). Handy knew how to *write* music, and he was the first to publish and copyright blues he had heard.

18.   Ortiz Walton, *Music: Black, White and Blue: A Sociological Survey of the Use and Misuse of Afro-American Music* (N.Y., Morrow, 1972). Addison Gayle (ed.), *The Black Aesthetic* (N.Y., Doubleday, 1971). Sidney Bechet writes in his autobiography *Treat It Gentle* (N.Y., Dacapo repr., 1960/78) 'And about the time they were making all these changes, some of the white musicianers had taken our style as best they could. They played things that were really our numbers. But, you understand, it wasn't our music. It wasn't us. . . . And in a way, you know, once you had a thing arranged and down like that, you got to owning it. You could put your name on it and almost believe it was yours. But you can't own a thing like that unless you understand a lot more about it than just repeating what's written down.' p. 114.

19.   Jim Haskins, *The Cotton Club. A Pictorial and Social History of the Most Famous Symbol in the Jazz Era* (N.Y., Random House, 1977).

20.   Lou Rawls, *Live in Chicago* (Capitol ST 2459). On it are renditions of Going to Chicago, Tobacco Road, Southside Blues, and Streetcorner Hustler's Blues.

21.   On the relation of culture and labor see Eugene Genovese, *Roll Jordan Roll. The World the Slaves Made* (NY., 1974).

22.   *Blues from the Delta* (London, Studio Vista, 1970). Dena Epstein, op. cit. shows that many blacks of the eighteenth-century practiced a musical bilingualism: they could switch musical codes and play white or black as the situation required.

23.   A typical example for whites playing New Orleans music are the New Orleans Rhythm Kings. Paul Mares admits 'We did our best to copy the colored music we'd heard at home. We did the best we could, but naturally we couldn't play real colored style'. *Hear Me Talkin' To Ya*, p. 123. A good demonstration of the difference in playing styles may be found on the record issued by Folkways 'Jazz Chicago No 2', Folkways FJ2806, which has the same tune played by King Oliver's Jazz Band and by the New Orleans Rhythm Kings.

24.   *Blues People*, p. 149.

25.   In *Hear Me Talkin' To Ya* the Austin gang tell their own story. See also Hoagy Carmichael, *The Stardust Road* (N.Y., Greenwood, 1946/69) and Mezz Mezzrow and Bernard Wolfe, *Really the Blues* (N.Y., Anchor, 1946/72).

26.   The best book on Bix Beiderbecke: Richard M. Sudhalter and Philip R. Evans with William Dean-Myatt, *Bix, Man and Legend* (New Rochelle, Arlington House, 1974).

27.   Eddie Condon, *The Eddie Condon Scrapbook of Jazz* (N.Y., St. Martin's Press, 1973) expresses the juvenile delight this group took in jazz.

28.   Whiteman's book *Jazz* (N.Y., J. H. Sears, 1926) is a curious document. Whiteman manages to write about jazz as if blacks had little or nothing to do with it.

29.   *Hear Me Talkin' To Ya*, p. 126.

30.   Cf. Neil Leonard, *Jazz and the White Americans*, and Chadwick Hansen, 'Social Influences on Jazz Style: Chicago 1920–1930'. A white cultural critic of the day, Gilbert Seldes, who was something of a trendsetter, refused to accept black musical originality as truly American. For him the center of the American Jazz tradition was occupied by Whiteman whose talent and 'originality' no black musician or orchestra leader had yet matched. No wonder that the black middle class or political leaders hesitated to champion black musical originality in the face of such entrenched listening habits and chauvinism. Cf. Harold Cruse, *The Crisis of the Negro Intellectual* (N.Y., Morrow, 1967), p. 98. Ralph Ellison found this middle-class craving for respectability still at work in 1964: 'So much of the modern experimentation in jazz springs — as far as Negro jazz modernists are concerned — from a misplaced shame over the so-called low-class origins of jazz. These are usually men of Negro middle-class background who have some formal training in music and who would like for jazz to be a 'respectable' form of expression tied up with other forms of revolt. They'd like to dry up the deep, rowdy stream of jazz until it becomes a very thin trickle of respectable sound indeed.' *Shadow and Act*, p. 8.

31.   Perry Bradford, *Born with the Blues. The True Story of the Pioneering Blues Singers and Musicians in the Early Days of Jazz* (N.Y., Oak, 1965).

32.   Cf. Leonard and Hensen. Leonard has listed some of the objections against jazz by cultural custodians. Professor Henry Van Dyke of Princeton thought jazz was not music at all (p. 21), music critic Sigmund Spaeth wrote that it was 'merely a raucus and inarticulate shouting of hoarse-throated instruments, with each player trying to outdo his fellows, in fantastic cacophony.' Concert pianist Ashley Pettis: 'Jazz is nothing more or less than the distortion of every aesthe-

tic principle', p. 24. A New York doctor, Dr. Elliott Rawlings, diagnosed 'Jazz music causes drunkenness. . . . Reason and reflection are
lost and the actions of the persons are directed by the stronger animal
passions.' The Illinois Vigilance Association led by Rev. Philip Yarrow
claimed that in 1921–22 alone jazz had caused the downfall of 1000
girls. H. E. Krehbiel held the theory that jazz brought the negro
brothels up North. And Minister A. W. Beaven saw early that jazz 'has
gotten beyond the dance and the music and is now an attitude toward
life in general. We are afflicted with a moral and spiritual anemia.' pp.
24ff.

33. Margulies, op. cit., writes: 'Its (Chicago jazz) emotion was desperate,
sometimes repressed and self-conscious, always unconsoled and
unconsolable. It was an authentic post-war expression, revealing alter-
nate flashes of despair, disillusion, and revolt. Ironically, Tin Pan Alley,
with its whole stock-in-trade of false emotion, vulgar publicity, and
big money manipulation, was the source of the Chicago style'. P. 211,
Theodore Maynard, a minor poet of the twenties, diagnosed jazz as an
affliction of the rich:

JAZZ

The band began its music, and I saw
A hundred people in the cabaret
Stand up in couples meekly to obey
The arbitrary and remorseless law
Of custom. And I wondered what could draw
Their weary wills to this fulfillment. Gay
They were not. They embraced without dismay,
Lovers who showed an awful lack of awe.

Then, as I sat and drank my wine apart,
I pondered on this new religion, which
Lay heavily on the faces of the rich,
Who, occupied with ritual, never smiled —
Because I heard, within my quiet heart,
Happiness laughing like a little child.

34. When Dvorak wrote 'In the Negro melodies of America I discover all
that is needed for a great, a noble school of music', a well-respected
music critic, Edward MacDowell 'laughed at the American national
musical costume' advocated by the 'Bohemian Dvorak' and demanded
to know what Negro music had to do with 'Americanism in art',
Leonard, p. 24–5.

35. *The Cultural Contradictions of Capitalism.* See also Cowley, *Exile's
Return.*

36. Phyl Garland, *The Sound of Soul* (Chicago, Regnery, 1969) has a
lengthy interview with B. B. King which should be required reading
for pop fans, pp. 91–2.

37. The newest general history of jazz is by James Lincoln Collier, *The
Making of Jazz* (N.Y., Delta, 1978). It lists books for further reading
and a discography.

38. Ross Russell, *Jazz Style in Kansas City and the Southwest* (Berkeley,
University of California Press, 1971).

V   ORAL TRADITION AND THE QUEST FOR LITERACY: THE CRISIS OF BLACK WRITERS FROM PHILLIS WHEATLEY TO RALPH ELLISON[1]

1770–1920

While inner-black folklore has always been an unideological, though often uncomfortable, expression of black reality, the earliest formal poetry by blacks is an example of upward cultural mimesis. Phillis Wheatley arrived from Africa in 1761, eight years old, and was raised in Puritan New England. She developed into a child prodigy and was handed around as a curious object. In 1773 she traveled to England; these are her lines to the University of Cambridge:

> 'T was not long since I left my native shore,
> The land of errors and Egyptian gloom;
> Father of mercy! 't was thy gracious hand
> Brought me in safety from those dark abodes.

Not all of her poetry is as blatantly anti-African as these lines, which contain all the stereotyped racial attitudes of the day couched in a neoclassical poetic register: land of errors, Egyptian gloom. But a facile dismissal of Phillis Wheatley would be irresponsible. She is an example of cultural mimicry. Her adaptation was proportionate to the social pressures which forced her to conform. She identifies with her oppressors to the point of repeating the racism of the late eighteenth century. Here is David Hume on the subject of race:

> I am apt to suspect the negroes, and in general all the other species of men (for there are four or five different kinds) to be naturally inferior to the whites. There never was a civilized nation of any other complexion than white, nor even any individual either in action or speculation.

This sentiment, which defines civilization by 'action and speculation,' may have been excusable in 1748 as the pinnacle of current enlightenment. However, it survived the emancipatory rhetoric of the American and French revolutions by going underground where it persisted as the tacit majority assumption. Black Cultural Nationalists and Muslims today are still fighting Hume by taking recourse to a 'superior' African tradition. Phillis Wheatley was denied this alternative; for the notion of cultural relativity, which today is preached but rarely practiced, did not exist in her time. She had to choose a lie for literary survival. This lie ruined her when she tried to make it on her own: she married a black scoundrel, John Peters, who left her and her small children to die in abject poverty. She lived the blues and didn't know it.

The evaluation of the formal tradition in black poetry has been attended to most assiduously by black and white critics, most of them conditioned in new critical thinking. Although their criticism is itself an interesting anthropological case study in the history of race relations, it would be futile to gather evidence or to track down naive new critical prejudice. The black poet was asked to 'transcend' his blackness and to enter into poetic universality.[2] Since even the most liberal critic knew subconsciously that this was an impossible order, poetic segregation could continue on formal excuses. Black poets rightly refused to talk to a universal void, but insisted upon speaking to their people and about themselves, using the particular code of their culture. This was exceedingly difficult in a social arena which was dominated by a certain class and a certain taste. Ralph Ellison sums it up:

> Now, the pathetic element in the history of Negro American writing is that it started out by reflecting the styles popular at the time, styles uninterested in the human complexity of Negroes. . . . And let's face it, these were times when white publishers and the white reading public only wished to encounter certain types of Negroes in poetry and fiction.[3]

Literary criticism was hardly interested in the struggle of black poets to find the style that was 'interested in the human complexity of the Negroes'; it fastened on the results and found them wanting. Measured with the yardstick of literate taste, practically all black poetry was regarded as 'not worth talking about.' The ongoing struggle of black poets with form and style, i.e. with their cultural code, was largely underestimated. Let us, therefore, select a few poets in the history of black formal poetry who have explored, or were caught in, the conflict between their cultural code and that of the white majority and who were torn between formal imitation (with its implicit danger of self-denial) and formal separatism (which lived dangerously close to minstrelsy) or between thematic imitation or rebellion. In general few black poets have committed themselves to an unequivocal choice which would belie their ambivalent history. Most of them have explored several 'layers' of their identity and have often shifted their allegiance in order to explore the full potential of their cultural reality. What to some white critics seemed like shiftlessness or shallowness in formal matters, had a historical basis in the 'shiftlessness' of the black cultural heritage, and a practical basis in the difficulty of finding an audience. Therefore much formal poetry has an exploratory and tentative character demonstrating a variety of styles and improvisational performances. Rather than deny the validity of this search for an authentic voice or question the value of experimentation, the ideal-type alternatives sketched above should serve to illustrate the tremendous odds and the constant danger of thematic and formal alienation which beset black poets. Often the conflict remained unresolved because time and place, audience and market-place did not permit a resolution. To the literary historian these form-theme contradictions are important landmarks in the evolution of an Afro-American formal culture within the dominant Euro-American scene.

Paul Laurence Dunbar is normally credited with being the first innovator and first truly gifted formal poet among blacks. William Dean Howells patronized him and called him 'the first man of pure African blood of American civilization to feel Negro life aesthetically and express it lyrically.' Dunbar was in a way revolutionary because he tried his hand at black vernacular poetry, thus choosing the road of formal separatism. This choice was both difficult and dangerous in terms of identity and integrity; for Dunbar tried the black idiom at the height of minstrelsy, i.e. at a time when white audiences were prepared to like black humorous speech for the wrong reasons. The reading public appreciated the work of Joel Chandler Harris, a white Southerner, who had collected and rewritten black folk stories, particularly those that encouraged paternalistic reactions. In theme Dunbar was equally caught in a trap. In keeping with the postbellum myth he sang of the good old plantation days. Thus Dunbar was caught between theme, form, and audience. His white readers would receive his poetry as a humorous confirmation of their assumptions, his black literate audience, though it always revered him for breaking through the barrier of race, was reminded of a class it had left and had learned to despise. Dunbar's critical instincts prevented him from being at ease with the 'jingle in the broken tongue'; in fact he was somewhat alarmed to find that his white readers preferred his black vernacular poetry to his rhymes in 'white' English. Despite these odds Dunbar continued the quest for poetic literacy. However, his sound intention — the emancipation of a black idiom for poetic use — was only partially successful.

At the turn of the century black formal poets were barred by external circumstances and the rigors of the market from discovering the resources of their folklore or, if they did, their public would misread them. Minstrelsy had spoiled the medium and at least the white and black literate public. But a change was at hand. The influx of a large rural population to the urban centers of the North and the adaptation of an oral tradition to Northern ghettos created a new social arena for a development of black cultural forms. The shift of blacks from rural to urban environments was accelerated by World War I: jobs were available, the army was open, a leap forward in political emancipation seemed at hand. Even DuBois, co-founder of the NAACP, called for a shift in strategy and for black support of the American war effort. The awakening after the war was twofold: blacks returning from the war found that they were still the labor reserve, first fired and last hired, and realized that there was little hope for any solidarity between black and white workers. But this political awakening was accompanied by a racial or ethnic awakening which was to have far-reaching consequences in the Garvey movement, the Crow Jim attitude of Black Muslims, and present day Nationalism. The urban matrix offered more spiritual freedom though black labor continued to depend on white capital. To be sure, the categorical division of the races hardened in the labor conflicts and defined patterns of settlement in the cities. This ghettoization perpetuated the oral culture of the rural South. And yet, even in these reduced circumstances the city offered greater anonymity and therefore more freedom to cultivate a life style and to assume whatever new identity was promoted by prophets such as Marcus Garvey or race leaders such as DuBois or Locke.

In the North energies are released and given intellectual channeliza-
tion — energies which in most Negroes in the South have been forced
to take either a physical form or . . . to be expressed as nervous
tension, anxiety and hysteria.[4]

White hegemony, though still much in evidence, was deper-
sonalized. The white master became the system. This meant
that the radical forms of double-conscious interaction such as
Samboism, Uncle Tomism, or Badness adjusted to the more
mediated urban variants of black-white interaction. This freedom also increased the chances of upward mobility and
institutionalized class stratification. While the rural South
knew only one class of blacks (the difference between house
and field niggers is vastly exaggerated), suddenly three classes
sprang up: the middle class, the working people, and the
underdogs. Booker T. Washington had told his rural public 'to
cast down your buckets where you are,' i.e. to advance *as one
class* of farmers, craftsmen, and laborers and merely to
improve their skills in these professions; W. E. B. DuBois
exhorted his urban public to produce a 'talented tenth,' a new
group of Afro-American leaders. Washington's advice,
though reactionary and Uncle Tomish, encouraged in-group
solidarity; DuBois's advice, though militant, entailed the
dangers of alienation within the black community, particularly between the literate and illiterate factions. Indeed the
ethnic awakening after World War I split into two movements: the literate public turned to the so-called Harlem
Renaissance; the illiterate proletariat listened to Marcus Garvey and his back-to-Africa promises.[5]

The new generation of literate Harlemites, their audience
politically disillusioned and ethnically alerted, struck a new
chord. Langston Hughes, James Weldon Johnson, Wallace
Thurman, Jean Toomer, and Claude McKay stand out from
the Renaissance group of poets. Langston Hughes' work is
symptomatic of the total achievement of the Renaissance, for
he began the necessary reconciliation of formal black poets to
their folk roots and grass roots audience. Due to the limitations dictated to poets by current taste and decorum he could
not go to the depth of folk truth and honesty, but he went far
enough to be called at different times and by different people
subversive, prurient, shallow, simplistic, racist, terms which
might well apply to oral folk culture when viewed from a
literate, formal perspective. Hughes wanted to be as honest as
the blues:

One of the most promising of the young Negro poets said to me once: 'I want to be a poet — not a Negro poet,' meaning, I believe, 'I want to write like a white poet,' meaning subconsciously 'I would like to be a white poet,' meaning behind that 'I would like to be white.' I was sorry the young man said that, for no great poet has ever been afraid of being himself.[6]

Being himself, Hughes realized, was no simple thing for a bi-cultural American with a double consciousness. And finding the appropriate audience was even more of a problem. His attitude towards the black middle class and their ability to respond to one of their own poets was expressed by Simple, the character which made Hughes famous: 'it also seems like he did not make any money because the white folks wouldn't buy his stuff and the Negroes didn't pay him no mind because he wasn't already famous.' Just as much as Hughes refused to fulfill white expectations of wildness and abandon, he refused to be 'just a poet — not a Negro poet.' He never withdrew into formal complexity for the sake of assimilation nor did he fall for a pseudo-African revival. He was only nineteen when he wrote his most anthologized and perhaps most haunting poem: 'The Negro Speaks of Rivers.' The river, a powerful poetic symbol in our culture, is of especial significance for Afro-Americans. Hughes, unconsciously I am sure, taps this rich connotative vein in the first lines:

I've known rivers
ancient as the world and older than the flow of human
              blood in human veins.

The flow of human blood in analogy to the flow of rivers, both a continuum and a constant renewal. Human veins surround the soul and body as rivers encompass the earth.

My soul has grown deep like the rivers.

Although Hughes could hardly foresee the semantic importance of the word 'soul' for future generations, he caught the spirit of solidarity inherent in the original meaning of the word. Here it appears in its metaphysical and universal sense, but its overtones reach into its present and more sensual meaning. The remainder of the poem refers to the senses, particularly to those sensual experiences meaningful to blacks in Africa and the Americas.

Hughes is best known for his attempts to adapt the forms of oral culture to literature. Despite the fact that literarization does violence to the true modality of these oral forms, which is spontaneous and improvised and which depends on the ephemeral act of performance and on the personality of the performer, he emancipated his culture more than others, particularly through books such as *The Weary Blues*. Measured against Eliot and Pound his contribution to American high culture may be slender, but given the cultural and social odds of his situation he may be called a revolutionary.

Not all Renaissance poets were as successful as Hughes. The problem of an assimilationist formal idiom against a separatist, radical theme is epitomized by the success of another poem of the Renaissance: Claude McKay's 'If We Must Die.' In content this is the first revolutionary formal poem, expressing the post-World-War-I anger of blacks. But McKay used the restrained and constricting form of the sonnet to drive his point home:

> If we must die, let it not be like hogs
> Hunted and penned in an inglorious spot,
> While round us bark the mad and hungry dogs,
> Making their mock at our accursed lot.

The final couplet reads:

> Like men we'll face the murderous, cowardly pack,
> Pressed to the wall, dying, but fighting back!

There is no whining here, but neither is there the blues feeling nor the suppleness of the urban idiom which Hughes mastered so well. The classical form 'universalizes' the immediacy of the issue and pushes it back into the nineteenth century pose of manful heroism, popularized by Henley or Kipling. Scholarly rumor has it that Winston Churchill, oblivious of the race and intention of the author, read these lines to parliament at the beginning of World War II to bolster courage.[7] Indeed the language positively roars, but the assimilationist form sends the reader off into a mistaken interpretation, as it did Churchill. When McKay did turn to urban black vernacular in his novel *Home to Harlem*, his bourgeois readers were enraged by what their antennae recorded as sexual levity. The dilemma of Renaissance poets between the requirements of theme and form and the expectations of their divided audience remained thus: the black poet should find his ethnic identity, but most available ethnic forms were stigmatized as low class for the very black audience that had moved into bourgeois literacy. While advocating black self-reliance, they expected poetry from their aspiring poets that did not endanger their precarious middle class identity. On the other hand, the white reading public which went slumming in Harlem sought the sensual richness of low class culture and expected to hear the tom-toms in the voices of black poets, whose supposedly naive African savagery they cherished more than the complexity of their Afro-American identity. Although white and black prejudice of what poetry should be did hamper the evolution of a truly black formal culture, the Renaissance marked tremendous gains: its legacy was a higher degree of racial consciousness, more freedom to deal with folk themes, it emancipated the blues and urban black speech, and it gave America black music and jazz, both of which were to stay as the most important black contribution to American culture. It is ironical that blues and jazz were by no means unanimously cheered by Renaissance artists. Only Hughes really allied himself with both these 'subcultural' forms. However important these changes were for black poets, they were largely ideological and did not affect black society at large. Few people in Harlem knew that a Renaissance was in progress. The blues people listened to Garvey's speeches extolling black pride and black virtues in terms of a radical-mystical Pan-Africanism which must have seemed as repulsive as it was unfeasible to the less desperate black middle class. Ultimately both Renaissance and Garveyism were dreams, and both were deferred. The Depression washed off the cultural and ethnic cosmetics, and the face of American social reality seemed unchanged. But an ideological heritage, however impotent when facing economic reality, does not merely evaporate. The dreams which inspired the Renaissance poets and the fervor of the grass roots people's belief in Garvey remained after Renaissance and Garvey had left. Both the nationalistic and ethnic sentiment, embryonically developed by the Renaissance among the literate and by Garvey among the grass roots public, touched on a common and collective black interest. Both the contemporary Black Cultural Nationalists and the radical movements have picked up where Renaissance and Garvey left off. Even Africa was affected by the Renaissance, for Senghor's 'negritude' was inspired by it, and Harlem was for a while the cultural center of blacks everywhere.

POST-HARLEM

In his essay 'Blueprint for Negro Writing' (1937) Richard Wright took black writers to task for seeing themselves in the mirror of white appreciation.[8] Instead of turning out white-inspired literature black artists should tap the two most important sources of folk art: religion and folklore and its 'social system of artistic communication.' Wright did not get around to practice what he preached. The folk aesthetic which he had in mind for black writing did not enter his major works which he continued to write in a manner that would 'shock banker's daughters'.

Wright's hesitation in following his own advice and taking up folklore as a basis for a black aesthetic has to do with the contradictory nature of the materials on the one hand and the ambiguous place of black folklore in the context of a white dominated American culture on the other. The materials of folklore cannot be divorced from the social and political context in which they arose. Thus the oral tradition is bound up with disenfranchisement, illiteracy and bondage; conversely, black folklore also stores fantasies and dreams, harbors that populist cussedness, so typical of all folklore, and counsels strategies of survival in an oppressive world. Depending on the situation in which it is put to use it may be reactionary or progressive, escapist or rebellious. The fact that general America was prepared to accept black folklore as minstrelsy surely did not endear it to black militants or writers trying to find a voice. Richard Wright's ritualized journey North which he recorded in *Black Boy* represents a flight from that symbolic South of folklore, and a quest for greater participation in a literate American culture. It is all the more striking that in theory he should have made that plea for a black aesthetic as early as he did. Ascent to literacy and immersion in the black group are, as Bob Stepto writes, the two drives characteristic of black literature. In practice Wright continued to write about the psychological and political inhibition of ascent. Fifteen years after his influential essay his literary descendants (Ellison says 'relatives') declared their artistic independence and substantiated their criticism of the one-sided thrust of Wright's fiction by showing that his blueprint could be met. James Baldwin captured the religion of the story front church — both its pleasure and its pain — and Ralph Ellison managed to work veritable lodes of folklore into his novel *Invisible Man* which combines a ritual of ascent and a ritual of immersion. Of the two Ellison has been indefatigable in translating the forms of black social ritual into artistic consciousness. Though in contrast to Wright Ellison's final assessment of black folklore would be more optimistic he does not belittle the pain that went into its making. Instead he would like to rescue the depth of experience, the energy, and ability to tolerate contradictions.[9] Though indebted to the modernist tradition of European literature, particularly to Hemingway, Conrad, Joyce, Eliot, and Malraux, whose distrust in socialist or other realism he shared, his chief allegiance is to his own untapped and rich cultural tradition: black folklore. Like Joyce he endeavors to recreate the consciousness of his race in its very forms and structures. He will not provide the security of a political vision or a rational orientation outside or above the forms of communication which its own black culture has produced in reaction to a long history of contradictions. Like his modernist masters Ellison has tried to recreate the 'webs of significance', the symbolic structures, and patterns of behavior of his specific culture. In other words, he has refused to arrange the data of black culture to fit a current world view, a political platform, or a sociological paradigm. Instead he seeks out the ambiguities and conflicts which have gone into the making of the modern and particularly the modern Afro-American identity and its social system of communication. The charge may be made, and has been made, that Ellison counsels reconciliation with the problem-solving strategies of black folklore and thus with the circumsribed social space of a folk horizon and that he existentializes the politics of slavery by equating the black condition with the 'human condition'. Ellison is, like Faulkner, ambiguous in his attitude toward Southern culture and black folklore. One suspects that Ellison, who grew up in an urban middle class home and received a larger than ordinary sense of entitlement from his mother, was socially and psychologically secure enough to accept the self-contradictory tradition of black folklore. This is a pattern that one may observe in the literature of many other ethnic groups as well: that only the most assimilated members of American minorities have been able to fully articulate what it means to be a 'minority' and to create an art out of the experience and 'privilege' of being a marginal man. In other words, the actual battle of 'integration' had to be won for those who wanted to write about their past in other than wound-worshipping terms. Those trapped in the actual political systems of oppression (e.g. the oral culture of the South) knew instinctively that their old culture was a barrier on the road toward American self-hood, and therefore used it only as a source of political energy.

They had to deny its redeeming function and had to let the next generation rescue it. Cultural identity, in other words, is the privilege of the socially secure. Thus the apparent paradox: the rural folk culture of blacks could only be rescued artistically from the *urban* perspective and by those who were not themselves trapped by it. Ellison brought that type of self-confidence into his work. Perhaps it had to do with a singular fact that he began as a musician. Of all black artists musicians have the strongest sense of self, and justifiably so. For musicians know first hand what America owes to blacks. With such a strong sense of self the quest for a past and the previous condition may invite celebration rather than self-hatred. Ellison describes his first contact with folk culture in *Shadow and Act* (p. 7):

> I was of the city, you see. But during the fall cotton-picking season certain kids left school and went with their parents to work in the cotton fields . . . those trips to the cotton patch seemed to me an enviable experience because the kids came back with such wonderful stories. And it wasn't the hard work which they stressed, but the communion, the playing, the eating, the dancing and the singing. And they brought back jokes, our Negro jokes — not those told about Negroes by whites — and they always returned with Negro folk stories which I'd never heard before and which couldn't be found in any books I know about. This was something to affirm and I felt there was a richness in it.

It is perhaps easier to celebrate that which does not enslave you, and indeed there are hints of pastoralism in his urban appreciation of rural folklore. But Ellison's political act lies elsewhere: first, in combatting the notion of pathology in black life (a sociological diagnosis with built-in therapeutic strategies that tend to perpetuate the disease of 'victimism'). Secondly, in making a conscious effort to rescue black folklore and folk consciousness, to open the shackles of folklore and to utilize the productive energy in it. Invisibility is the key metaphor of his novel, but it explains his aesthetic and his social criticism as well. The thrust of his art is toward literacy and consciousness. By recreating the deep structures of black oral culture as literature, he makes them both visible and available outside the social organization which created them. It may have been an advantage that Ellison was not trapped in the folk culture that he so lovingly (and optimistically) restores. And his ability may explain Richard Wright's inability or hesitation to deal affirmatively with folk materials; for Wright carried the scars of his Southern folk tradition into exile. Perhaps Wright knew the sedentary and conservative power of folklore only too well and therefore created a Bigger Thomas who lacked the compensatory resources and the escape mechanisms of a folk culture — imagine Bigger singing the Blues! Wright radicalized the psychological aspect of blackness and racism. Ellison, on the other hand, realized that preaching pathology perpetuates it and worshipping wounds ultimately leads to 'victimism'. Instead he has tried to bolster black pride and self-respect by stressing the celebration, the self-help and survival wisdom in black life. Ellison and Wright are — as relatives — two chips off the same block of black history and experience.

The modernist authors, whom Ellison often cites as his teachers, used universal or mythological 'codes' and therefore encouraged readings which stressed the universal or apolitical appeal of their work. Inspired by T. S. Eliot's directives on reading Joyce, an entire generation of critics joined the exodus from the nightmare of history into mythic universality and spatial form.[11] Ellison, though not denying the universal substratum of his folkloristic code, would insist on its historical singularity. Black folklore, which is an ironic commentary on some of the most cherished background assumptions or myths of American history, refuses to be reduced to purely archetypal or universal paradigms. To wit, Oedipus and Brer Rabbit represent paradigmatic patterns of behavior and ritual which are part of a larger cultural 'web of significance', but the former is now truly universal whereas the latter is still rooted in Afro-American history. In other words, Brer Rabbit may well have oedipal features, but Oedipus lacks the specific *historical* wisdom of Brer Rabbit.

Black folklore represents a sedimentation of behavior and ritual developed in labor and perfected in play. In a world of necessity it carved out areas of freedom. Ellison, in keeping with his childhood encounter with folklore, stresses the celebration. He writes 'It (folklore) announced the Negro's willingness to trust his own experience, his own sensibilities as to the definition of reality, rather than allow his masters to define these crucial matters for him.' Yet, neither his experience nor his sensibility were shaped outside the range of his master's voice or influence. The color line demarcated also the area of safety for fantasy and consciousness. Fantasy had to be put on a leash as animal story, consciousness was camouflaged as 'lie', and rebellion masqueraded as self-irony. These strategies of *Verfremdung* guaranteed survival in an oppressive symbolic universe, but the strategy itself was also a mark of oppression. They sharpened the appreciation of style and ingenuity, but they also counseled evasion and deception. Its 'grammar' is double-edged. Today these strategies and their cultural results do not always appeal to militant readers who tend to underestimate the radical edge in them. But as Ellison says, Sambo, Jack and Uncle Tom were in their own way heroic, given the circumstances in which they had to operate. They were determined to maintain a sense of self beyond the definition which the white man forced on them. Black folklore could not ignore the white man's definition of reality, but it could lampoon and transcend it. Though not unburdened by the white presence, it was never unhinged by it. Ellison writes:

> It preserves mainly those situations which have repeated themselves again and again in the history of any given group. It describes those rites, manners, customs, and so forth, which insure the good life, or destroy it; and it describes those boundaries of feeling, thought and action which that particular group had found to be the limitation of the human condition. It projects this wisdom in symbols which express the group's will to survive; it embodies those values by which the group lives and dies.

But for the black folk in the South 'the limitations of the human condition' were largely man-made, they were political, and not existential nor anthropological. The group's will to survive is evident in folklore, but those rituals in preservation of the caste line and in protection from violence 'were thoughtlessly accepted by blacks and whites.' The adverb is significant. It indicates the rigorous social determination of these forms and the taboo or ban on a conscious exploration of the 'human condition'. The revolutionary message of black folklore had to stay in allegorical hiding, had to be displaced as comedy, must hibernate in invisibility, until a poet of consciousness would come and rescue it.

Ever since the Greeks freed art from its mythical shackles its grammar of forms has moved toward consciousness. Though the evolution of poetic and social forms of communication has always been interdependent, poetry has constantly transcended the purely social. The emancipatory promise of art is its ability to explore the not-yet-conscious and not-yet-possible on the one hand, and its drive towards ever greater self-consciousness on the other. Literary fantasy and the dreams of poets are infinite, bounded by their adventurous spirit, but folklore and myth are by comparison finite provinces of communally sanctioned behavior and meaning. Unlike forms of private fantasy they are moored to the context and dynamics of lived reality. Though the highest praise has often been given to those Western artists who have become the antennae or conscience of their race, they did not merely 'reproduce' the folklore of their people, but brought it into self-critical light. Moreover, these modernist authors took the freedom to ransack the arsenal of formal and thematic archetypes of literate and oral traditions anywhere and transform them into private systems of aesthetic communication. In contrast, neither the form nor content of myth or folklore may be changed at the whim of a creative individual. Aristotle warned his contemporary artists not to tamper with ancient myths since these had achieved a paradigmatic perfection. Folklore, far less venerable, but equally public, is subject to what Jakobson called 'die Präventivzensur der Gemeinschaft'. It is an intersubjectively controlled sedimentation of experience and therefore answerable to a shared horizon. Consequently it exerts strong social control, a power which it loses as it becomes 'poeticized' and turns into fiction (One is reminded of Heraclitus' complaint that Homer destroyed the power of the Olympians by turning them into a fiction.) A member of a folk group may not treat the oral forms or traditions of his community disrespectfully. In art the poet is in control of his fantasy — like a God paring his fingernails — as much as the reader is in control of his response.

Within its social organization folklore promotes solidarity and in-group cohesion by providing a set of solutions to common, not individual, problems. It creates and maintains survival strategies and provides protection for the individual as long as he remains loyal to the group and its horizon. As was noted above, this protection may also turn into a trap. Unless made conscious, 'the patterns of behavior maintained by folklore tend to reproduce the pathology of sociopsychological bondage even after the material causes of this pathology have been changed and removed.' This is the conservative and sedentary force of folklore. At the same time folklore may be liberating in another respect. While restrictive in conceptual freedom, it emancipates the senses and liberates through rituals of catharsis. There is a potentially emancipatory force in folklore, which is often lacking in our Victorian notion of high cultural response. This is its unabashed delight in innocent carnality and its ability to squeeze a large measure of freedom from the enjoyment and acceptance of the here and now. Though freedom of choice and poetic license, so typical of Western art, are lacking in folklore, it enjoys a wealth of collective rituals of catharsis, rituals which may seem compulsive to the uninitiated but which provide quite another area of freedom, an area where the folk artist can enjoy his licence: this is in terms of performance and style. Individual talent in folk art surfaces as style. It is in this area that folk-trained artists have most to offer. This talent has carried over into literature: public poetry readings by black poets are probably the most successful branch of black literary activity.

Ellison's function as a writer, his social act, is to counteract the repressive forces of ritualized behavior by lifting it from thoughtlessness into consciousness, from social habit into poetic form. At the same time Ellison has tried to salvage the affirmative and cathartic power of folklore, its delight in histrionics, and its supple, jazz-like style. The importance of performance and style is evident in all forms of black folklore, and Ellison freely draws on these resources of his culture. In short, the function of folklore in Ellison's fiction is neither ornamental, nor purely comical, nor universal. Folklore is his semiotic cultural code, a system of shared meanings and a pragmatic charter of behavior. Its forms are sedimentations of historical consciousness and deeply rooted cultural mores. Characteristic of these forms is a persistent ambivalence toward white America. They teach a strategy of suspending affirmation or rejection and withholding judgement until the situation in which they are used either forces, permits, or invites it. Some folk stories cherished most by the folk for their deep truths are told as lies. The label 'lie' is the visa which permits their being told at large. This licencing mechanism is similar in folklore or fiction; for fiction, as the French say, is a form of *mentir vrai*, of lying truthfully. The subterfuge is particularly called for at those times or in those places which render telling the truth dangerous.

The short story 'Flying Home' (1944) which is based on one such folk lie is an excellent vehicle to illustrate Ellison's use of black folklore.[15] A close examination of this story will show why so much praise and criticism of his work, particularly of *Invisible Man* (1953) which is remarkably similar, is based on an inadequate and incomplete understanding of black folk forms.[16]

The title 'Flying Home' is full of irony; it alludes to black history, myth, and current politics. 'Flying' is an old metaphor of freedom, popularized by spirituals and politicized by the underground railway. Richard Wright picked this symbol as a metaphor of Bigger's crude aspirations, and Jesse B. Semple playfully links NASA and freedom.[17] Flying also recalls the hope which blacks had placed in the air force as an agency of integration, and what became of that hope. The title is identical with that of a popular tune which Lionel Hampton wrote as a tribute to a largely white air force. Archetypal burrowers have come up with a number of mythological allusions, all of which are irreverently and ironically deflated by the folk tale (the lie) within the story:[18] Todd-Icarus, the black pilot, tries to reach the light, that is, whiteness. The *hubris* of his aspirations causes his downfall and he returns 'home' as the prodigal son. But, as the folk tale underlines, his homecoming is ambivalent. He returns to the repressed history of the 'previous' (folk) tradition and to that class from which he had fled for the sake of a white bourgeois mirage. The very title unites various contexts of meaning under one multilayered symbol. 'Flying Home' is meaningful in the context of mythology, black folklore, black history, current politics, psychology, and jazz. Of all these contexts folklore has the last word, for it comments and reflects upon every other possible analogy in an ironical manner. The high seriousness of the mythological tale, the depressing facts of black history, the sociology of race relations, the aspirations of the middle class — all these are lampooned and deflated by the wisdom of the folk tale. Ellison uses the affirmation and rejection of the folk tale for ironic purposes; a sort of double fiction built into his fiction. Folklore is — so to speak — his metafiction. The folk story Ellison makes use of acquired shape and meaning through generations of shared experience. It was shaped by the 'Präventivzensur der Gemeinschaft'. Thus its structure is the product of spontaneous social interaction; in Ellison's word a 'thoughtless' process. Ellison's method of artistic composition is that of the modernist poets, that is, it is highly conscious. Though his story is manifestly simple, it has a deliberate structure, a substratum of symbolic correspondences and parallelisms. But this deliberate structure stays close to the folk experience. Ellison merely parallels and thus concentrates folk forms by finding the appropriate connection in action, incident, and character. His story is folklore in poetically condensed form. His remarkable talent lies in making the right choice from black folk forms and themes and combining them into a new coherent symbolic system.

The episode and its prehistory are short. A black pilot named Todd is stationed in a training camp in Alabama impatiently waiting for his call to active duty. Caught between the 'ignorant black men' of his past and the condescending white officers of his present situation, he expects to achieve his manhood and identity by meeting the enemy. (Todd seems to have internalized the practice of transferring inner-societal conflicts to an outside enemy.) On a practice run with an airplane which is appropriately called 'advanced trainer,' he pulls the plane into a steep climb and loses control. Before he can correct his error by going into a dive, a buzzard hits the propeller, blurs his vision, and he panicks into an emergency landing. All this is prehistory. The story begins as Todd regains consciousness. A black sharecropper with the historically significant name of Jefferson and his son find him and try to help him up, but his foot is broken. While the son runs for help, the old man helps Todd pass the time. A conversation ensues between this old, resigned, but eminently wise sharecropper and the achievement-oriented Todd, a conversation which gradually unveils the repressed identity conflicts in Todd and his mindless overassimilation to a white world which rejects him. Todd feels the danger instinctively: 'It came to him suddenly that there was something sinister about the conversation, that he was flying unwilling into unsafe and uncharted regions,' namely into his repressed knowledge of racial reality which had anticipated the inevitable wreck of his ambitions. Todd believes that he is one hundred years ahead of Jefferson in terms of consciousness and civil liberties ('that buzzard knocked me back a hundred years') and he rationalizes this difference as a negative definition of his identity. 'Sure he's all right. Nice and kind and helpful. But he's not you.'

This social advancement, which has alienated him from the spontaneous racial solidarity of his group and which feeds his subconscious anxiety and panic, forbids him to accept Jefferson's rather relentless folk wisdom.[19] Jefferson, to be sure, is proud of Todd's achievement, but he knows its limitations better than Todd. His rather naive attempt to kill time and entertain Todd turns into a Freudian blunder, which triggers the conflict; for the tale of the 'Flying Fool' is an allegory of the hopes generated by the Emancipation and the sobering experiences of Reconstruction which uses the concrete metaphors of flight to drive its point home. Todd is doubly affected by this tale: allegorically he is a member of that group whose aspiration the tale calls 'foolish', concretely he is trying to fly into a higher class. Todd does not want to be reminded of the tale's moral which Jefferson specifies as 'you have to come by the white folks, too.' It is the 'too' implied in the story which angers him, since he would like to be taken as an individual person with unalienable rights rather than as a member of a group, a class, or a race.

Todd's rage surprises Jefferson who had not intended any harm. The unresolved tension between Jefferson and Todd is then interrupted by the white landowner, Graves, accompanied by two attendants from a lunatic asylum who threaten to put him into a strait jacket. Now the presumptive threat to his identity by a member of his race turns into a real threat to his life by a racist; Todd's resistance to the moral of Jefferson's story explodes into hysteria, an indication that Todd has totally lost control of himself and his ambivalent situation.[20] At the same time the confirmation of Jeff's wisdom by Graves' act forces Todd's repressed knowledge back into his consciousness: 'And then a part of him stood behind it all, watching the surprise in Graves' red face and his own hysteria.' The threat to identity and life is then resolved by Jefferson who becomes his 'sole salvation in an insane world of outrage and humiliation.' Jefferson's subtle act of Tomism deflects Graves' aggression by humoring his prejudice. The story ends with a scene, not totally convincing in its latent optimism, which takes the return of the prodigal son more or less seriously. Against the backdrop of harmonious nature, which has always been a hackneyed cipher of human peace and solidarity, Todd is carried away by Jefferson and his son. The structural necessity of having to put a story to bed seems to have gotten the better of reality.

STRUCTURE, POINT OF VIEW, AND AUTHOR'S STANCE

In the tradition of the modern novel, Ellison chose a central intelligence whose consciousness controls and reproduces direct speech or action and whose personal feelings and emotions blend in free indirect style and interior monologue. This mixture is a stylistic means to dramatize both the schizoid consciousness of Blacks, which DuBois characterized as 'double consciousness', and the tension between affective experience and analytical narration. Double consciousness refers to the psychological dilemma of having to look at oneself using the linguistic and metaphorical conventions of a racist language. Free indirect style refers to an analogous formal convention of a dual focus: namely to the narrative process in which the protagonist describes his experience using the narrative conventions of an external narrator. Though feeling as an 'I' he refers to himself as a 'he'. This convention which has been largely internalized by the reading public creates an ironic distance between the experiencer and the narrator, though both are lodged in one person. This is the formal analogue to a real split in the human personality, dramatically aggravated in the black experience, namely the split between having a body and being a body.

The irony generated by this split in the human psyche was perfected by James, Joyce, Faulkner, and other modern writers. In the case of black writers this 'technical device' loudly proclaims its social basis. Here the irony and ambivalence inherent in the discrepancy between their achieved and ascribed status, between their virtual and real identities, remains socially active no matter how high Blacks climb up the social ladder. In the present story Todd's preoccupation with his body signals (anguish, panic, dread, sweat, hysteria, pounding blood, shame) bears out his precarious body consciousness. The split between bodily experience — which is a direct and unmediated expression of his anxieties — and analytic, narrative distance — which tries to control these anxieties by explanation — is particularly obvious in Ellison's use of this ironic convention. (My italics for direct speech and interior monologue.)

> *That buzzard knocked me back a hundred years*, he thought. Irony danced within him like the gnats circling the old man's head. *With all I've learned I'm dependent upon this 'peasant's' sense of time and space.* His leg throbbed. In the plane, instead of time being measured by the rhythms of pain and a kid's legs, the instruments would have told him at a glance. Twisting upon his elbows he saw where dust had powdered the plane's fuselage, feeling the lump form in his throat that was always there when he thought of flight. *It's crouched there*, he thought, *like the abandoned shell of a locust. I'm naked without it. Not a machine, a suit of clothes you wear.* And with a sudden embarrassment and wonder he whispered, *'It's the only dignity I have . . .'*

The mixture of unmediated experience in interior monologue or direct speech (dependence, nakedness, dignity) and the ironic distance of free indirect style (irony, lump in his throat, embarrassment, wonder) permits Ellison to contrast immediacy and distance without ever appearing as a narrator or author in the text. This stylistic variation is further heightened by his use of different levels of discourse and their attendant registers: Jefferson's warm and ironic black idiom, Todd's meticulously neutral, and Graves' aggressively racist diction. By contrasting them Ellison identifies the linguistic markers of oppression (Graves), survival mimicry (Jefferson) and isolation (Todd).

Ellison's dramatization of time as a process of consciousness, in which representational and represented time are one, underlines Todd's impatience and fear. Moreover, he has lost the safety of physical time (his instruments) and is dependent on psychological time (pain). His impatience is a perfect structural stimulus for the flashbacks and the tale; however, these are not merely structural ornament. His memories of his childhood give us his prehistory including his socialization. We find out that he knows just as much about racism as Jefferson, but he doesn't want this knowledge to interfere with his social advancement. Jefferson's tale merely adds a collective sanction to Todd's private, but repressed experience. Both flashback and tale are woven into Todd's painful present and invite constant comparison. Thus this short story not only mirrors the surface of Afro-American experience, but demonstrates the sociopsychological dynamism of these conflicts which are buried in the forms of behavior and language. Irony suffuses all; it is the common denominator and the formal analogue to a persistent contradiction in black reality and identity.

MYTHOLOGICAL ARCHETYPE AND AFRO-AMERICAN SIGNATURE[21]

A. The Fall

Todd's fall from heaven is an ironic version of the fortunate fall. Like the fall of Ikarus and Adam it is a fall into knowledge which his middle class aspirations required him to repress. Todd's *hubris* is his desire to be accepted as a full citizen and individual rather than being typecast as a black and implicitly being blamed for the 'backwardness' of the black folk. However, this black folk — like the choir of Greek tragedy — maintains and preserves the collective problem-solving strategies. This function carries a measure of authority and power, much to Todd's irritation, for it is Jefferson, as the spokesman of this tradition, who wields this power and control.[22] Todd cannot explain why the old man should intimidate him so much. Todd, who suffers from that amnesia which the Greeks called *hamartia* and which modern psychology calls repression, stumbles into the *peripeteia* which is caused by folk wisdom. Todd's fall on Jefferson's land permits a host of analogies: mythologically it is a fall from self-deception into knowledge; psychologically from Ego into Id; socially from the achieved status (he can fly) into the ascribed status (he is not supposed to); geographically from North into South; and in imagery from white into black ('The closer I spin toward the earth the blacker I become').[23] It is significant that this fall should have been caused by a stimulus of his childhood: he spots a kite and seeks the boy (himself) at the end of the line. This 'unguarded' behavior then prompts him to go into a steep climb ('in exultation' at having come so far in this world) and he crashes. The unruly behavior points to a complex chain of motifs: *hubris*, freedom, madness, folly, and fall.

B. Hubris

As a child, Todd's dearest wish was to own a model airplane. In his naiveté he confused model planes (appearance) with real planes (reality) and tried to grab one as it flew overhead, assuming that a white boy had lost it. When this attempt failed he experienced his first fall into knowledge. His mother, he remembers, took this as a sign of incipient insanity. Later on in the story the racist Graves will connect flying and madness: 'You all know you cain't let the Nigguh get up that high without his going crazy. The nigguh brain ain't built right for high altitudes. . . .' This motif is picked up by Jefferson's tale: blacks who have made it to heaven (freedom) are so inordinately foolish in their flying that they become a danger to the heavenly community and have to be put into a harness. Likewise Graves intends to save the white South from Todd's folly by putting him into a 'white' strait jacket. The strait jacket motif, which suggests oppression, is dialectically connected to Todd's idea of safety and protection. For Todd his plane is his shell and character armour, without which he loses his identity. Todd does not realize that the plane is his ideological strait jacket and a much more powerful harness because its control function escapes him. However, he senses that he may be flying blind, i.e. according to the compass of white norms.

C. Flying, birds, bad luck

Another chain of motifs connects flying with bad luck. Black folklore calls bad luck 'buzzard luck.'[24] A buzzard causes Todd's downfall. Jefferson's son has named these birds jimcrows which is also the folk term for racial discrimination. Thus a buzzard = jimcrow = racial discrimination causes his 'fortunate' fall. Indeed Jefferson says, 'the white folks round here don't like to see you boys up there in the sky,' and Todd, who lamely replies 'no one has bothered us' gives himself the lie, for the jimcrows already got him. Jefferson tells him a folk anecdote about buzzards:

> They the damnedest birds. Once I seen a hoss all stretched out like he was sick, you know. So I hollers, 'Gid up from there, suh!' Just to make sho! An' doggone, son, if I don't see two ole jimcrows come flying right up outa that hoss's insides! Yessuh! The sun was shinin' on 'em and they couldn't a been no greasier if they'd been eating barbecue.

This anecdote with its hyperbolic (and typical rural-black) twist turns his stomach. It also picks up a motif mentioned in a letter by Todd's girlfriend. For her the whites' strategy of keeping these pilots in permanent training by humoring their pride is a covert form of racism: they are 'beating that dead horse.' Todd picks this up: 'Maybe we are a bunch of buzzards feeding on a dead horse, but we can hope to be eagles, can't we?' Graves kills this hope as he completes this particular chain of motifs by saying, 'I want you to take this here black eagle over to that nigguh airfield. . . .' Ellison uses universal and mythical archetypes, but undermines their harmless meaning by contrasting them with a not so harmless reality. This ironic demythification does not entirely deny the relevance of the myth of the fall, but its truth turns into mockery when placed in the specific black context.

EXPERIENCE, ROLE, AND IDENTITY
The donnée of the story is based on a controversial incident during World War II. Marcus Klein writes:

> A Negro air school had been established at Tuskeegee during the war, apparently as a sop to civil libertarians. Its pilots never got out of training. The school became sufficient issue for Judge Hastie to resign from the War Department in protest over it. . . .[25]

This political event, which neatly summarizes the structure of the conflict between American promise and black reality, is also the basic theme of the folk tale. The backdrop of political reality and folk wisdom is the dramatic frame of reference for the development of character and of black role behavior. Todd, who carries the burden of the black bourgeoisie, hopes to achieve his social identity by accommodating himself to white authority and expectations. Jefferson has had to carve out a strategy for survival in a racist world. His strategy may show an element of resignation but it has not dulled his sense of self. His accommodation, though politically conservative, remains constant play whereas Todd, who seeks political advancement, is imprisoned in his frozen role. Ellison, speaking of the grandfather in *Invisible Man*, called his behavior a 'kind of jiujitsu of the spirit, a denial and rejection through agreement.' Indeed, 'jeffing' in black English is a 'low level con.'[26] Todd, on the other hand, has internalized what he assumes to be a higher social role, nervously oblivious of its attendant anti-black prejudices. Thus he calls Jefferson a weak clown though he instinctively feels the black farmer's power over him. Indeed, Jefferson's weakness, his conscious role playing, will be Todd's salvation.

The very opening of the story hints at Todd's problem. The sun has blinded him, and he can no longer distinguish whether the faces staring at him are white or black. It is typical that his vision should be impaired, since he had measured himself for too long 'in the mirror of other men's appreciation.' Indeed, color constitutes his particular stigma.[27] While his vision has gone bourgeois, his sense of touch and his hearing have retained a measure of spontaneity. He dreads the touch of whites and relaxes only as he hears the comforting black idiom. Once he is fully conscious, his spontaneous body reactions are overruled by his bourgeois role which now rejects Jefferson's touch. Jefferson is a strong representative of the previous condition; therefore Todd's body 'refuses to laugh' when Jefferson tells his lie. Laughter would have documented his physical solidarity with Jefferson and therefore admission of his failure. On the other hand residual echoes of his black folk memory constantly invite him to laugh at Jefferson's excellent performance. Jefferson stimulates in him the memory of that particular mood created by the survival strategy of the blues. The blues not only catch the oppressive and painful 'details and episodes of a brutal experience' in their 'plots,' they also externalize and overcome them by a hyperbolic and self-ironic performance.[28] In order for the blues or the folk tale to be successful the listener has to be willing to 'ratify' its experience (tell it like it is) and to share the moment of ritual catharsis. The performer draws a stronger identity from his performance, but only when his performance is appreciated. The bourgeois Todd has repressed this particular interaction ritual, for the physical acknowledgement of Jefferson's tale would bring into question his new identity. Should he affirm the tale by laughter he would give himself the bodily lie and at the same time acknowledge Jefferson's power over him. Thus he has to reject the very instinctive force of solidarity which invites him to laugh.

Todd feels this double bind quite intensely since Jefferson is an excellent raconteur. When asked, whether he is going to tell one of those lies of folklore, he answers with the sly disclaimer: 'Well I ain't so sho', on account of it took place when I was dead.' This is his story in partial paraphrase: 'Well I went to heaven and right away started to sproutin' me some wings.' Doubtful at first whether his freedom may not be another trick of whitey, he soon starts flying with foolish abandon. Other black angels convince him of the truth of his liberation, but they also warn him that he will have to wear a special harness over his wings. 'That was how come they wasn't flyin'. Oh yes, an' you had to be extra strong for a black man even, to fly with one of them harnesses. . . .' He chooses to disregard this rule of white heaven for the moment. 'I was raisin' hell. Not that I meant any harm, son. But I was just feeling good. It was so good to know I was free at last.' Soon his behavior comes to the attention of Saint Peter, who reprimands him. Jefferson 'cons' himself out of punishment and even solicits some praise about his ability to fly ('beating that dead horse'). Saint Peter will grant him permission to fly without a harness if he will stick to the rules of white heaven. Soon Jeff forgets his promise and raises enough hell to knock off the tips of some stars (Stars Fell On Alabama!) and — so it is alleged — to cause a race riot in Alabama. Saint Peter says:

> 'Jeff, you and that speedin' is a danger to the heavenly community. If I was to let you keep on flyin', heaven wouldn't be nothin' but uproar. Jeff, you got to go!' Son, I argued and pleaded with that old white man, but it didn't do a bit of good. They rushed me straight to them pearly gates and gimme a parachute and a map of the state of Alabama. . . .

(At this point Jefferson cracks up at his own performance). He is merely permitted a few parting words: 'Well, you done took my wings. And you puttin' me out. You got charge of things so's I can't do nothin' about it. But you got to admit just this: While I was up here I was the flyinest sonofabitch that ever hit heaven!'

Jefferson is so caught up in his own narrative style that the political dimension of its plot escapes him, but not Todd, in whom it provokes a rather violent reaction. The ironic movement both in the story and the act of narration is quite confusing. First there is the irony inherent in the story: behind the humorous and concrete facade of this lie there is a political folk wisdom which articulates its own negative potential by calling its truth a 'lie.' Heaven is the symbol of freedom and getting to heaven is an old formula for emancipation or flight.

This new freedom, however, continues to be controlled by whites. The black man who indulges in this freedom in a manner unacceptable to whites is put into a harness — as happened during Reconstruction. The irony deepens when Jefferson repeats the negative prejudices of whites against blacks in justifying his eviction: that blacks tend to exaggerate and that, like children, they will forget rules, that they are a danger when left to their own devices and that they are to be blamed for lynchings. This negative role expectancy is picked up by the final line and turned into its opposite: 'While I was up there I was the flyinest sonofabitch that ever hit heaven!' (Other versions are 'While I was up here in yo place I wuz the flyinest fool you had' or 'Yeah they may not let no colored folks in, but while I was there I was a flyin' fool!').[29] Behind this punch line there is a dialectical folk consciousness which exposes white prejudice by exaggerating it (viz., 'of all those who did not follow your racist laws I was the worst, the flyinest fool'). His villany consists in desiring his freedom. It is playfully underlined by his lack of respect for proper grammar and his creation of a new form: the superlative participle.

Todd, who rejects his instinctive urge to participate in order to be able to consciously reject the truth of his story, does not understand the implicit rejection and mockery of white behavior. He fears that Jefferson is calling him a fool. This misinterpretation creates another level of irony, that of the situation. Jefferson would like to entertain Todd. His motives are naive and honest, but he 'thoughtlessly' chooses the wrong story. Todd must harbor the suspicion that behind the objective and folkloristic front of the lie there lurks the subjective and conscious jive of the narrator. He feels that Jefferson wields an enormous power over him and he is annoyed that this man should make him feel as uncomfortable as white officers do. He then screams, 'go tell your tales to the white folks,' oblivious that this command has fulfilled itself, for Jefferson did tell his story to Todd's whitened identity.

For many years Ralph Ellison has been fighting singlehandedly to rescue the black usable past which is stored in folklore. In interviews, essays, addresses and seminars all over the United States he has been arguing for a respect and appreciation of black folklore which according to him it has not received at the hands of white or black poets or critics. He does not want to minimize slavery by romantically praising its cultural results, but he argues that this culture is not only a 'mark of oppression' but primarily a celebration of survival. Although Jefferson is caught in a pattern of behavior which is, to a certain degree, thoughtless and although the wisdom of his folk tale is so much part of his 'thoughtless' behavior that its actuality escapes him, his accommodation to the situation has not unhinged his identity. Todd, on the other hand, is alienated from his group heritage and clings to a pseudo-identity which he can only maintain at the cost of blindness, self-hatred and self-deception. Not being himself, he cannot laugh about himself, as can Jefferson who draws pleasure from narrating painful truths. Jefferson's is the power of the blues; he can create catharsis out of conflict and oppression. This human power is a dialectical result of his political weakness. Todd, who is painfully made aware of his own weakness, lost this power when he moved up and away from his group. His 'fortunate fall' results in a new solidarity between Jefferson and himself and a deeper understanding of what his real buried self may be. Thus oral culture, particularly when it meets with false consciousness, may become an agent of de-alienation.

Ellison has explored the richness of the black oral tradition. Ironically this makes him a forerunner of the very cultural nationalism whose militant fringe has been rejecting him for years as an Uncle Tom. It should satisfy his sense of irony that this state of affairs forms the main theme of his work.

NOTES

1.   Standard anthologies: Langston Hughes and Arna Bontemps, eds., *The Poetry of the Negro 1746–1970* (New York, 1970); Dudley Randall, *The Black Poets* (New York, 1971); Stephen Henderson, *Understanding the New Black Poetry: Black Speech and Black Music as Poetic References* (New York, 1973); Abraham Chapman, ed., *Black Voices* (New York, 1968) and *New Black Voices* (New York, 1972); Bernhard Bell, ed., *Modern and Contemporary Afro-American Poetry* (Boston, 1972). The most comprehensive critical work is Jean Wagner, *Black Poets of the United States*, translated from the 1962 French edition (Urbana, 1973). More articles of an introductory nature in: Addison Gayle, ed., *Black Expression: Essays By and About Black Americans in the Creative Arts* (New York, 1969), particularly those by Sterling Brown, Saunders Redding, Arna Bontemps, James Emanuel. Roger Whitlow, *Black American Literature: A Critical History* (Chicago, 1973), does not live up to the adjective of its subtitle. It contains a very useful and nearly complete bibliography of fiction, poetry, drama, and criticism up to 1972.

2.   Cf. Chapman, *Black Voices*, p. 42. Though some black cultural militants exaggerate the prevalence of racism in literary academia, one is hard put to explain why the 1972 edition of *Everyman's Dictionary of Literary Biography* with its policy of keeping the range of the volume 'as catholic as possible' does list Rex Stout, but not Chester Himes or Frank Yerby, does list Harriet Beecher Stowe but not Frederick Douglass, does list Alan Drury, William Manchester, James Michener, Leon Uris but leaves out Gwendolyn Brooks, James Weldon Johnson, Ralph Ellison, W. E. B. DuBois, Claude McKay, LeRoi Jones and a host of others. It may not be intentional, but there is a systematic purity about it (certainly not the result of editorial negligence), which requires a strong subconscious resistance. Certainly no one in his right mind would argue that Drury is a better writer than Ellison.

3.   'A Very Stern Discipline: An Interview with Ralph Ellison,' *Harpers*, 234 (March, 1967), 79.

4.   *Shadow and Act*, p. 99.

5.   Francis L. Broderick and August Meier, eds., *Negro Protest Thought in the Twentieth Century* (New York, 1965). Nathan I. Huggins. *The Harlem Renaissance* (New York, 1971).

6.   Hughes, 'The Negro Artist and the Racial Mountain,' in: Gayle, *Black Expression*, p. 258.

7.   Churchill's misreading is reported by Stephen Bronz, *Roots of Negro Racial Consciousness* (New York, 1964).

8.   Richard Wright called black folklore a 'social system of artistic communication' and suggested that black artists take greater note of it. His 'Blueprint for a Negro Writing' was reprinted in *The Black Aesthetic*, ed. Addison Gayle Jr. (New York, 1971). Ellison's use of folklore was commented upon by George Kent, 'Ralph Ellison and Afro-American Folk and Cultural Tradition,' *Blackness and the Adventure of Western Culture* (Chicago, 1972) and Larry Neal, 'Ellison's Zoot Suit,' in *Ralph Ellison: A Collection of Critical Essays*, ed. John Hersey (Englewood Cliffs, 1974).

9.   Robert Stepto, *From Behind the Veil* (Urbana, University of Illinois Press, 1979). Stanley Edgar Hyman and Ralph Ellison, 'The Negro Writer in America: An Exchange,' *Partisan Review* (Spring, 1958), reprinted in: *Mother Wit From the Laughing Barrel*, ed. Alan Dundes (Englewood Cliffs, 1973). Ellison's rejoinder to Howe is in 'The World and the Jug,' *Shadow and Act* (New York, 1966).

10.   George Kent (op. cit.) looks at Ellison's use of folklore with 'a certain unease' and Larry Neal (op. cit.) praises Ellison's return to folk roots, but finds it hard to swallow his appeals to universality. Susan Blake, 'Ritual and Rationalization: Black Folklore in the Works of Ralph Ellison', *PMLA*, vol. 94, No. 1 (January 1979), 121–35, blames Ellison for ignoring, minimizing, distorting and denying the true folk expression. Though her analysis is the most probing to date she seems to miss the irony and conscious jive in Ellison's use of folklore. Ultimately she will not and cannot stand ambivalence and contradiction. Black folklore is not universalized into myth; myth is teased by folklore, and reality is teased by both.

11.   The conservative bias of the modernist tradition is discussed in Ostendorf, *Der Mythos in der Neuen Welt: Eine Untersuchung zum amerikani-*

schen *Myth Criticism* (Frankfurt, 1971) and in Robert Weimann, *Literaturgeschichte und Mythologie* (Berlin und Weimar, 1971).

12. *Shadow and Act*, p. 175.

13. Lucien Goldman, *Pour une sociologie du roman* (Paris, 1964), p. 27.

14. P. Bogatyrev and R. Jakobson, 'Die Folklore als eine besondere Form des Schaffens,' *Donum Natalicium Schrijnen* (Utrecht, 1929). See also Roger D. Abrahams on the social control function of folklore in 'Personal Power and Social Restraint in the Definition of Folklore,' *Journal of American Folklore* 84 (1971): 16–30; and Richard Bauman, 'Differential Identity and the Social Base of Folklore,' *Journal of American Folklore* 84 (1971): 31–41. Useful suggestions are made by Peter L. Berger and Thomas Luckmann, *The Social Construction of Reality: A Treatise in the Sociology of Knowledge* (New York, 1966), particularly on 'Sedimentation and Tradition' and on the 'Origins of Symbolic Universes.'

15. The story may be found in the following anthologies: E. Seaver, ed., *Cross Section* (New York, 1944); C. A. Fenton, ed., *Best Short Stories of World War II* (New York, 1957); Langston Hughes, ed., *The Best Short Stories by Negro Writers* (Boston, 1967); James Emanuel and Theodore Gross, eds., *Dark Symphony: Negro Literature in America* (New York, 1968); Darwin Turner, ed., *Black American Literature: Fiction* (New York, 1969); Eva Kissin, ed., *Stories in Black and White* (Philadelphia, 1970); Francis Dearns, ed., *Black Identity* (New York, 1970); William Adams et al., eds., *Afro-American Literature: Fiction* (Boston, 1970).

16. The deceptive quality of black folklore has sent liberals, militants, and well meaning translators in all directions of arbitrary interpretation. Liberals tend to universalize its meaning thus pulling its teeth, militants call it 'irrelevant for the cause of black liberation', and translators simply ignore it. Ellison, who seemed content that in Germany his novel was read and treated as a novel, not as protest fiction, would be appalled by the translation of his work: folklore gets knocked straight out of the picture. 'Blues' is translated as 'sad song', and Brer Rabbit or Brer Bear don't make it at all into German. This is unfortunate, for German has by now acculturated the Blues and there is a perfectly fine tradition of animal tales that could have been utilized for the folkloric resonances of his novel. It simply did not seem important enough to the translator. The story 'Flying Home' was literally massacred at the hands of the translator. None of the folkloric allusions survive the translation into German. Heinz Politzer (ed) *Amerika erzählt* (Frankfurt, 1971).

17. Langston Hughes is quoted in Dundes, ed., *Mother Wit*, p. 52: 'The sky would be my roadway and the stars my stopping place. Man if I had a rocket plane, I would rock off into space and be solid gone. Gone. Real gone! I mean *gone*.' The hyperbolic finale is reminiscent of the folk tale within the story.

18. Joseph Trimmer, 'Ralph Ellison's "Flying Home",' *Studies in Short Fiction* 9 (1972): 175–82.

19. On anxiety and panic due to isolation from the group see Ellison, *Shadow and Act*, p. 99ff.; also William Greer and Price Cobbs, *Black Rage* (New York, 1968), and Francois Raveau, 'An Outline of the Role

of Color in Adaptation Phenomena,' in *Color and Race*, ed. John Hope Franklin (Boston, 1968). See also Erik H. Erikson, 'The Concept of Identity in Race Relations,' in *The Negro American*, eds. Talcott Parsons and Kenneth Clarke (Boston, 1965). On the strategies of repression required for a 'change' or 'alternation' of consciousness see Berger and Luckmann, *The Social Construction of Reality*, pp. 180–81.

20. Ellison, *Shadow and Act*, p. 99ff.

21. See Leslie Fiedler's 'Archetype and Signature: A Study of the Relationship between Biography and Poetry,' *Sewanee Review* 60 (1952): 253–273. My use of both terms is less Jungian than Fiedler's. See Ostendorf, *Der Mythos in der Neuen Welt*, pp. 27ff. and 129ff.

22. Roger D. Abrahams, 'Personal Power and Social Restraint.'

23. This essay is indebted to Martin Christadler's interpretation of *Invisible Man* in *Der amerikanische Roman*, ed. H. J. Lang (Düsseldorf, 1972).

24. Rap Brown, *Die Nigger Die* (New York, 1969), p. 29 goes into some signifying:
    Man, I can't win for losing.
    If it wasn't for bad luck, I wouldn't have no luck at all.
    I been having buzzard luck
    Can't kill nothin' and won't nothin' die.

25. Marcus Klein, *After Alienation: American Novels in Mid-Century* (New York, 1964), pp. 102–103.

26. Iceberg Slim, *Pimp: The Story of My Life* (Los Angeles, 1969), p. 315.

27. A discussion of schizoid phenomena caused by race can be found in Erving Goffman, *Stigma: Notes on the Management of Spoiled Identity* (Englewood Cliffs, 1963) and in Joseph Gabel, *Ideologie und Schizophrenie* (Frankfurt, 1967). Dan Aaron draws parallels between various minority groups and their acculturation patterns in 'The Hyphenate Writer and American Letters,' *Smith Alumnae Quarterly* (July, 1964): 213–217.

28. Ellison's definition of the blues in 'Richard Wright's Blues,' *Shadow and Act*, pp. 89–104.

29. B. A. Botkin, *A Treasury of Southern Folklore* (New York, 1949), p. 111 and Roger D. Abrahams, *Positively Black* (Englewood Cliffs, 1970) list different versions.

30. On the transcendence of the negative stereotype see Constance Rourke, *American Humor* (New York, 1931). Friedrich Engel's theory that there would be no Western civilization without Greek slavery has found a persuasive advocate in Eugene Genovese, who has applied this dialectic to black culture in *Roll Jordan, Roll: The World the Slaves Made* (New York, 1974).

VI CONTEMPORARY AFRO-AMERICAN CULTURE: THE SIXTIES AND SEVENTIES

The sixties and seventies will go down in American history as that period when America discovered the richness of black oral tradition; when America discovered the affirmative and celebratory elements in that culture; when linguists pointed out the wit and 'logic of non-standard English';[1] when folklorists discovered the 'invisible' culture of the black ghetto streets;[2] when a hitherto stigmatized life-style became fashionable; when the mystique of soul caught on in the young white population;[3] when crinkly hair — until then quite undesirable — was stylized into a beauty mark: the Afro spawned the Jew-fro and the Wasp-fro.[4]

The sixties will also be remembered for a musical revolution: white popular musical culture acknowledged the Afro-American style as its chief inspiration. There had been constant borrowing all along. Phyl Garland writes: 'Unfortunately, it has been a part of the American pattern for the originators of black music to be shunted into the background once their creations have been adopted by whites and made lucrative as well as popular'. In the fifties Bill Haley and Elvis Presley built a white Rock'n Roll culture on the basis of black models, but it remained a *white* culture. It coexisted with a black Rhythm and Blues culture which was largely invisible to the white market. In the sixties white taste graduated from the white imitators to the black creators. In 1967 Otis Redding toppled Elvis Presley in the British charts. Suddenly black soul music became the pervasive musical taste of white and black Americans, with B. B. King, Ray Charles, Otis Redding, and Aretha Franklin in the lead. Rock music moved closer to Jazz from whose loins it had originally sprung, and jazz musicians taught incipient rock artists what rock can sound like with a little style and musical inspiration.

Our understanding of black culture today is not assured once we have identified possible sources of prejudice. For one thing we cannot experience black culture first hand. We perceive black culture through texts and through electronic chan-

nels. These media (texts, news, records, TV, film) are themselves achievements of Western literate culture. They have
given a certain structure to our culture and have influenced its
forms. To wit, our culture is strongly text-oriented, it is a
culture of literacy. Black culture (like other low class or folk
cultures) is strongly oral and performance-directed.

The context of ongoing black culture (as everyday praxis) is
largely unavailable to us. We no longer live in an oral tradition,
we were raised in different kinship systems, and our 'social
construction of reality' differs from that of blacks.[6] Moreover,
whatever we know of black culture is handed down on the
basis of a selection which is not our own and which is not the
selection of blacks, either. The selection is made for them and
us by cultural custodians: impresarios, a. and r. men, literary
magazines, film distributors, record companies, publishing
houses, field workers, human and social scientists. Whatever
we know of black culture has been preselected by those in
control of the media and the human and social sciences.
Although a critical revolution has occurred in the media and
the sciences and stereotypes have diminished, only a few
blacks have managed to get control over these mind-
managing channels. One of the frequent complaints of blacks
is that they are being misrepresented, and that a pre-
structured, abstract version of their world makes it into the
press, into the school books, into TV, and into film. This has
to be taken into account when we look at individual items
from that culture.

When Southern whites of the nineteenth century said 'those
niggers sure can sing and dance' or commented on the loose
and easy manners and morals of their slaves they felt reassured
in their social and cultural Darwinism. Rhythm, song, and
dance were to them symptoms of the animalism and inferiority of blacks and of their adaptability to slavery. In the sixties
young blacks proclaimed a new black aesthetic: In contrast to
whites, blacks are said to be more sensual, do not suffer from
the rigors of a puritan work ethic, have a more natural body
control, show less constraint in motor behavior, and do not
suffer from that typical western alienation from the human
body — in short, blacks have rhythm; they sure can sing and
dance. The new black aesthetic claims as distinctive what
white racists saw as a stigma.[7] This tells us that cultural
behavior may be interpreted and used for a variety of political

purposes. As long as we do not understand culture as a static essence, but as a social resource, it follows that the use of culture will be adapted to the changing political needs of the situation.

In the nineteenth and early twentieth century the loss of ethnic differences was a desirable goal. Today ethnicity and folk tradition are in vogue, partly as a result of the black civil rights movement and the black cultural nationalism. Other interest groups, too, discovered that ethnicity could become a political weapon. One need not be a Marxist or a student of German history to comprehend the inherent dangers of such ethnic politics, i.e. the danger of orienting political struggle along race rather than class lines. Surely the 'mystique of soul' which is said to unite all blacks posits this unity on the basis of ascription rather than achievement. Dahrendorf points out the conservatism of such ethnicity by calling it a refeudalization of society; for as in feudal society ascription (on the basis of status, race, or pedigree), not achievement determine social stratification and political action. However, it must be remembered that black ethnicity is a consequence of a long historical lesson: that the avenues of upward mobility (class advancement or personal advancement through achievement), though forever a promise, were never a reality for blacks. The contradiction is more American than Afro-American: for American ideology and American religion kept promising mobility, and political practice refused it. Thus blacks were forced to fall back on their own resources and quietly strengthened in-group solidarity. In a process which may be observed in many ethnic or class minorities blacks turned negative ascription (racist slurs made by whites) into a positive virtue (ethnicity and soul). But the analogy to pre-industrial societies is illuminating. There is a strong anti-bourgeois and aristocratic element in the Afro-American life style, in the black attitude toward work (which in black English is still called 'a slave'), toward money, toward leisure, toward clothes and last but not least in their penchant for aristocratic nicknames (Duke, Count, Earl, Lords, Princess). Those who want to break out of a distinctively black world and want to enter the American bourgeoisie overcompensate in formality and decorum. In the twenties Marcus Garvey shaped his movement along feudal lines, complete with court etiquette, titles and costumes. However fanciful black ethnicity and its aristocratic front may seem to us, we should note the important element of protest in it, protest against false promises and against the destruction of their older race and class ties in the name of an achievement oriented enlightenment. Black ethnicity (even that of Garvey or the Muslims) cannot be explained away as an expression of backwardness or as an escape into irrational fantasies. The success of both movements, and the lack of success of achievement-oriented groups (DuBois, NAACP) among the black grass roots people is witness to the black folk belief that the avenues of achievement have been and will be blocked, no matter what Mr. Charlie says. Blacks in America have been excluded from formulating the norms by which they had to live — and to achieve. Ethnicity is a conscious effort to reverse that process: it is an effort to create norms for group behavior (*Gemeinschaft*) to compensate for lack of participation in the larger decision-making (*Gesellschaft*) and at the same time to reaffirm forms of behavior which hitherto has been stigmatized as deviant (soul food, soul talk, soul music). This type of black ethnicity has been quite successful since these subcultural forms and norms of behavior have indeed had a powerful effect on shaping the consciousness and behavior of the white majority. The influence has always been there; for as Ellison writes 'Southern whites cannot walk, talk, sing, conceive of laws or justice, think of sex, love, the family or freedom without responding to the presence of Negroes'.[8] New is the acknowledgement of this influence by the open conversion of American youth to black talk, dress behavior and music. Unfortunately, the pattern of financial exploitation has not been reversed. Thus the success of black culture in the sixties is noted by black artists with pride and with bitterness. B. B. King expresses this ambivalence well: on the one hand white musicians who copy black music still make more money than blacks; on the other hand, had it not been for the reimporting of black blues via Britain King would not have been as famous as he is today. It adds to the bitterness that music next to sport has been one of the few avenues of upward mobility open to blacks. Therefore they resent it if these avenues are blocked by young whites who have so many more chances in life than they ever had.

This brings us to the many-faceted relationship between black culture and white need and use of that culture. Politically and socially the master needed his Jacques to take care of *les choses*; culturally and psychologically Prospero needed Caliban. Jacques, the servant, became Jacques the patient. Ugly Caliban became Caliban the beautiful, but the pattern of dependence persisted. Euro-America has always had a secret longing for the uncivilized pastoral freshness of Caliban and those in power have always liked to go 'slumming' with Jacques. Blacks in literature have often been romanticized (Uncle Tom, Nigger Jim, Dilsey) as a pastoral alternative to being 'sivilized', as Huck Finn calls it. The white self-image changed accordingly: the white oppressor turned into the white emancipator — but still on top. This was the crux of the goodwilled civil rights activism in the Sixties: too often white Northern liberals who came to work for the cause were locked in a role over which they had no control and for which they surely could not be held responsible, but a role which nonetheless irritated blacks. Therefore black militants called for an all black political action and rejected whites who came to help from a position of cultural and social superiority.

The melting pot assumption of the liberal political credo (i.e. that in the long run ethnic, religious and linguistic difference would or ought to disappear) has led scientists to look at black history as a progress report in acculturation. Sidney Mintz and Ralph Ellison have suggested to reverse the question: how much have the Americans become Africanized? And how much the Europeans via America? Without Afro-Americans we would have Brassens and Piaf, Heino and Heintje, but no Beatles, no Stones, no Martial Solal, and surely an impoverished radio and TV. Admittedly many Europeans would rather do without these cultural imports and would prefer to keep Europe at an *Académie-française* level of cultural purity. But cultures grow by borrowing and exchanging and not by legislation. The black infusion into our own cultures is a reality, whether we like it or not.

What does this mean in terms of our interpretation of current black culture? We already know — even experience — a lot of 'borrowed' black culture, albeit in whitened form. However, we know these individual forms and items, say the blues or jazz, in the context of our own culture and our own experience, not in the cultural and sociopolitical context of black life. Thus many European listeners will instinctively prefer the 'reconstructed, whitened' black culture to the real article when they are offered side by side. Our white European blues are prettier, as it were, and far less ambivalent. The blues have been 'good to us' — certainly to the Stones or to Tom Jones. For us the blues are 'counter culture', an alternative to our own culture which we are free to take or leave; for blacks the blues are an overcoming of choicelessness.

It is a most remarkable fact, however, that the white dominant youth culture of the USA, which for years tried to leave suffering behind in a mad pursuit of happiness, should have adopted the popular culture of Afro-Americans, a culture of suffering and survival, a culture which manages to squeeze celebration from adversity.

AN INVENTORY OF CONTEMPORARY BLACK CULTURE

It will be impossible to deal with all aspects of black culture in the sixties and seventies. In keeping with the larger, anthropological definition of culture we would have to look at the following aspects: literature and the arts, music, film, sports, religion, fashion, and everyday life, all of which saw marked changes in the sixties.

(1) Black literature, particularly poetry, consciously moved away from a formal to an oral-ethnic style.

(2) Black music went through a formative phase. Building on Charlie Parker, the younger generation of John Coltrane, Ornette Coleman and Cecil Taylor took giant steps in jazz. In the popular scene black musicians moved to the limelight and seem ready to stay there.

(3) In film black Sambo became Superspade. Unfortunately, before black film could develop, it was in the hands of manipulators and con-artists: minstrelsy became 'blaxploitation'.[11]

(4) In sports blacks stopped being good colored boys and introduced the world to black power and black rhetoric (Muhammad Ali).

(5) The black church saw major changes. James Baldwin in 1962 could call black religion a 'mask of self-hatred'; and the church often was a safety valve for black aggressions which were bottled up and muted in self-denial and stoicism. The shooting of Martin Luther King marked the point in his development from passive to active civil disobedience at which he became too dangerous for certain white racists. Today many black ministers opt for political participation, a good example being Jesse Jackson, and the churches are full.[12]

On an average Sunday in May 1976 I found that the congregation of the African-Methodist-Episcopalian church at Cambridge, Mass., consisted mostly of young blacks aged fifteen
to forty.

(6) Fashion, says philosopher v.d. Leeuw, is a key to anthropology and culture. The high premium which is on style
and performance in everyday black life has given rise to a
fastidious attention to clothes and fashion. Several reasons
may be given for this. One is anthropological and existential:
clothes are the outer shell of man, an extension of his skin, and
thus important in the presentation or *mise en scène* of self. In
proportion to the negative ascription which blacks had to
endure because of their skin, they compensated in terms of
their 'second skin'. Thus the presentation of the black self in a
white world followed an extreme traditionalism. Those who
wanted to rise into the bourgeois class would try to outdress
managers and executives in their attention to Brooks Brothers
sobriety and muted property. (Cf. Invisible Man on first coming to New York.) Within the black world this bourgeois
white shell is considered 'lame', 'stiff', or 'square', words
connoting the psychological paralysis that goes along with
such dress. A second reason is that here — as well as in Africa
— the element of play and role-playing is quite pronounced
and carries over into dress and fashion. Black street culture has
always been conspicuously flamboyant with an abandon
which the white Anglo-Saxon Protestant world had never
known (except to some degree in Southern plantation culture). This abandon is nowhere as visible as in the 'front' of the
hustler, in the extravagance of the black musician, or in the
robes of the preacher on the make. The norm, says Kochman,
is to be dressed in the extreme.[13] The black penchant for
costumes and masquerade and for the colorful presentation of
self remind us — as do certain interaction rituals and games of
insult — of pre-industrial and pre-bourgeois phases of European history. (Cf. Huizinga, *Homo Ludens*, 1938).

Since all cultural items and cultural areas are part of the same
on-going praxis they share some of the fundamental structural
features. Therefore it may be permissible if we single out the
first two areas for a closer scrutiny of some of those structural
peculiarities: black poetry and black music.

THE NEW BLACK AESTHETIC IN POETRY AND MUSIC

Christopher Caudwell once said that 'in poetry the affective associations are organized by the *structure of the language*, while in the novel they are organized by the *structure of the outer reality* portrayed.' Poetry seeks out the social character of language, it explores the continuous and unending structuring activity of man through language. This is very true for black literature. The search for an adequate code has occupied black poets for a long time. The high literary English style could not do justice to black reality, in fact was its enemy, as Paul Laurence Dunbar found out. On the other hand the code of subculture was considered a sign of pathology and was being monopolized by minstrelsy and show business. The new black literature of the sixties uses non-standard black English without restraint and with a lot of pride. Knowledge of the black code is *de rigueur* in certain white subcultural circles: 'groove', 'cat', 'jive', 'drag', 'strung out', 'outa sight', 'like crazy, man' etc. A quick survey of black English tells us that there is a large number of interaction rituals and verbal strategies which our culture lacks or which existed in older periods of our history. In terms of dialogue alone black speech behavior differentiates between jive, joning, woofing, preaching, bopping, sounding, signifying, rapping, running it down, jeffing, etc. These strategies not only refer to language but also to motor behavior and kinesis. Most of these peculiar oral structures have found their way into modern black poetry. Next to these very basic interaction rituals there are many 'simple forms' in black culture which have also influenced both formal and popular mass-culture: proverb, tale, blues, spiritual, gospel, toast, dozens, lies and boasts. What is characteristic of these forms?

Due to a long history of enforced orality black culture has remained strongly agonistic.[15] The premium is on performance and style rather than on discursive logic. Black English prefers hyperbole and expressive metaphor to symbolic density or hermetic meaning. Black English is strongly interactive, and therefore favors kinetic over static terms. In short, it favors the expressive, affective and conative functions over the cognitive and self-reflexive functions of language. This expressive culture, however, is the result of a history of *enforced* illiteracy. Thus black English lacks civilized sophistication and it also lacks the honing and channeling which goes on in a culture of literacy. Black English is in the original sense of the word 'uncultivated'. Therefore it has maintained a semantic playfulness and an expressive exuberance which we were taught to admire in earlier phases of Western culture, e.g. Chaucer and Shakespeare, but which we rarely appreciate in current subcultures, except perhaps as comedy. Because of its roots in orality black poetry is best when performed.

Of these simple forms the *proverb* (often recognizably African) has a stabilizing function; it is concentrated teaching, a minimum common denominator of collective resignative wisdom. The *folk tale* often has the character of a parable which presents political experience in the harmless disguise of an animal tale or lie. The camouflage was necessary to circumvent white censorship. Often these animal stories — popularized by Chandler Harris, who added Uncle Remus as narrator — bring into focus the structure of the black-white relationship. They couch in irony what is a bitter historical truth: the victimization of the weak by the strong. But they also project hope by endowing the weak with an extraordinary wit and stamina. Thus the rabbit has learned to outtalk anyone in the animal kingdom — surely a realistic mirror of the actual importance of linguistic wit in black survival. The *blues* are best known among Europeans. They have had strong influence on poetry from Langston Hughes' *Weary Blues* onward. Similarly the *spiritual*, which is at the same time the whitest and blackest form of black subculture depending on which church it has come from. The contemporary soul culture has drawn from both these traditions and has fused the secular and sacred traditions into one mass cultural stream. The *dozens* are particularly difficult to stomach for bourgeois audiences: they are a ritual of verbal aggression which tries to touch on the most sensitive, stigmatized and traumatized areas of black experience. Played mostly by adolescents, but not unknown among adults, they are a game of one-up-manship in which the antagonists try to outdo each other in insults testing not only their inventiveness, but also the opponent's stamina. Non-blacks tend to forget that they are indeed a game and are shocked. Residues of the dozens may be heard in Muhammad Ali's ritualized insults against his opponents, also in the rhetoric of some militants. The dozens seem to have gone into some of the revolutionary poetry of Imamu Amiri Baraka (LeRoi Jones). *Toasts* are an interesting form of improvised folk art. These are long poems or ballads about the deeds of mythogenic black figures such as John Henry, Stagolee (Stagger Lee), Slim, Shine, and the Signifying Monkey. Most of these stories are well known in the black world. During the performance the narrator has to demonstrate his talent for improvisation by improving on the basic version in terms of wit, delivery, and embellishment (cf. improvisation in jazz). A twofold talent is required: first the mnemonic feat of presenting a longish plot; second, the interactionist feat of keeping the attention of the onlookers by wit and speed.

But is not a poet by definition a member of the middle class? Surely once a black youngster has elected to become a poet he is bound for middle class goals? But in contrast to the white world the border lines between black subculture and black middle class are not rigidly defined. Most black poets know both the formal code of proper, received American and the jazz talk of the street. Rarely will we find a contemporary poet who has moved too far away from the ghetto to understand or use its code. Often we find two types of poetry from one poet: Gwendolyn Brooks, for example, has written poetry which measures up well to the general American standards of language or poetic excellence. But she also writes in black English. Her choice of the code was dependent on time and place: in the fifties she had a hard time publishing her Euro-American poems. Today she no longer needs to assert her poetic competence and she prefers to write in Black English, bitter, direct, and unideological poetry:

> *We Real Cool*
>> The Pool Players
>> Seven at the Golden Shovel.
> We real cool. We
> Left school. We
> Lurk late. We
> Strike straight. We
> Sing sin. We
> Thin gin. We
> Jazz June. We
> Die soon.

Carolyn Rodgers, herself an accomplished poet, has presented a typology of contemporary black poetry, which is based on black speech and communication patterns.[16] It is a typology of poetic pragmatics, as it were, based on interactions rather than on texts. Though she shifts the locus from text to performance, from immanence to pragmatics, she would not claim that black poetry *is* the actual street code. Black poetry, though it builds on black orality, is highly complex and literate. However, its structure and literate complexity will be understood only by those who understand the structure of the underlying street code. These are her types:

1. *signifying*
    a. open
    b. sly
    c. with or about
2. *teachin'/rappin'*
3. *covers-off*
    a. rundown
    b. hipto
    c. digup
    d. coatpull
4. *spaced* (spiritual)
    a. mindblower (fantasy)
    b. coolout
5. *bein'* (self/reflective)
    a. upinself
    b. uptight
    c. dealin'/swingin'
6. *love*
    a. skin
    b. space (spiritual)
    c. cosmic (ancestral)
7. *shoutin'* (angry/cathartic)
    a. badmouth
    b. facetoface (warning/confrontation)
    c. two-faced (irony)
8. *jazz*
    a. riffin'
    b. cosmic ('Trane)
    c. grounded (Lewis)
9. *du-wah*
    a. dittybop
    b. bebop
10. *pyramid* (getting us together/building/nationhood)

This typology may seem eccentric or arbitrary, but only to those who forget that genres and types have a linguistic and historical basis. Rodgers' basis is black English and black behavior. She admits that this typology may be changed, modified, and enlarged. Many of her types overlap, others could easily be renamed or dropped. The most important category is the first — signifying — which is an underhanded strategy of mockery and criticism. It seems to me the verbal analogue to double consciousness, the interaction ritual which manages to put double vision into words. It may be directed at the opponent, but it may also include the speaker (with or about). It may be open or sly. This irony and inversion characterizes the groundbass of black folklore. We know it from the 'Massa and John' tales, from animal stories and from the toasts. A good example of the latter is the 'Signifying Monkey' who manages to involve the lion in a fight with the elephant by claiming that the elephant had made sexual insinuations about the lion's mother. The lion, who believes this, attacks the elephant, who badly mangles him. The lion realizes that he has been had and takes revenge on the monkey. The monkey manages to talk himself out of the lion's paws, jumps up on a tree and continues his jive. Signifying in black poetry is difficult to pinpoint if one does not know this particular tradition of black oral culture. It is this tradition which gives resonance to Don L. Lee's two-liner:

> Wallace for president
> his mamma for vice-president

With a pokerface Don L. Lee suggests Wallace for president. Coming from a black this alone would be a form of signifying. The second line may be misunderstood by European readers: the pure denotation seems to suggest Wallace's mother for vice-president. This would insinuate Oedipal relations, but no more. However, 'mamma' which is equidistant from 'momma' and 'mammy' connotes a lot more. In the South young wealthy whites often had a black mammy — a black mammy for vice-president? Secondly, the dozens, the game of ritual insults, often begins with the formula 'yo momma. . . .' In many instances the game is on by just saying 'yo momma. . . .' For black listeners the second line has a host of cathartic connotations which they may enjoy with impunity.

Mom's Mabley, a veteran stand-up comedian and the Greek choir of Harlem, puts it more bluntly when she says that she is going to move into the White House as 'the first common-law First Lady', thus putting the history of miscegenation into a nut-shell. 'Signifying is a way of saying the truth that hurts with a laugh, a way of "capping on" (shutting up) someone.' And also: 'It's a four to four balanced way of making love to — while poking hurt/fun at — one's self and one's lifestyles.' Imamu Amiri Baraka comments on Western Whigs favored by blacks:

> why don't you take that thing
> off yo haid
> you look like Miss Muffet in a
> runaway ugly machine, I mean,
> like that.

This combines criticism of Western standards of beauty (Shirley Temple as Miss Muffet) with an exaggeration of black ugliness which is quite common in the black world. The contrast and the hyperbole create positive release. Again there is resonance in the term 'ugly'. 'Nigger you been whupped with an ugly stick' or 'Yo mother raise you on ugly milk' or 'Nigger, you so ugly you can open a branch face' are ways of putting someone 'in the dozens'. Negative hyperbole is pervasive in the blues as well. B. B. King sings about the notorious evil and difficult women:

I gave you a brand new Ford, you said you want a Cadillac,
I bought you a ten dollar dinner, you said 'thanks for the snack',
I let you live in my penthouse, you said it was just a shack.
B. B. King pokes fun at the conspicuous consumption of his woman and at his inability to satisfy her and convince her of his worth. The black audience in this live performance answers with 'Tell it brother' and with appreciative cat-calls. The house hits the ceiling as he includes himself and his life-style in the signifying:

I gave you seven children, and now you want to give them back.
The second type, teachin'/rappin', is related to didactic poetry. It is enlightenment without mockery. Rapping is according to Kochman the least ambivalent or ritualized, and

thus the most referential and personal type of communication. The third category is didactic with a critical edge: 'These poets hip you to something, pull the covers off something, or run it down to you, or ask you to just dig it — your coat is being pulled.' Spaced poetry according to Rodgers is 'a mystical and positive way of looking at the black man's relationship to the universe.' This tradition includes religious metaphysics, the spirituals, Langston Hughes' 'A Negro Speaks of Rivers', and Ishmael Reed's Voodoo poetry. The closest western analogy may be the hymn. This tradition is particularly strong in jazz, e.g. in Coltrane's 'A Love Supreme' or in Sun Ra's cosmic music. The American vogue of 'consciousness–expansion' surely has its dubious ideological recesses though it may have begun for valid countercultural reasons. In black culture this tradition is not *counter*cultural, it is not a search for *new* states of consciousness, but it is merely a renaissance of an old tradition moored in the spirituality of black religion, the mysticism and superstition of black oral tradition. This traditional reference will not make black poets immune to dangerous and irrational political ideologies, but in many cases fantasy and surrealism go along well with political enlightenment as in Jewel Latimore's 'Folk Fable', in Ebon's 'The Statue of Liberty Has Her Back to Harlem' and in Ishmael Reed's novels.

Bein' or love poetry need little introduction or justification. One should add, however, that the historical deformation of black subjectivity rarely permitted the luxury of 'bein' or 'love'. Nina Simone admits that she would like to compose love songs, but she doesn't as long as the need for protest songs is urgent. For her it is 'Mississippi Goddam.' But love poems are multiplying, examples are Hoaglund's 'love child — a black aesthetic' or Rodger's own 'Songs of a Blackbird.' At times a misguided political activism attacks this type of poetry for its escapism, but its emergence is evidence of the reconvalescence of a traumatized black self. Love poetry may after all be much better social therapy than 'shouting' poems, a category which has become notorious in the sixties, particularly through Baraka, Giovanni, and Sanchez. There is an element of catharsis in being able to say things now which would have caused a lynching several decades ago. However, this type of poetry has a built-in obsolescence proportionate to the ability of society to assimilate and incorporate protest. Protest poems, or novels, have been severely criticized for being short-cuts into dead-ends. Repressive tolerance is at an all-time high in America, and protest, for a time anyway, was quite marketable. During the early sixties it may have served the function of liberation, of cutting the umbilical cord. Soon thereafter it became food for liberal masochism and titillated the bad conscience of white America. In answer to Giovanni's 'Nigger Can You Kill' and Baraka's 'Black Art' and Sanchez' 'Homecoming' Al Young turns his signifying on 'Militant Dilettantes':

Don't nobody want no nice nigger no more
these honkies man that put out
these books and things
they want an angry splib
a furious nigrah
they don want no bourgeois woogie
they want them a militant nigger
in a fiji haircut
fresh out of some secret boot camp
with a bad book in one hand
and a molotov cocktail in the other
subject to turn up at one of their conferences
or soirees
and shake the shit out of them

The next two types are difficult to pinpoint. Here we might follow Ellison's advice and look at America's debt to jazz:

> Without the presence of the Negro American style, our jokes, our tall tales, even our sports would be lacking in the sudden turns, the shocks, the swift changes of pace (all jazz-shaped) that serve to remind us that the world is ever unexplored, and that while a complete mastery of life is mere illusion, the real secret of the game is to make life swing. It is its ability to articulate this tragic-comic attitude toward life that explains much of the mysterious power and attractiveness of that quality of Negro American style known as 'soul'.[17]

Michael Harper's *Dear John, Dear Coltrane* captures the spirit of jazz in poetry as do the records of the Last Poets. In music, as was said before, Afro-Americans have made the most substantial and influential contribution to American culture. The sixties were perhaps not as crucial for the liberation of black American music as for poetry, folklore, and everyday life-styles. For in music the cultural emancipation of blacks had begun much earlier and progressed much further than in any other area of culture. Indeed jazz may be said to have been in the vanguard of Afro-American cultural liberation, though the creative achievement of many jazz musicians was not matched by gains in status or wealth. Between New Orleans in 1920 and today there have been a number of musical revolutions, many of which were nipped in the bud by commercialization and imitation. It speaks for the regenerative powers of this art and the creativity of its musicians that each period of commercialization was followed by a new creative burst. One of the most consequential — particularly in terms of black pride — occurred during the early forties when Charlie Parker, Dizzy Gillespie, Bud Powell, Charlie Mingus, Max Roach and others ushered in a new black music which 'one could not dance to' and which 'had no melody', as many listeners protested. These bebop musicians refused to be song and dance men or minstrels. They recoded the blues and evergreens and turned them into defiant gestures of self-authentication. In Europe, where critics have often tended towards purism, Hugues Panassié accused these black musicians of being traitors to their musical tradition when they moved from swing and jump to bebop. American critics, too, found this music unacceptable and applauded the wholesale revival of dixieland during the middle forties. Little did they realize that Parker was truer to his heritage than the Yerba Buena Jazz Band (a white dixie band) ever could be. One should add here that the categorical purism so typical of many European jazz aficionados is totally lacking in the black musical world. 'All music gotta be folk music, I ain't never heard a horse sing a song,' Louis Armstrong is reported to have answered to a query concerning the difference between folk and jazz music, and Ellington always refused to make evaluative distinctions in music. Musical socialization in the black world has a catholic and *total* character; thus Ornette Coleman won his musical spurs in a Texas blues band and Charlie Parker played in Jay McShann's jump band before they struck out for new territory. In bebop black culture submitted its declaration of independence with Charlie Parker as the new hero. His role — as Baldwin writes in the jazz story 'Sonny's Blues' — was that of the revolté and outsider; he had gone *beyond* the melting pot. Parker's death took the form of a cultural-revolutionary suicide, a form of self-sacrifice which was later politicized by the Soledad brothers and the 'Black Panthers'. A. B. Spellman, black musician and critic, writes:

> The jazz musicians who produced bebop in the Forties may be said to have been the artistic vanguard of the dynamic social action that the later decades were to experience, ranging from the court actions of the NAACP all the way to the Watts riots.[20]

Undoubtedly minstrelsy continued to exist — particularly in the massive export of dixieland to Europe where it became the young music of the fifties. And minstrelsy continues in popular culture where many black artists have a hard time keeping clear of the lucrative vertigo of minstrelsy. But jazz, which like the novel has been declared defunct many times and which indeed went into a decline after Parker's death in the early fifties, was revitalized by Miles Davis, John Coltrane, Ornette Coleman, Cecil Taylor, and Archie Shepp in the late fifties and early sixties. Again white purists kept telling Coltrane that he was on the wrong track and that he was deserting jazz. Today Coltrane's music represents the key tradition of the sixties, and he has become model and teacher for a generation of young musicians. Charlie Parker broke new ground and carved out a new role for jazz musicians. He paid for it with his life; he died from an 'overdose of dues'. His stance was that of an outsider. Coltrane expanded the ground of jazz and solidified the house of jazz. In contrast to Parker he was not a bitter man, not a loner, but a universalist and, as Shepp says, 'a bridge' who brought black musicians 'to a kind of unity'.

Du Bois was indeed prophetic when he wrote about the leading role of black music some seventy years ago. He claimed that some day black music would shape and influence white music. Who would doubt this after the sixties? Ellison quotes an anonymous musician: 'No one ever thinks of the possibility that Duke Ellington might well have been a first-rate classical composer, but that he was looking for something better.' Or as the Duke said it himself in song: 'it don't mean a thing if it ain't got that swing.'

NOTHING LIKE BEIN' US

After being chevied and chased through a series of prefabricated identities, after trying on a variety of masks from Sambo to the 'angry splib', many blacks of the sixties and seventies are tired of playing roles and wearing masks forced upon them and designed for them by the dominant culture. They want to be left alone. Black poets, musicians, politicians today reject progressive paternalism as well as conservative racism. They realize that as long as whites set the norms for their behavior, in politics or in culture, they will continue to be dependents. For blacks the past decade was a period of coming to terms with this fact and with the norms of their own black culture. Blacks — and whites — have learned to respect that tradition and to evaluate it on its own terms. In this new attitude of black self-respect and white acknowledgement of this self-respect lies the important legacy of this decade. Blacks can now say in earnest what black folk used to say with bitter-sweet irony: Nothing like bein us.[21]

NOTES

1. William Labov, et. al., *A Study of the Non-Standard English of Negro and Puerto Rican Speakers in New York City*, Office of Education, Washington, 1969.
2. Roger D. Abrahams, *Deep Down in the Jungle: Negro Narrative Folklore from the Streets of Philadelphia*, rev. edn. Aldine, Chicago, 1970.
3. Claude Brown, 'The Language of Soul', in Kochman, *Rappin'*.
4. Eldridge Cleaver, 'As Crinkly as Yours', in Dundes, *Mother Wit*.
5. See also LeRoi Jones, *Blues People: The Negro Experience in White America and the Music that Developed From It*, William Morrow, New York, 1963.
6. Peter L. Berger and Thomas Luckmann, *The Social Construction of Reality*, Penguin, London, 1967.
7. Addison Gayle, Jr., ed., *The Black Aesthetic*. Baldwin, too, claims that blacks are more 'sensual' than whites: *The Fire Next Time*, p. 62.
8. Ellison, p. 123
9. Garland, p. 32, 83–99.
10. Mintz in Whitten/Szwed, *Afro-American Anthropology*.
11. Daniel J. Leab, *From Sambo to Superspade: The Black Experience in Motion Pictures*, Houghton Mifflin, Boston, 1975. Donald Bogle, *Toms, Coons, Mulattoes, Mammies, and Bucks: An Interpretive History of Blacks in American Films*, Viking, New York, 1973.
12. Cf. Jesse Jackson, 'Give the People a Vision', *The New York Times Magazine*, April 18, 1976. Grace Sims Holt, 'Stylin' Outta the Black Pulpit', Kochmann, p. 189–204.
13. Kochman, p. 165. Cf. Lou Rawls describes the 'front' of a hustler in a live performance *Live in Chicago*, Capitol records ST 2459. See also James Maryland, 'Shoe-shine on 63rd', in Kochman for a vivid description of the difference between the clothes of a pimp and a black power activist.

14. Works in black literature are too numerous to list. Cf. the bibliographies referred to in note 1, chapter V.

15. Oral subcultures are often 'warrior cultures'. Black culture is particularly agonistic since blacks have always had to fight 'the man'. 'The Negro boys and girls who are facing mobs today come out of a long line of improbable aristocrats — the only genuine aristocrats this country has produced'. Baldwin, *The Fire Next Time*, p. 134. One should add here that medieval 'warrior culture' knew games of ritual insult quite comparable to those of black subculture.

16. In Kochman, p. 336–45. On the new black poetry see Abraham Chapman, ed., *New Black Voices*, Mentor, New York, 1972; and Stephen Henderson, *Understanding the New Black Poetry: Black Speech and Black Music as Poetic References* (New York, Morrow, 1973). More references are obtainable from articles and books cited in notes 1 and 2, chapter V.

17. *Time*, April 6, 1970.

18. Bernard Jacquin puts it succinctly: 'Besides the stigma of immorality, it [the word 'jazz'] implies economic dispossession'. University de Lille III, 1976, 237. Jacquin includes a useful bibliography of works on free jazz in French in Régis Durand, ed., *Myth and Ideology in American Culture*. General histories of jazz were written by André Hodeir and Lucien Malson.

19. Biographies and autobiographies provide a better introduction to black culture than many scholarly works, e.g. the biographies of Bessie Smith by Chris Albertson, of Charlie Parker by Ross Russell, and of Coltrane by C. O. Simpkins M.D. Many black artists (Mahalia Jackson, Billie Holiday, Dick Gregory, Maya Angelou, Ethel Waters, Charlie Mingus et. al.) or public figures (Malcolm X, Iceberg Slim, et. al.) have written or dictated their autobiographies. Cf. Russell C. Brignano, *Black Americans in Autobiography. An Annotated Bibliography of Autobiographies and Autobiographical Works since the Civil War* (Durham, Duke University Press, 1974).

20. *Black Music*, 16.

21. It is telling that recent black scholarship stresses the theme of cultural self-authentication or self-legitimation. Robert Stepto. *From Behind the Veil. A Study of Afro-American Narrative* (Urbana, University of Illinois Press, 1979).

INDEX

Aaron, Daniel, viii, 147
Abrahams, Roger D., 9, 10, 58, 60, 61, 62, 146, 147, 165
Adams, William, 146
Adorno, Theodor, 96
Albertson, Chris, 166
Allen, William Francis, 54, 64
Angelou, Maya, 166
Armstrong, Louis, vii, 8, 77, 84, 90, 99ff, 106, 107, 110, 112, 114, 163

Baez, Joan, 6
Baldwin, James, 11, 31, 38, 51, 60, 127, 153, 163, 166
Banks, Frank, 40, 61
Baquet, George, 114
Barber, John, 57
Barker, Danny, 115
Barnum, P.T., 83
Basie, Count, 112
Baumann, Richard, 10, 58, 60, 146
Baumann, Zygmunt, 16, 55
Bausinger, Hermann, 11, 60
Beaven, A.W., 117
Bechet, Sidney, 114, 115
Beecher Stowe, Harriet, 145
Beiderbecke, Bix, 87, 104, 116
Bell, Bernard, viii, 144
Bell, Daniel, 109, 114
Bellah, Robert, 63
Benedict, Ruth, 30
Benjamin, Walter, 2
Bercovitch, Sacvan, 11
Berendt, Joachim Ernst, vii
Berger, Peter L., 55, 60, 146, 147, 165
Bernstein, Leonard, 7
Bigsby, Chris, vii
Binderman, Murray B., 61
Black Panthers, 164
Blake, Susan, 145
Blake, Eubie, 110
Blesh, Rudi, 81, 84, 94, 114
Böhmer, Peter, 57
Bogatyrev, P., 146

Bogle, Donald, 58, 165
Bontemps, Arna, 60, 144
Bornemann, Ernst, 94
Botkin, B.A., 147
Bourdieu, P., 55, 60, 114
Bourgignon, Erika, 49
Bradford, Perry, 105, 117
Braudel, Fernand, 2, 7, 11, 55
Brearly, H.C., 61
Brignano, Russel C., 166
Broderick, Francis L., 145
Bronz, Stephen, 145
Brooks, Gwendolyn, 145, 157
Brown, Claude, 165
Brown, James, 30
Brown, H. Rap, 147
Brown, Sterling, 144
Burke, Kenneth, 68

Carmichael, Hoagy, 87, 103–4, 116
Carroll, Pete, 88
Cash, W.J., 80
Caudwell, Christopher, 155
Chametzky, Jules, viii, 57
Chapman, Abraham, 60, 144, 145, 166
Charles, Ray, 64, 148
Charters, Samuel, 72, 92
Chaucer, Geoffry, 156
Christadler, Martin, viii, 147
Churchill, Winston, 124, 145
Clarke, Kenneth, 54, 147
Cleaver, Eldridge, 165
Cobbs, Price, 58, 146
Coleman, Ornette, 153, 163, 164
Coles, Robert, 63, 114
Collier, James Lincoln, 117
Coltrane, John, 153, 161, 164, 166
Condon, Eddie, 87, 103, 116
Connover, Willis, vii
Conrad, Joseph, 127
Cowley, Malcolm, 114, 117
Crouch, Stanley, 43
Cruse, Harold, 116

Dahrendorf, Ralf, 150
Dalby, David, 57
Dathorne, O.R., 64
Dauer, Alfons, 113
Davis, Miles, 164
Dean-Myatt, William, 116
Dearns, Francis, 146
Devereux, George, 11
Diamond, Stanley, 7
Dickens, Charles, 80
Dickson, Bruce Jr., 61
Diderot, Denis, 74, 92
Dillard, J.L., 55, 57
Dodds, E.R., 15, 30–1, 55, 60
Dollard, John, 40–1, 61
Dorson, Richard, viii, 60, 63
Douglas, Ann, 79, 93
Douglass, Frederick, 35–6, 52, 145
Dreitzel, Hans Peter, 57
Drury, Alan, 145
DuBois, W.E.B., viii, 11, 14ff, 36, 54, 90, 105, 121, 122, 136, 145, 151, 164
Dunbar, Paul Laurence, 74, 120, 121, 155
Dundes, Alan, 9, 55, 57, 60, 61, 62, 63, 114, 145, 146
Durand, Régis, 166
Dvorak, Anton, 117
Dylan, Bob, 6

Ebon (Thomas Dooley), 161
Eliot, T.S., 114, 124, 127, 129
Elkins, Stanley, 1, 10, 17, 24, 55
Ellington, Duke, vii, 100–1, 106, 110, 112, 163, 164
Ellison, Ralph, vii, viii, 4–5, 7, 11, 12, 15, 16, 18–19, 25–6, 30–1, 45–8, 55, 56, 57, 58, 59, 60, 62, 66, 88, 90, 91, 116, 118, 119, 126, 127, 128f, 130, 132f, 134, 136, 137, 140, 143, 144, 145, 146, 147, 151, 152, 162, 164, 165
Emanuel, James, 144, 146
Engels, Friedrich, 147
Engerman, Stanley, 1, 10, 55
Epstein, Dena, 64, 91, 115
Erikson, Erik, 54, 147
Evans, David, 48, 62
Evans, Philip R., 116

Fabre, Michel, vii
Fass, Paula S., 113
Faulkner, William, 29, 36, 127, 136
Fenton, C.A., 146
Ferris, Bill, 102
Fiedler, Leslie, 7, 29, 147
Finnegan, Ruth, 59
Fisher, Miles Mark, 64
Fitzgerald, F. Scott, 95
Fogel, Robert, 1, 10, 55
Foster, Pops, 114
Foster, Stephen, 77, 80
Franklin, Aretha, 30, 64, 148
Frazier, Franklin, 2–3, 12, 17
Frye, Northrop, 7
Fuchs, Eduard, 93

Gabel, Joseph, 147
Garland, Phyl, 117, 148, 165
Garrison, Lucy McKim, 54, 64
Garvey, Marcus, 59, 61, 121, 122, 125, 150, 151
Gayle, Addison, 12, 60, 62, 115, 144, 145, 165
Geertz, Clifford, 5, 12
Genovese, Eugene, 9, 10, 30, 51, 55, 59, 60, 63, 64, 92, 115, 147
Gershwin, George, 7, 87
Gillespie, Dizzy, 54, 163
Giovanni, Niki, 161, 162
Glazer, Nathan, 4, 12
Goffman, Erving, 25, 57, 60, 75, 94, 147
Goldman, Lucien, 146
Goodman, Benny, 103–4, 107, 112
Goody, J., 58
Gorer, Geoffrey, 90
Gramsci, Antonio, 26, 59
Green, Alan W., 94
Gregory, Dick, 41, 62, 166
Grier, William, 58
Grimstead, David, 82
Gross, Theodore, 146
Gutman, Herbert, viii, 3–4, 9, 10, 11, 16, 31, 55, 59, 60, 63, 93, 94

Hadlock, Richard, 114
Haley, Bill, 148
Hall, Basil, 80
Hall, Robert, 57

Hampton, Lionel, 133
Handy, W.C., 75, 85–6, 88, 94, 99, 115
Hannerz, Ulf, 60, 61
Hansen, Chadwick, 114, 116
Harding, Walter, 91
Hareven, Tamara, 11, 12, 94
Harper, Michael, viii, 162
Harris, Joel Chandler, 120, 156
Harte, Bret, 75
Haskins, Jim, 115
Hemingway, Ernest, 127
Henderson, Stephen, 61, 144, 166
Hentoff, Nat, 94, 114
Hersey, John, 58, 145
Herskovits, Melville, 4, 12, 19–20, 54, 55, 56, 57
Hesse, Eva, vii
Hesse, Hermann, 95, 113
Himes, Chester, 145
Hoaglund, Evrett, 161
Hobsbawm, Eric, vii, 113
Hodeir, André, vii, 166
Hoggart, Richard, 58
Holiday, Billie, 8, 166
Holt, Grace Sims, 165
Horn, David, 115
Howe, Irving, 145
Howells, William Dean, 120
Hudson, Julius, 59
Huggins, Nathan I., 9, 10, 57, 91, 94, 145
Hughes, Langston, 11, 60, 61, 62, 122ff, 125, 144, 145, 146, 156, 161
Huizinga, Jan, 154
Hume, David, 118f
Hurston, Zora Neale, 40, 61
Hyman, Stanley Edgar, 91, 145
Hymes, Dell, 9, 10, 12

Iceberg Slim, 24, 147, 166

Jackson, Bruce, 10, 43, 58, 60, 61–2, 93
Jackson, Jesse, 153, 165
Jackson, Mahalia, 166
Jacquin, Bernard, 166
Jahn, Janheinz, vii, 51, 58
Jakobson, R., 131, 146
James, Henry, 136

Janis, Harriet, 114
Jason, Heda, 59
Jefferson, Thomas, 74
Johnson, Bunk, 100, 114
Johnson, James Weldon, 122, 145
Jones, Le Roi (Imamu Amiri Baraka), 1, 56, 62, 103, 106, 113, 145, 156, 160, 161, 162, 165
Joplin, Janis, 6, 7
Joplin, Scott, 110, 111
Jordan, Winthrop, 67
Joyce, James, 127, 129, 136
Jung, Carl G., 88

Kammen, Michael, 57
Kaplan, Sidney, 57
Karenga, Ron, 12, 62
Kealy, Gregory, 11
Keil, Charlie, 10, 11, 60, 61, 62
Kelly, Robert, 12
Kennedy, John and Robert, 6
Kent, George, 145
Keppard, Freddie, 100, 111
Kersaud, Billy, 84
King, B.B., 48, 110, 117, 148, 151, 160
King, Martin Luther, 6, 42, 153
Kinnard, J., 93
Kipling, Rudyard, 124
Kissin, Eva, 146
Klein, Marcus, 140, 147
Kluckhohn, Clyde, 56
Kmen, Henry A., 93
Kochman, Thomas, 54, 56, 58, 59, 60, 61, 62, 154, 160, 165, 166
Krehbiel, H.E., 117

Labov, William, 9, 10, 61, 165
Laing, R.D., 57
Lang, H.J., 147
Larcy, Rubin, 61
Latimore, Jewel, 161
Leab, Daniel J., 165
Lee, Don L., 159
v.d. Leeuw, Gerardus, 154
Leonhard, Neil, 114, 116, 117
Levi-Strauss, Claude, 7
Levine, Lawrence, 3, 8–9, 10, 60, 64
Lindsay, Joe, 90
Lippe, Rudolf zur, 93

Lipset, Seymour Martin, 92
Locke, Alain, 121
Lomax, Alan, 60, 114
Lord, Albert, 58
Lovell, John Jr., 64
Luckmann, Thomas, 55, 60, 146, 147, 165

McCarthy, Albert, 94
McCue, George, 114
MacDowell, Edward, 117
McKay, Claude, 122, 124, 145
McPartland, Jimmy, 103, 115
McPherson, Alan, 56, 58
McShann, Jay, 163
Madden, Richard P., 92
Maher, James T., 114
Malcolm X, 31, 166
Malraux, André, 127
Malson, Lucien, 166
Manchester, William, 145
Marcuse, Herbert, 55
Mares, Paul, 116
Margulies, Max, 96, 113, 117
Marsala, Marty, 115
Martineau, Harriett, 67, 71
Maryland, James, 165
Mayfield, Curtis, 48
Maynard, Theodore, 117
Mbiti, John, 59, 62, 63
Meier, August, 145
Melnick, Mimi Clar, 61
Mezzrow, Mezz, 81, 93, 103–4, 111, 116
Michener, James, 145
Mingus, Charlie, 163, 166
Mintz, Sidney, 16, 18, 54, 55, 56, 57, 88, 90, 152
Mom's Mabley, 160
Montell, William L., 10, 11
Moody, Anne, 59
Moore, Rudy Ray, 61
Morgenstern, Dan, 114
Morrison, George, 114
Morton, Jelly Roll, 98, 101, 103, 111, 114
Moten, Benny, 112
Moynihan, David, 3–4, 12
Muhammad Ali, 153, 156
Muslims, 151
Myrdal, Gunnar, 3–5, 12, 17, 91

NAACP, 151, 164
Nathan, Hans, 91
Neal, Larry, 55, 145
Newman, Ronald B., 61
New Orleans Rhythm Kings, 116
Newton, Francis, 113
Newton, Huey, 16, 56
Nichols, Thomas Low, 83
Nipperdey, Thomas, 54
Noble, David, 88

O'Connor, Ortrun, viii
Oliver, King, 111, 114, 116
Oliver, Paul, vii, 62
Osofsky, Gilbert, 60
Ostendorf, Berndt, 145, 147

Panassié, Hugues, vii, 163
Paredes, A., 10, 60
Parker, Charlie, vii, 4, 23–4, 57, 153, 163, 164, 166
Parrish, Lydia, 63
Parsons, Talcott, 54, 147
Patterson, Orlando, 63
Perez, Manuel, 114
Peters, John, 119
Pettis, Ashley, 116
Picou, Alphonse, 114
Piersen, William, 91
Pike, James, 73, 92
Piron, Armand, 114
Politzer, Heinz, 146
Pope, Alexander, 65
Pound, Ezra, 124
Powell, Adam Clayton, 61, 63
Powell, Bud, vii, 163
Presley, Elvis, 7, 90, 148
Pynchon, Thomas, 93

Randall, Dudley, 144
Raveau, Francois, 146
Rawlings, Elliott, 117
Rawls, Lou, 45, 101, 115, 165
Redding, Otis, 30, 148
Redding, Saunders, 144
Reed, Ishmael, 84, 161
Rehin, George, 91
Rice, Phil, 72
Ricoeur, P., 64
Roach, Max, 163

Robichaux, John, 114
Rodgers, Carolyn, 157, 159, 161
Rolling Stones, The, 6, 90, 110, 152, 153
Rosenberg, Bruce, 61
Rosengarten, Theodore, 36, 60, 61
Rourke, Constance, 62, 147
Russell, Ross, 23–5, 57, 117, 166

Sanchez, Sonia, 39, 161, 162
Saxton, Alexander, 92, 93
Schafer, William, 114
Schuller, Gunther, 62, 88, 92, 113, 114
Schwendter, Rolf, 55
Seaver, E., 146
Seldes, Gilbert, 116
Senghor, Léopold, 126
Shapiro, Nat, 114
Sharp, Cecil, 7–8
Shaw, Nate, 36–9, 60
Shepp, Archie, 164
Sidran, Ben, 26
Silberman, Charles, 38, 62
Simone, Nina, 48, 161
Simpkins, C.O., 166
Smiley, Portia, 40
Smith, Bessie, 112, 166
Smith, Charles Edward, 85
Solal, Martial, 152
Soledad brothers, 164
Southern, Eileen, 89, 93, 94
Spaeth, Sigmund, 116
Spellman, A.B., 164
Stearn, Marshall and Jean, 113
Stepto, Robert, viii, 126, 145, 166
Stoddard, Tom, 114
Stoephasius, Rita, viii
Stout, Rex, 145
Stuckey, Sterling, 64
Sudhalter, Richard M., 116
Sun Ra, 161
Szwed, John, 10, 12, 42, 54, 55, 56, 62, 63, 64, 165

Taylor, Cecil, 153, 164
Teschemacher, Frank, 103
Thernstrom, Stephen, 11, 20, 57
Thompson, E.P., 15, 55, 59
Thurman, Wallace, 122
Tocqueville, Alexis de, 66, 70, 73

Toll, Robert, 9, 10, 58, 63–4, 91, 93
Toomer, Jean, 122
Townsend, Henry, 47
Trimmer, Joseph, 146
Trollope, Frances, 67, 73, 80, 92
Turner, Darwin, 146
Turner, Lorenzo, 57
Turner, Nat, 39, 73
Tuveson, Ernest Lee, 11
Twain, Mark, 73, 75–6, 78, 80

Uris, Leon, 145

Valentine, Charles, 56
Van Dyke, Henry, 116
Van Vechten, Carl, 73, 92
Vann Woodward, C., 2, 59
Veblen, Thornstein, 18
Vesey, Denmark, 39

Wagner, Jean, vii, 144
Walters, Ethel, 166
Walton, Ortiz, 115
Ware, Charles Pickard, 54, 64
Washington, Booker, T., 28, 31, 59, 122
Watt, Ian, 58
Webb, Chick, 112
Weimann, Robert, 146
Wepman, Dennis, 61
Wheatley, Phillis, 118f
White, Newman, 94
Whiteman, Paul, 87, 101, 104, 105, 110, 112, 116
Whitlow, Roger, 144
Whitten, Norman, 10, 12, 42, 54, 55, 56, 62, 63, 64, 165
Wilde, Oscar, 2
Wilder, Alec, 114
Williams, Bert, 82, 83, 84, 92
Williams, Raymond, 11, 62
Wolf, Eric, 16, 59
Wolfe, Bernard, 93, 116
Wood, Peter, 10, 22–4, 63, 91
Wright, Richard, 11, 24, 32, 59, 126, 127, 129, 133, 145, 147

Yarrow, Philip, 117
Yerby, Frank, 145
Young, Al, 162
Young, Lester, vii